P9-DXZ-331

April, 1992

159 - Think about
161 - Golden Rule
* 167 - 1st Look at "Market Adventure"
182 - Job Interviewing Questions
186 - Red flags during interview
188 - Asking past employer
203 - obsolescence

THE UNNATURAL ACT OF MANAGEMENT

WHEN THE GREAT LEADER'S WORK IS DONE, THE PEOPLE SAY, "WE DID IT OURSELVES"

Everett T. Suters

HarperBusiness

A Division of HarperCollins*Publishers*

THE UNNATURAL ACT OF MANAGEMENT. Copyright © 1992 by Everett T. Suters. All rights reserved. Printed in the United States of America. No part of this book may be used or reproduced in any manner whatsoever without written permission except in the case of brief quotations embodied in critical articles and reviews. For information address HarperCollins Publishers, Inc., 10 East 53rd Street, New York, NY 10022.

HarperCollins books may be purchased for educational, business, or sales promotional use. For information, please call or write: Special Markets Department, HarperCollins Publishers, Inc., 10 East 53rd Street, New York, NY 10022. Telephone: (212) 207-7528; Fax: (212) 207-7222.

FIRST EDITION

Library of Congress Cataloging-in-Publication Data
Suters, Everett T. (Everett Thomas), 1931–
    The unnatural act of management : when the great leader's work is
done, the people say "We did it ourselves" / Everett T. Suters.
        p.   cm.
    Includes index.
    ISBN 0-88730-551-2
    1. Corporate turnarounds—Management—Case studies. 2. Industrial
management—Case studies. I. Title.
HD58.8.S88   1992
658.1'6–dc20   91-40225
                                                                   CIP

92 93 94 95 96 PS/HC 10 9 8 7 6 5 4 3 2 1

To my mother
Bessie Suters Boeke
With love

To my good friend
Hal W. Lamb III
With thanks

The Management
of
Enfield Manufacturing Company

Scott Wilson	President and CEO
Richard Thompkins	Executive Vice President
Alan Braswell	Financial Vice President
Gordon Block	Administrative Vice President
Barbara Lansing	Sales Manager
Mike Cline	Plant Manager

Contents

SECTION FOUR
THE THREE MOST COMMON MANAGERIAL PITFALLS AND HOW TO AVOID THEM   63

SECTION FIVE
HOW TO MAINTAIN OPEN AND EFFECTIVE COMMUNICATIONS   89

SECTION THIRTEEN
MANAGING YOURSELF AND YOUR LIFE   225

SECTION FOURTEEN
THE CONCLUSION OF A TURNAROUND   235

Foreword
by Stew Leonard

I can heartily recommend *The Unnatural Act of Management* to anyone who is a manager, aspires to be a manager, or answers to a manager. You will benefit immediately from the author's unique ability to simplify the complexities of management; and then provide the reader with provocative and practical advice for dealing with them.

This interesting book is written in a unique story form, and as I began reading, I recognized the main character as the thinly disguised alter ego of Everett Suters. This very believable author has over 30 years of experience as a CEO/entrepreneur, and he has met over 2,500 payrolls in computer services, manufacturing, and real estate organizations that he has either founded or acquired. As a result he has the qualifications to present strong evidence to the reader why the challenges and problems of managers in all organizations are more alike than they are different.

Everett knows what it's like to start a business from scratch, and to have his back against the wall. He has lived the situations, problems, and human relations challenges that Brent Powell, the main character, encounters as he attempts to salvage a failing company. The subtitle—"When the great leader's work is done, the people say, 'We did it ourselves'"—echoes the unnatural "hands-off" management philosophy Everett suddenly discovered after eight years of struggling as an overworked, "hands-on" manager in his first company, as he was on the verge of liquidating that business. He describes the two most important, but simple, management lessons he ever learned that enabled him to become an effective "hands-off" manager. The first was to develop an understanding of what management really is, and the second was to develop an understanding of when you are managing and when you are not. I believe you will be intrigued by Everett's unique concept of management as a decision-based, thinking job, and by the irony that, although managers are ultimately judged on their results, they aren't directly producing results when managing. Managers are managing only when they are producing results indirectly through their people and other resources.

This concept is consistent with the only justification for any organization, which is that members of a group can accomplish more by working together than they ever could as individual performers.

You will read about how you can identify and avoid the three greatest managerial pitfalls: being overcommitted, being irreplaceable, and allowing "intruders on your turf." I was fascinated by Everett's view of management as a bifocal process, and his assertion that we can be more effective by keeping the two time components of management in proper perspective. He shares with us how we can deal with the intrusion of the more immediate and demanding work of today while giving a higher priority to the more important work of tomorrow.

This book describes why inspiration, or the lack of inspiration, is a reflection of the atmosphere and the attitude that is generated within higher management and inevitably seeps down throughout the organization. You will read how your associates generate their own inspiration when you sincerely display an attitude of caring about, appreciating, and believing in them by maintaining a low profile and by giving them guidance in the form of advice on courses of action instead of giving them directions.

Everett provides sound evidence that hiring the right people is not a form of "Russian roulette," but rather a skill that can be learned by following the few simple procedures that he describes. He also explains why periodic performance reviews are counterproductive for "decision makers," and how we can more effectively evaluate our associates continuously based on the assumptions they make about their own decisions

This book identifies the human relations challenges that confront all managers, and it provides sound advice for the various ways of dealing with them. In addition, you will learn how to use the five "Golden Rules" of criticism and how to terminate, without the usual trauma, those who don't work out. To me, one of the most interesting and helpful sections of the book deals with how we can successfully manage our personal lives and eliminate much of the stress by following sound management principles. Everett points out that pressure in the management job is a fact, but stress is an emotion, and whether this pressure results in counterproductive stress or in a positive motivational force depends largely on our attitudes toward our jobs. You will also learn a clever technique, referred to as "stress transfer," that will enable you to transfer the stress others have caused you back to them.

I have benefited greatly from Everett's insight and experience as he has consulted with me about management. I continue to be amazed at the vast amount of information he is able to absorb, intelligently analyze, and evaluate. His advice has been invaluable to me, as I believe this book will be to you. I feel privileged to be invited to share with you my feelings about *The Unnatural Act of Management*, and I know you will benefit from this fascinating book.

> Stew Leonard
> Chairman
> Stew Leonard's, World's Largest Dairy Store

(Editor's note: Stew Leonard received the Presidential Award for Entrepreneurial Excellence from President Ronald Reagan at the White House in 1986.)

Preface

As a CEO/entrepreneur for over thiry years, I have met over 2,500 payrolls in organizations I have either founded or acquired. I have experienced successes, as well as the pain, frustration and stress from some of my mistakes and failures. The *unnatural acts* and other lessons I have learned about management from these experiences are a part of this story.

I have discovered that in spite of our individual differences, all managers are confronted with similar situations, challenges, and problems, and we tend to make the same mistakes. This book provides you with the opportunity to benefit immediately from what it took me many years to learn . . . too often the hard way.

This is not a textbook filled with charts, graphs, footnotes, and statistics. Although the story is fictional, there are no fictional approaches to management based on abstract theories or fads. Instead, you will find simple, common sense management practices that have worked successfully for me, and that you can begin using immediately.

To refer to management as an *unnatural act* is perhaps a misnomer. However, it is an unnatural process when you are able to achieve *your* objectives through your people, and they will say: "We did it ourselves." This story is about that process.

I hope you will benefit as much by reading this book, as I have by writing it.

Everett T. Suters
February 1, 1992

Acknowledgements

I am grateful to Mark Greenberg, Publisher of the HarperBusiness division of HarperCollins, and to Virginia Smith, Executive Editor, for believing in this book. I am particularly indebted to Virginia for her diligence in dealing with the unusual format of this book, and for her patience with me.

My sincere appreciation to my good friends at *INC.* and *Success* magazines for their encouragement and support, and to David Asman, Editor of the "Managers' Journal" column in *The Wall Street Journal*, who originally convinced me to continue writing about management.

Many thanks to Mitch Tuchman for his editorial contributions and very helpful constructive criticism. Also to John Varley, retired Vice-President of Johnson and Johnson, New Brunswick, New Jersey, for reading the manuscript and for his helpful suggestions and objectivity.

Finally, warm gratitude to my good friend Stew Leonard who is a continuous source of inspiration to me and has given me encouragement and support when I have needed it most.

• •

The Beginning of a Turnaround

●●●●●●●●●●●●●●●●●●●●●●●●●●●●●●●●●●●●●

Advice from a Stranger

As Brent Powell and his accountant, Matthew Dawkins, were concluding their meeting in the conference room of Dawkins and Rowe, Brent received a call from the receptionist. "Mr. Powell, your answering service phoned. Mrs. Stanley Wilson wants you to call her. She said it's urgent."

Dawkins suggested that Brent use the conference room phone. As Brent dialed the number, he was puzzled by the call because he hardly knew Helen Wilson. They had rarely seen each other during his long friendship with her husband, Stanley, and they had not spoken since Stanley's funeral more than three years earlier.

Helen was obviously upset when she answered the phone. "Brent, my son, Scott, had a heart attack last night, and he's in intensive care. We don't know how serious his condition is yet, but it doesn't look favorable. I called because I need your help."

"Just tell me what I can do," Brent responded, though he wondered what he could possibly do for Helen Wilson.

"You're probably surprised to hear from me, and I do feel awkward calling you after all this time, but Enfield Manufacturing is in trouble. Scott has been under a lot of stress, and that's probably the cause of his heart attack. I'm calling to see if there's any way you might be able to help us at the plant."

"Helen, I'll do anything I can, but what about Richard Thompkins? If he's still the executive vice-president, can't he keep things going until Scott is able to come back?"

"Apparently not, and I'm very disappointed in him. Richard said we should bring in someone else."

Brent was tempted to ask why but decided not to. "Helen, try to calm down. I'm only ten minutes from Grand Central, and I can be on the next train to Westport."

As Brent walked down Park Avenue toward Grand Central Station, he thought back to the day 19 years earlier when he had walked along this same street just after meeting Stanley Wilson. That casual meeting on a commuter train from Connecticut had had a dramatic impact on Brent's life.

At the time, Brent was the 28-year old president of a computerized payroll service. He had founded the company two years previously, after leaving IBM, where he had been a sales representative. Running the company was his first management experience, and he found the pressures and challenges overwhelming. At IBM, he had taken management for granted, assuming that it was simply a matter of combining common sense with his sales experience. Later he realized how wrong he had been.

On that bright April day, as the train stopped in Grand Central, Brent had closed the management book he was reading. The distinguished-looking stranger seated next to him had glanced at the title and asked, "Are you a manager?"

"I'm supposed to be," Brent replied. The stranger smiled and nodded sympathetically.

As they stood up to leave, the stranger had turned to Brent and said matter-of-factly, "Management, like acting, should usually only be noticed when it's bad. Lao-tse, the Chinese philosopher, wrote, 'When the great leader's work is done, the people say, "We did it ourselves." ' " The stranger added, "You can be effective if you will learn that good management is an *unnatural* act."

Brent had followed the stranger onto the platform and asked, "Do you have a card?"

The stranger had handed Brent his card as he said, "Give me a ring if I can ever help you."

Walking along Park Avenue, Brent had reflected on the stranger's words: "Management is only noticed when it's bad.... When the great leader's work is done, the people say, 'We did it ourselves.'" Before he realized it, Brent had walked the 16 blocks to 58th Street. Then he recalled the stranger's parting words: "You can be effective if you will learn that good management is an *unnatural* act."

Suddenly he had realized what he was doing wrong. He had been doing what was *natural* for him: keeping a high profile, managing with a strong hand, taking credit for good results, and blaming his people when things went wrong. He should have been doing what was *unnatural* for him: keeping a low profile, teaching his people to manage themselves, giving them more of the credit when things went well, and accepting more of the responsibility when they did not. It all made sense. The stranger was right. Good management is indeed an *unnatural act*.

Two weeks later, Brent had contacted Stanley Wilson, and this was the beginning of a long and mutually rewarding relationship.

Brent's thoughts returned to the present as he hurried to catch the 11:18 to Westport. The one-hour ride gave him the opportunity to reflect on what Helen had said. It came as no surprise to Brent that Enfield Manufacturing was in trouble. He had known when Scott took over at Enfield after his father's death that he was not qualified to be president. Stanley and Brent had never discussed Scott's deficiencies as a manager; now Brent wondered if Stanley had ever discussed them with Helen.

Brent and Scott were both 47 years old, and although Scott had always appeared friendly, Brent had detected a feeling of sibling rivalry. It was obvious to both that Stanley Wilson had looked on Brent as a surrogate son with qualities his own son lacked. Scott knew that Brent had responded to his father's management advice and had learned a great deal from him, whereas Scott went out of his way to disagree with his father, even when he knew Stanley was right.

"Westport Station . . . Westport Station." The announcement interrupted Brent's thoughts. As he looked up, he saw Helen walking across the parking lot. She was stylishly dressed, and she was taller than Brent had remembered. Stanley would have been 72 now, and Helen appeared to be in her late sixties. Brent could understand Helen's concern about Enfield Manufacturing because of her lack of involvement in the business. Stanley had always made a practice of separating his business life from his family life, and he rarely discussed Enfield with his wife.

"You didn't have to meet me, Helen," Brent said, as she approached him on the station platform. "I could have taken a cab."

"I was glad to," she replied. "Besides, I wanted to leave the house and try to get my mind off Scott."

"How is he?"

"Not very well. The doctors say it will probably be three to six months before he can return to work." They continued to discuss Scott's heart attack as they walked to Helen's car.

As they drove out of the parking lot, she said, "Brent, I called you because Stanley used to tell me that I should get in touch with you if the company was ever in trouble. I almost called you several times, but I didn't see how you could do anything without hurting Scott and alienating him from the rest of our family.

"The truth is that Scott isn't cut out to be president, and I don't want him to ever come back. If he did, I'm sure the job would eventually kill him.

"Stanley had serious reservations about Scott being able to run the business, but I never realized it until shortly before his death. We had a long discussion one day, and Stanley told me he had never admitted Scott's deficiencies to you, but he knew you were aware of them. Stanley always hoped Scott might change, but I believe he knew Scott never would."

She fell silent, and Brent asked, "When we spoke this morning, you seemed upset with Richard. Do you mind telling me why?"

"I feel he's letting me down just when I need him the most. Last night at the hospital, I told him I didn't want Scott back in the business. Then when I asked him to take over as president, he said he was flattered but wasn't interested in the job. So I asked if he would run the business until we could find somebody else. Richard's response was that Enfield is on the verge of bankruptcy and the problems are too serious for him to deal with. I really thought he had more ambition and more confidence in his own ability.

"When I told him about Stanley's advice to get in touch with you if the company was ever in trouble, Richard encouraged me to call you. He said he didn't know of anyone more qualified to help us."

"I appreciate that, Helen, but I'm concerned about your feelings toward Richard. How well do you know him?"

"Not very well. Stanley rarely discussed the people at the plant. I know that Richard is from a wealthy old Boston family, and that he and his wife are both tennis buffs, enjoy sailing, and are interested in the arts and civic affairs. I've been very impressed with Richard the few times I've been with him, and if I were picking someone to play the role of a corporate executive in a movie, he would be my choice. I just don't understand why he doesn't want to be president, because he always seems so sure of himself."

"Helen, I know Richard very well, and he *is* sure of himself. He's ambitious, an excellent manager, and is particularly good at training other managers. However, I'm not surprised that he doesn't want to be president, because he doesn't like being out on the cutting edge."

"I don't know what you mean by that."

"Stanley was an entrepreneur, a risk taker. He was future ori-ented with the vision to know when to make a move and when not to. Richard isn't that type. He is more today oriented and is better at carrying out the objectives others have established. That's the reason he and Stanley worked so well together. Richard focused on today's work while Stanley was focusing on the future, establishing new objectives, and planning how to achieve them. Richard is uncomfortable with this type of activity, and this is what it will probably take to solve Enfield's problems."

"I didn't realize that was the case. I probably owe Richard an apology. I was upset last night, and I believe I overreacted."

"I wouldn't give it another thought," Brent said. Then he deliberately changed the subject. "Since Scott has majority control of the stock, I'm concerned about how he can be convinced that something different should be done."

"Oh, but he doesn't have majority control. Stanley was planning to leave Scott controlling interest, but he changed his will the week before he died. He was so concerned about Scott's ability to run the business that when he divided his 70 percent of the stock, he left 15 percent to Scott, 15 percent to each of our two daughters, and 25 percent to me. So the girls and I control 55 percent."

"Do the employees still own the remaining 30 percent of the stock?"

"Yes, it's held in an employee stock-ownership trust. Scott is the trustee, but even with the additional 15 percent he personally owns, he still controls only 45 percent of the stock."

"Was Scott upset that Stanley changed his will?"

"No. He never knew how it was previously written."

Helen looked concerned and added, "Ever since Enfield has been in trouble, Scott's been very sensitive about having to deal with his sisters and me as stockholders. Now that he has had a heart attack, I feel I must be particularly careful not to do anything regarding the company that will upset him. That's why I was hesitant to call you, but I didn't know of anything else I could do."

"How do your daughters feel about Scott?"

"They don't know much about the business, but they do know Scott, and they blame him for their stock dividends being discontinued. This has created a financial hardship for them and been a cause of friction within our family.

"The girls have no confidence in Scott as a businessman, and they've been pressuring me to do something, but his heart attack is not the way I would have chosen to resolve the problem. However, both of my daughters have already called this morning, asking how we can make sure he doesn't come back to the company, for his own good as well as ours.

"Brent, I'm trying to do what is best for Scott, and this is the most difficult decision I've ever made, but I'd like for you to replace Scott as president of Enfield if you'll accept."

"Helen, I'm sincerely honored by your offer, and I want to do what I can to help. Stanley did more for me than I could ever repay. Nevertheless, because of my other commitments and plans for the future, I'm not able, or willing, to assume a full-time job, or even a part time job on a permanent basis."

Tears came into Helen's eyes as she said, "But what can I do? I don't know where else to turn."

"Wait, Helen, hear me out. I didn't say I couldn't help you. Stanley knew my plans when he told you to contact me if the company was ever in trouble, and I seriously doubt he meant to imply that I would be a candidate to become president of Enfield.

"Even though I'm committed to a series of management seminars starting in June, I can spend a great deal of time at Enfield during the next 90 days. Then I can look in periodically after that if I'm needed."

"But would 90 days really do that much good?"

● ●

The Phenomenon of the 90-Day Turnaround

"Helen, Stanley used to talk to me about the way organizations often get themselves into or out of trouble in about three months. I don't know how serious the problems are at Enfield, but within 90 days we can probably determine where the company will go from there, for better or for worse."

"That sounds like some sort of superstitious theory."

Brent smiled. "That was my opinion when Stanley first described the phenomenon to me. Three months is not an exact time frame but rather approximates the cause and effect cycle of six important factors in business:

- Level of sales activity
- Backlog of outstanding orders
- Cash and accounts receivable positions
- Gain or loss of key personnel

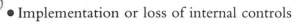

- Implementation or loss of internal controls
- Effects of good or bad management decisions

These and other factors can work for or against an organization, and they don't show up overnight. However, within approximately 90 days, their combined effects usually announce loud and clear whether a trend is changing."

"If that's the case, when can you start?"

"Well, this is Friday. I can be there when the plant opens Monday morning."

"That would be wonderful. Now we need to decide on how you should be compensated."

"Let's just consider any contribution I can make as partial repayment of an outstanding debt to Stanley for everything that I learned from him."

"I wouldn't consider letting you help us without any financial consideration."

"Sorry, Helen, it's the only way I would be comfortable doing so. I also believe I can be more effective with the management group at Enfield if they know I have no financial interest in the company."

"Whatever you say, Brent, and I'm very grateful."

Brent laughed. "I haven't done anything yet."

Helen and Brent drove to the Post Road Restaurant in Darien. After they were seated, Helen said "Brent, although you and I have spent very little time together, I know quite a lot about you from talking with Stanley. He didn't like to talk about business at home, but you were one of his favorite subjects. You were a real curiosity to him, and he apparently was to you.

"Stanley considered you to be his closest friend. He said you both tended to be loners, with a large number of friendly acquaintances but very few close friends. He also felt that because of the 25 years difference in your ages, you probably wouldn't have become such close friends without the strong mutual interest you had in management. He found management discussions with you to be very provocative because of your different styles and viewpoints.

"Stanley saw himself as being more inside focused. He liked the production side of the business and said he wanted to know how things were done. He said your focus was more on management and marketing, and you were never particularly interested in how things were done as long as they were done right. He also said you didn't like details but could be very good at them when they involved a new venture or had anything to do with financial information.

"Stanley seemed to take his work more seriously, and he envied your ability to enjoy your work like it was a game, even when things weren't going well. Even though you were both tough minded, Stanley felt you were deceptively so because of your laid-back appearance. Although you worked a lot of hours, he said you paced yourself well, never seemed to be particularly busy, and did a lot of your work away from the office, where you wouldn't be distracted. He learned from you that it wasn't necessary for him to always be at the plant to do his work, and I believe he regretted not learning this during his younger years when our children were growing up.

"Stanley said management was only a means to an end for him, whereas you were interested in management as an end in itself and tended to think more deeply about the philosophy of management. This is why he liked to expose you to new management ideas, because after thinking about them, you usually came back with a different slant, and he would learn from you.

"He felt that he taught you a great deal and was flattered by your obvious respect for him as a manager. However, he said that as you matured as a manager there was more of a mutual respect between you, even though you never discussed it.

"It seems odd that he drew comparisons between himself and you but never compared himself with Scott, though the two of them were different in even more ways."

In spite of Brent's serious reservations about Scott's qualifications to be president of Enfield, he wanted Helen's viewpoint, so he decided to pursue her comment. "I only saw Scott a few times, and although he and Stanley resembled each other physically, their personalities were obviously quite different. It might help me at Enfield if you would tell me more about these differences."

Helen thought briefly, then said, "Stanley was very practical and wanted to see things written down in black and white. Scott is highly creative and seems to formulate things in his head, and that's where they often remain, according to Stanley. Scott studied industrial design at the University of Washington, much to Stanley's chagrin. He wanted Scott to go to Yale, as he had, and study engineering.

"After Scott came into the business, Stanley's biggest complaint was that Scott had a strong tendency to redesign or change things even when it wasn't necessary. Scott would also come up with wild ideas without thinking through how they could be implemented, or whether they even had any practical value.

"Stanley was concerned that Scott wasn't tough-minded enough to be an effective manager. He acts tough-minded at times, but he turns it on and off like a faucet, and Stanley felt that this inconsistency is disconcerting to others.

"Competition was the biggest problem between Stanley and Scott. If Stanley wanted to go to the right, Scott wanted to go to the left. They played golf together until Stanley quit because he said it was no longer a game—it was war!

"They loved each other but never really liked each other. They didn't have a common bond to hold them together, as you and Stanley did with your mutual interest in management."

Helen and Brent fell silent as they reflected on their respective relationships with Stanley Wilson. Then Brent said, "If I'm going to be at the plant on Monday, I'd like to go to Scott's office tomorrow to review his files and do some homework over the weekend."

Helen paused as she was suddenly hit with the realization that an outsider would be going through her son's files and would occupy the office that had been her husband's for more than 40 years.

"All right, I'll call Richard and arrange to have the weekend security guard let you into the plant. Scott won't be that happy when he discovers you've gone through his files, but I know you must."

2

● ●

A Nostalgic Return

Enfield was located in buildings that were more than 100 years old and had previously housed the Wilson family's carriage business. The original brick walls, arched windows, high ceilings, and wooden floors were just as they had been when the plant was built. By design, Stanley's unpretentious but comfortable office was far removed from the offices of those who had reported to him.

Brent had not been in this office for almost four years. Although he had once been a frequent visitor, he had never been invited back after Stanley's death. From habit, he sat in the same visitor's chair he had used when he was with Stanley, but now he looked across the table at the empty leather-covered swivel chair and beyond to Stanley's rolltop desk, which sat against one wall. Above it hung the framed quote he had gazed at many times before: "When the great leader's work is done, the people say, 'We did it ourselves.' " Brent stared at it once more.

Mementos were all around the office, and the brick walls were covered with photographs of people and places that had been important to Stanley. The office had the pleasant smell of an old library.

Stanley had been as unconcerned about his surroundings as he was meticulous about his papers, which he never put in drawers. When they weren't in file cabinets, they were visible on the desk, on the table, and even on the floor. The piles of papers on his table were usually in apparent disarray, leaving just enough space for him to work. Even though they were constantly being rearranged, Stanley had an uncanny ability to reach into the middle of a pile and pull out just the paper he wanted. In the far corner of the room, he always had several bulging briefcases, and he usually had one in his hand when he entered or left the building.

Now the paperwork was gone, and the desk and table appeared sadly barren. His clutter had made the office feel comfortable to visitors; it was clearly a working area, without the imposing appearance of many executive offices.

Brent felt strange, as he realized he had never been in this office when Stanley had not been there. Then he stood up slowly and walked around the table. Running his hand across the top of the old leather-covered chair, he thought of Stanley sitting there. Then, with a feeling of irreverence, he sat in his mentor's chair for the first time.

He smiled, thinking of how Stanley had often used the expression, "This is what I would do if I were sitting in your chair." Now Brent was sitting in Stanley's chair, and he asked aloud, "Well, Stanley, what would you do if you were sitting in your chair now?" He answered his own question: "I know what you would do, because you taught me."

Brent settled back against the comfortable leather and stared out at the snow-covered hills. He was confident that he could indeed save Enfield, and it seemed as though his old friend was calling in his marker from beyond the grave and asking Brent for help.

Brent watched the falling snow for several more minutes. Then he swung the chair around to the work table and said to himself, "Well, let's get started."

●●●●●●●●●●●●●●●●●●●●●●●●●●●●●●●●●●●●●

The Team and the Challenge

Brent stopped at the front gate of Enfield. Charlie MacIntyre, the plant guard, who had known Brent ever since he first begain visiting Stanley at Enfield, walked over to the car. "Hello, Brent, it's nice to see you again after so long a time. We've really missed seeing you around here, and I understand you're going to fill in for Scott while he's out sick. I think you'll find that things are running as smoothly as ever at Enfield."

"That's good to hear, Charlie. It's nice seeing you again."

Richard Thompkins was waiting in Stanley's old office when Brent arrived at 7:35. As they shook hands, Brent said, "Richard, it's been a long time."

"Too long, Brent, much too long. The last time I saw you at Enfield, Stanley was still with us. We've really missed him, and I wish he was here now."

For the next few minutes they reminisced pleasantly about the days when Brent was a regular visitor. Then Richard became very serious. "Brent, we're in trouble, and I mean big trouble."

Richard was not prone to exaggeration, and Brent had hoped he would have a more moderate view of the condition of Enfield Manufacturing. He wasn't surprised, however, since he had reviewed Enfield's financial statements over the weekend.

Brent smiled, "Richard, you really know how to cheer up a guy on a cold Monday morning."

"I'm sorry, Brent." Richard replied, and he looked embarrassed.

"I'm pulling your leg, Richard. I would have been surprised if you had said things were going well."

"I spoke to Helen Friday night," Richard said, "and she told me about her conversation with you. Her biggest concern was that if you could only commit to working with us for the next three months, would that really be enough time to do us any good?

"I told her that within three months I believe we will either have filed for bankruptcy or will be well on our way out of trouble. I also indicated that I couldn't think of anyone better qualified than you to save Enfield."

"That's nice of you to say, Richard."

"You know I really mean it. Besides, having you aboard is almost like having the old man back at the helm. Even though you two had extremely different styles, you were very similar in your management philosophy. That's probably why Scott resented you, and this brings to mind a concern I have about the degree of acceptance you'll find here. In spite of our problems, Scott has built up considerable loyalty among some of those in the management group. In addition, he doesn't want to accept the responsibility for our problems and is reluctant to be critical of his own father. This is why he has blamed you indirectly several times in management meetings for the problems we're now having."

Brent stared at Richard in disbelief. "How the hell could Scott accuse me of having anything to do with Enfield's problems?"

"He has suggested that you influenced Stanley to make bad decisions, and now we're paying the price for those decisions."

"That's a bum rap! Stanley and I spent a lot of time talking together, but when the subject was Enfield Manufacturing, I was merely playing devil's advocate. Although I never hesitated to tell him when I disagreed with him, Stanley always made his own decisions."

"But tell me," Brent continued, "how's your relationship with Scott?"

"Oh, we get along well enough because he knows I don't want his job and pose no threat to him. He also knows I'll give my best efforts to implement his decisions, even the ones that are obviously bad. I point these out to him with regularity, but he won't listen to any opinion that's contrary to his own. Stanley made some bad decisions too, but I had considerably more respect for his ability because of his excellent batting average.

"Scott likes to refer to himself as a forward thinker, but as far as I'm concerned that's just a euphemism for being a dreamer. He just won't face reality."

"You sound bitter. That's uncharacteristic of you."

"I suppose I am because in my opinion what has happened to Enfield was totally unnecessary. We had a good company with a respectable history of increasing sales and earnings. Then, in my estimation, we blew it. What has occurred here is our own doing. We've blamed the marketplace, foreign competition, the government, high costs, and everything else except ourselves. The sad truth is that our problems were created within the walls of this plant."

Brent responded, "I would agree with your assessment because in almost all organizations, regardless of size, and no matter how good the product or service, there are usually only five to seven people whose decisions will determine their success or failure."

Richard nodded in agreement and asked, "Brent, how do you plan to start working with us?"

"On Saturday, I started reviewing the financial statements in Scott's files. I'm concerned about your ratios of costs to sales on an overall basis, as well as on each of your product lines, and how costs break down between labor and materials. I'm particularly concerned about the numbers I've seen on your #4000 series of products.

"I'd like to have a breakdown of your fixed manufacturing costs and your overhead costs, including the costs of management, marketing, and sales. For the sales department specifically I'd like to look at your performance reports, to see if your salespeople are meeting their quotas.

"Finally, I want to look at your cash-flow projections for the next 90 days. This will tell me how much tighter your cash may get before we see an improvement."

"I'll have all of that for you by this afternoon."

"Good. Now tell me more about your top management group."

"Well, Mike Cline, the plant manager, is the only one you already know. Then there's Barbara Lansing, our sales manager. She was a sales representative the last time you were here. The other two key people are Gordon Block and Alan Braswell.

"You can depend on Mike and me to be your allies. Mike and Scott are always at cross purposes, so he'll be relieved to have you here."

● ● ● ● ● ● ● ● ● ● ● ● ● ● ● ●
Mike Cline, Plant Manager

"As I remember Mike," Brent commented, "he's about five-seven and built like a tank. He's probably in his late thirties."

"Yes, he's 38, from Scranton, Pennsylvania. His father is a retired steel worker. His wife, Sarah, was his high school sweetheart. They spend a lot of time with their three sons, camping, working with Little League, that sort of thing. Mike worked his way through college at night, has a degree in industrial management, and is extremely self-confident, not intimidated by anyone. He's totally honest, unpretentious, and a hard worker. He's endowed with good common sense and relates well to his people because he came from a background similar to theirs. He's usually dressed in khakis and looks the part of a plant manager. When he wears a suit he seems out of uniform.

"Nevertheless, Mike is quite intellectual, although at first he may not appear to be so because of his manner. He's always working to better himself and his plant operations. He loves what he is doing and says he wouldn't want to go any higher in management if it meant having to leave operations. In summary, he's a solid citizen and a real asset to the company."

● ●

Gordon Block, Vice-President/Administration

"Gordon Block is vice-president in charge of office administration, which encompasses accounting, personnel, purchasing, and the computer operations. You'll like him. He's a nice fellow and enormously popular around the company. He's single, grew up in Baltimore, and graduated with honors from the University of Maryland.

"Some people don't take him very seriously because he's only 29 and looks even younger. He probably has the highest I.Q. of anyone in the group. He's the sort of person who amuses himself by writing computer programs, but I am sometimes concerned about the extent of his common sense. However, this may only be because of his age and lack of experience.

"Gordon probably will feel rather neutral about you being here, but once he determines you can help us, I'm sure he'll be very much on your side."

● ● ● ● ● ● ● ● ● ● ● ● ● ● ● ● ● ● ●

Barbara Lansing, Sales Manager

"Barbara Lansing is loyal to Scott and I believe she'll resent you because of Scott's attitude about the influence he felt you exerted on his father.

"She's very intense, something of a workaholic. She takes strong positions and aggressively defends them; there's seldom any middle ground with her.

"Barbara is extremely effective in dealing with prospects and customers and she had an outstanding record as a sales representative. Scott promoted her to sales manager about two years ago. She has excellent leadership skills, but at first some of the men in the sales department resented answering to a woman. Nevertheless, she soon gained their respect, and she has told me that being a female has not hampered her career.

"Barbara is 38, a graduate of the University of Kentucky with a degree in psychology. Both of her parents are physicians. She told me they were deeply disappointed when she elected not to follow in their footsteps.

"I see her as a complex personality: outgoing, yet private about her personal life. Her husband is a low-key electrical engineer, and she makes no bones about being the more dominant of the two. They have two daughters, and although Barbara is decidedly career oriented, she does a fine job of balancing her career with being a wife and mother.

"Perhaps I should point out Barbara's tendency to be too idealistic. Alan Braswell is the same way. Maybe that's why they get along so well together. They both feel Scott knows what he's doing, and he has them convinced that if Stanley had lived and continued to run the company, Enfield would have soon failed."

Brent asked, "What would you say is Barbara's strongest attribute?"

"I'd say she has two. One is her ability to read the political winds in our customers' organizations and respond accordingly. The other is her flair for assessing the marketplace, and she has come up with some outstanding marketing ideas. That, along with her good sales record, were the reasons Scott promoted her to sales manager."

"Why didn't he make her marketing manager?"

"One of the few things Stanley and Scott ever agreed upon," Richard said as he laughed, "was that we didn't need a marketing manager. As you know, Stanley placed very little value on marketing and felt that the sales manager should handle the responsibility. Scott of course disagreed on this point, and felt he was best qualified to handle the job himself along with his other responsibilities. I remember very well the lively discussions that you, Stanley, and I had

about your strong belief that Enfield needed a full-time marketing manager."

● ●

Alan Braswell, Vice-President/Finance

"That brings us to Alan Braswell, the financial vice-president. Technically, he answers to me, but he started informally answering to Scott when we began the original feasibility study for the #4000 series.

"He's 37 and married to a freelance commercial artist. They have a son and a daughter, both teenagers. Alan graduated with honors from the University of Pennsylvania, then went to the Wharton School of Finance. He's bright enough, perhaps too bright, because he tends to be impatient with people who don't grasp matters as quickly as he does.

"I'm afraid Alan is going to give you some real problems. Helen even thinks we should get rid of him."

"How do you know Helen feels that way?"

"She said so at the hospital on Thursday night. She even said that if it weren't for Alan, Scott might not have had a heart attack."

"As little as she knows about the business, why would she have thought that?"

"After Stanley's death, Scott decided to begin having annual stockholders' meetings with Helen and his sisters right after the end of our fiscal year. He felt this would keep them out of his hair for the remainder of the year, and he wanted Alan and me at the meetings to give him support.

"At our last meeting we had an extremely unfortunate situation. It was partially Scott's fault and partially because of Alan's abrasiveness. The new equipment for the #4000 series had recently been installed, and as a result we were beginning to have profit and cash-flow problems. Scott delegated to Alan the unpleasant task of explaining to his mother and his sisters why we discontinued their dividends.

"Although Helen and her daughter Sandra are low-key, there's absolutely nothing low-key about her daughter Connie. She criticized Alan during the meeting for installing the new equipment and blamed him for Enfield's financial problems. Then the two of them got into an embarrassing argument over the #4000 series. This made Alan look bad because in addition to his abrasiveness, he's somewhat naive about the marketplace. As a result, he did a rather poor job of trying to justify why we installed the new equipment.

"The whole time, Scott sat there like a clam, letting Alan take the heat when the whole project was Scott's idea. Alan's only responsibility for the #4000 series was to orchestrate the financing and installation of the equipment, and I must say he did an excellent job.

"I hope I haven't sounded overly critical of Alan because fundamentally he's a nice fellow, and he has a lot of potential as a manager, but he's undeniably his own worst enemy because of his abrasiveness.

"Scott hired Alan shortly before Stanley's death. By then, Stanley was working only two or three hours a day, and he never really got to know Alan. It's a pity because he could have helped him considerably. I'm sure you can help him if you are able to neutralize his loyalty to Scott.

"I'll say this for Alan. When anyone gives him constructive criticism, he listens and reflects on it. Then, if he agrees, he will respond positively."

"How does Alan get along with the rest of the group?"

"Actually rather well. We all respect his ability and accept and make allowances for his abrasiveness. He gets along particularly well with Barbara and Scott. Scott has given Alan a free rein, and I get the impression that they both believe I'm a conservative old fogey who was hand-molded by Stanley."

Richard glanced at his watch as the members of the management group appeared at the office door. "Enfield has had so many problems and distractions lately that we haven't held regular management meetings, but as you requested, I scheduled one for 8:30."

Brent stood as the members of the management group entered the room. Alan Braswell was the first to introduce himself. "I'm Alan Braswell, Mr. Powell."

"It's nice to meet you, Alan. Please call me Brent."

Gordon Block and Barbara Lansing shook hands with Brent and hesitantly called him "Brent."

Mike Cline smiled warmly as he shook hands. "It's great seeing you again, Brent, and I'm looking forward to working with you. Let me know any way I can help you."

"Thanks, Mike. I appreciate that!"

After everyone was seated, Alan looked at Richard and asked, "How is Scott?"

"I talked to Helen this morning," Richard responded. "The doctors still say it will probably be at least three or four months before he'll be able to work again."

"What do we do in the meantime?" asked Alan, again directing his question to Richard.

Richard was uneasy being the focal point of the meeting, and he shifted the attention to Brent by saying, "The easiest way to answer that question is for Brent to explain why he's here."

"As you probably know," Brent began, "Scott's father and I were close friends, and although I've never known Scott very well, Helen asked me to fill in for him for the next three months."

Disregarding Brent's request to be referred to by his first name, Alan commented, "I mean no offense, Mr. Powell, but you haven't been involved with this business for more than three years. A lot has changed since then, and I'm concerned that by the time you are up to speed, Scott will be back, and all the time you've invested and the time we've invested in you will be to no avail."

Brent responded, "I'm the first to admit I don't know very much about the details of what Enfield is now doing. However, I've discovered that organizations are a lot more alike than they are different, and I believe a good manager can manage anything within reason if he has sufficient resources.

"We should all know very shortly if my presence here is counterproductive. If it is, I'll be the first to admit it, and I'll leave, because I'm not here by desire but at the request of Helen Wilson."

"No offense meant to Mrs. Wilson," Alan continued, "but she isn't close enough to this business to understand our situation."

Brent bristled at Alan's persistence. "Helen may not understand your situation, but she knows Enfield has significant problems as evidenced by the dividends being discontinued."

Alan became defensive. "That proves my point. She doesn't understand how we're being hurt by foreign competition, and how we're having to sacrifice profits, at least over the near term, to become state of the art in our technological capability."

"You may be right, but she is a concerned major stockholder who asked me to do what I can in Scott's absence. Rather than get into a debate at this point about your opinion, which I happen to disagree with, let me describe how I see my role. First, I'm not looking for another job. I already have plenty to keep me busy, and I'll be here for no longer than three months. Second, I'm not a pawn in the hands of Helen Wilson. I have no vested interest in Enfield Manufacturing because I've refused to accept any financial compensation. I'm not on the board, not a stockholder, and not an officer of the company. Although Helen has asked me to temporarily assume Scott's authority, I'm accountable to her and the implementation of any significant decisions I make are subject to her prior approval.

"Even though Helen and Scott's sisters control 55 percent of the stock, they have no interest in meddling in the management of the company. They simply want to protect their interests. My allegiance is to the friendship I had with Stanley, who had told Helen to contact me if she ever felt I was needed.

"Now, I'd like to hear from you. What do you think your problems are?"

Alan quickly responded. "The most immediate problem is in dealing with the pressure from vendors to pay our bills, and from the First Enfield Bank to bring our loan payments current. I'm afraid the bank will call our loan when it discovers that Scott has had a heart attack."

Brent answered calmly, "I don't think the bank will, but let's talk more about that later. What other problems do you have?"

Barbara said, "Alan mentioned foreign competition. I believe that's our biggest problem, particularly with our high-tech products. We're better at marketing, but they're better at producing comparable products at a much lower cost."

Richard added, "Although our sales are up, our costs of sales have gone up even higher. We're losing money, and we're beginning to be in a cash bind."

"Your descriptions of the bank and foreign competition sound like symptoms of the problem," Brent responded, "and are outside the confines of this plant. From my perspective, your problems are within the walls of Enfield, and more specifically, have been caused by some of those within the top management of this company."

"What do you mean by that?" Barbara snapped.

"I don't know of any better way to say it. So let me summarize my view of the current situation here. I don't see Enfield as being in trouble yet, but there are some serious problems that need to be corrected as soon as possible. It's not unusual for organizations to find themselves in this position from time to time. This is particularly true if they've been successful for a sustained period, and then begin suffering from the inertia of this success to the extent that they've gotten complacent and are out of sync with the marketplace.

"Management's job is to recognize and then solve these problems before they grow to the point that the organization is at risk. My focus will be on the solutions, not on the problems themselves or on those who might have caused them. On the contrary, those who cause problems are often the best qualified to solve them because of their familiarity with these situations.

"I believe in addressing the problems managers are having by first looking for less obvious solutions on the inside of their organizations, rather than focusing on the more obvious symptoms of the problems that are found outside of the organizations, which in your case is the pressure from your creditors and from foreign competition.

"I'd been a manager for several years before I learned the *unnatural* wisdom of taking simplistic approaches to most management problems, instead of taking what is basically simple and making it complicated. I believe what we need to do at Enfield should be relatively simple, and with your cooperation, we can and will do it.

"I have to be out of town for the next two days, but Richard is going to meet with you and put together prioritized lists of what you believe should be Enfield's major objectives and the objectives in each of your areas of responsibility. I would also like to know about any significant problems each of you is having, and later I will discuss them with you individually."

Brent was satisfied that with the exceptions of Alan Braswell and Barbara Lansing the group would support him. Whereas Alan had openly disagreed with him on several points, Barbara's criticism was in the form of innuendo, if not outright sarcasm. It was clear to Brent that she was strongly influenced by Scott's bias against him. Brent was concerned that this could make him less effective in working with the group, so as the meeting adjourned he asked Barbara to remain after the others left.

"Barbara, may I assume you're interested in this company getting back on solid ground and that you would like to be a part of making this happen?" he asked.

"Of course," she answered quizzically.

"Fine," Brent said. "From some of your comments during the meeting it appears that you resent my being here, and that's your prerogative, but I'd appreciate a fair chance before you judge me.

"In any event, I want to make my position very clear, and please don't take this as a threat, but as a simple statement of fact. I badly need the help of the entire management group, but if anyone displays an air of resentment toward me to the extent I decide it is counterproductive to our combined efforts, I'll make it my business to get that person out of Enfield Manufacturing."

It was difficult for Brent to read Barbara's reaction, because she stared at him without comment. Then she asked, "Is there anything else?"

"Yes, there's one thing. If you do resent my being here and would care to tell me why, perhaps we can clear the air."

"What I resent is that instead of trying to continue being state of the art in our industry, you want to move us backwards. You say Enfield has problems, and I agree with you, but I believe we're heading for even more problems."

"That's an interesting observation," Brent said. "This is the second time I've heard the expression '*state of the art*' since I've been here. Why is there such a compulsion about this?"

"We have to be state of the art to remain competitive."

"How did you arrive at that conclusion?"

"Scott is convinced of it, and I think he's right."

"What makes you think I would disagree?"

"Scott told me you had convinced his father that we shouldn't spend the money that was necessary to upgrade our capacity, and now we're three years behind the foreign competition."

"For what it's worth, I didn't convince Stanley Wilson. I didn't have to. *He* decided not to spend the money to upgrade the production facilities. The fact that I happened to agree with him is beside the point."

"How could you and Stanley Wilson possibly have justified taking such a radical position?"

"I don't see that position as being radical at all. What Stanley and I both feared would happen, has happened."

"What is that?" she asked curiously.

"By upgrading the equipment, it became necessary to focus your marketing efforts on selling larger orders, which require longer production runs but yield lower profit margins. You can't justify short runs on the newer equipment because of the high set-up costs. You're competing with foreign companies on the larger orders, and this is where they have a solid niche."

"What alternatives do we have?"

"One possibility is to discontinue the #4000 series and continue to penetrate the market that made Enfield successful—the smaller orders from large *and* small customers, where the competition can't touch us. We can fill the needs of these users with our older, smaller equipment, which is paid for, fully depreciated, and has a very low obsolescence factor."

Barbara was still skeptical. "What would happen to our new equipment?"

"We'd sell it. We can probably get almost 60 cents on the dollar of the original costs. As our volume of business increases, we can buy new, smaller equipment."

"But discontinuing the #4000 series will make our profits and cash-flow position even worse."

"Why is that?"

"Because the #4000 series represents 30 percent of our sales volume."

"Yes, but look at the bottom line. There's a big difference between sales volume and profits. I'm sure you're aware that the company is losing a significant amount of money on the #4000 series."

"What makes you think I would be aware of that?"

"By reading the financial statements."

"We don't receive copies of the financial statements."

"Since when?" Brent asked with a surprised look.

"Since Scott took over."

"Well, starting next week you'll have copies, and we'll discuss them in management meetings."

As Barbara rose, Brent said, "Barbara, I hope we'll be able to work together harmoniously."

She left without further comment.

4

● ●

How to Deal with Creditors When You're on the Defensive

After Barbara left, Brent phoned Alan and Richard and asked them to come to his office to discuss the Enfield Bank situation. When they arrived, Brent opened the discussion.

"Alan, you said that your immediate concern is with the bank, and I believe I can help you. Even though the First Enfield Bank has a reputation for being tough on borrowers who get into trouble, I read the loan documents over the weekend, and I'm confident we have the power to deal with the bank effectively."

Alan settled back in his chair. Because of the pressure he and Scott had been getting from the bank, he was relieved that Brent had volunteered to help. Nevertheless, with a hint of sarcasm, he asked if Brent had any suggestions for dealing effectively with the vendors who had been pressuring him to bring their accounts current. Some of them had put Enfield on a C.O.D. basis, and there were others who would no longer even sell to the company.

Brent smiled. "Alan, when you're in financial trouble, vendors are the best source for the equivalent of interest-free loans. They also have short memories. No matter how much pressure they put on you or how mad they may get, if you can keep them in a position where they don't become any worse off by continuing to do business with you, they usually will. This assumes you don't give them any reason to question your character.

"If you convince them they can improve their position by working with you, all the better. They 'shoot themselves in the foot' by cutting you off because you'll go elsewhere and be lost as a customer. This doesn't improve their indebtedness from you, and reduces the chances you'll eventually pay them.

"What you might want to do is to dangle the carrot of improvement in front of them. Every time you place an order, pay for it C.O.D. and also pay a little toward the past due balance until you're current.

"Although I'm convinced I can help buy you some time with the vendors, since our immediate concern is the bank, let's focus on that. After going through the file on the Enfield Bank, I believe it's in a weak collateral position."

Alan interrupted. "How can you say that? The bank has a lien on the equipment that produces the #4000 series, and by foreclosing, it could shut down that part of the business tomorrow."

"Not really. The bank can't just seize the equipment. It has to give us notice of demand for payment of its loan and of its intention to foreclose. If we don't pay, the bank has to go through the process of disposing of the equipment at a fair market value. If we don't receive credit for the fair market value, the bank runs the risk of our filing a lawsuit against it for the difference, so the loan officers probably won't act hastily.

"I've had a lot of dealings with banks. I know our rights and how we can make life unpleasant for them. Banks become very uncomfortable when they have to deal with enlightened borrowers because it eliminates what is usually their biggest weapon."

"What's that?" Alan asked.

"Intimidation. When loans are in trouble, most loan officers use intimidation as a strong weapon. They come at borrowers from an assumed position of power. Acting powerfully is often as good as having power. Borrowers are often the ones with the real power, but they don't realize it, so they lose it by not using it."

Alan argued, "But there's a stand-off if we both think we have the power."

"Your point is well taken," Brent replied. "Let me put it another way. Perceiving you have power very often makes it become reality. I'm suggesting that at the very least we don't let the First Enfield Bank's perception of power become reality."

Alan still argued. "Okay, I'll buy your concept of perception, but how do we have power over the bank when it can foreclose on us? Even if we file for protection under Chapter Eleven of the bankruptcy code, the bank would ultimately prevail."

"Not necessarily. John Maynard Keynes, the British economist, said, 'If you owe your bank a hundred pounds, you have a problem. But if you owe your bank a million, it has a problem.' When a bank is in a position where it will come out significantly less than whole by calling a loan, it has ceased to be your lender and has become your partner. By not cooperating and working with you, the bank only hurts itself.

"Technically, the bank might win by putting us out of business, but it would lose more than it would gain because it would receive only a fraction of the amount we owe.

"Everything I've said assumes the bank will make rational decisions. Therefore, never rub its nose in the plight you've put it in or give it any reason to question your character. If this happens, a bank will tend to act irrationally, and then you're in trouble. Our challenge is to lead the loan officers through logical decisions about how to deal with us."

After discussing the bank situation for the next few minutes, Brent said, "Scott had a note on his calendar to call Paul Harrell at the Enfield Bank today. I think I should call him now while you two are here in case he raises any questions I can't answer."

"Might as well," answered Alan. "We'd better break the news to him about Scott before he hears about it indirectly."

"I agree," Brent responded. "Instead of avoiding a bank when you're in trouble, I've found it's best to go on the offensive and not show any sign of weakness."

Brent dialed Harrell's direct line and when he answered, Brent said, "Mr. Harrell, my name is Brent Powell. I'm doing some work with Enfield Manufacturing. Do you have a minute to talk?"

"Certainly, Mr. Powell. What can I do for you?"

"There's a note on Scott Wilson's calendar to call you today, and I thought I should give you a ring.

"Unfortunately, Mr. Wilson has had a heart attack. It might be several months before he'll be able to work again, and his family has asked me to fill in for him."

There was a pause before Harrell said rather solemnly, "Mr. Powell, I believe we should have a meeting as soon as possible. Can you come to my office this afternoon?"

"Mr. Harrell, since this is my first day at Enfield, my schedule is rather uncertain. Maybe it would be better if you came out here."

Brent smiled to himself as Harrell paused before responding. "Well, er . . . I suppose I could do that. How about around three?"

When Harrell arrived shortly before three, Brent met him in the reception area and escorted him to his office.

"May I call you Paul?" Brent asked as he motioned the banker to the visitor's chair.

"Certainly."

"Would you care for a cup of coffee?"

"No, thanks," Harrell answered stiffly.

Alan and Richard arrived, and after they were seated, Harrell began. "Mr. Powell, my bank is very concerned about the financial condition of Enfield, particularly now that Mr. Wilson is in the hospital. Could you bring me up to date?"

Alan and Richard watched Brent with interest, wondering what he would tell Harrell. Casually, but deliberately, Brent leaned back in his chair, stared at Harrell for a few seconds, then said very seriously, "Paul, I can't believe how bad things are here at Enfield, and I'm not sure we're going to make it."

Harrell leaned forward and said, "But just last week Mr. Wilson said the company was doing better."

"You were either misinformed, or Mr. Wilson doesn't view the situation as I do."

Harrell found himself on the defensive and attempted to establish a position of power. "Mr. Powell, three months ago my bank agreed to give Enfield Manufacturing a moratorium on the principal payments on our loan with the understanding that the company would keep the interest payments current. Now the interest payments are in arrears, and as a minimum I must insist that these payments are brought current immediately."

Brent was aware that the company did not have the available cash, but he turned to Alan and asked, "Can we give Paul a check to cover our past due interest payments?"

Alan felt Brent had put him on the spot and he answered uneasily, "I really don't see any way that we can and still have enough cash to meet the payroll next Tuesday."

Brent turned back to Harrell and said calmly, "I'm sorry, Paul, but we just can't do it, and I haven't been here long enough to determine when, or even if, we will be able to bring your loan current."

In a tone of implied threat, Harrell said, "I'm afraid that when I report this to my loan committee, they'll decide to call your loan and start foreclosure proceedings."

Without a hint of concern Brent responded, "Paul, I can fully appreciate your position, and I realize you must do what you believe is best for the bank."

There were several seconds of awkward silence as Harrell waited for Brent to continue, but Brent volunteered nothing further.

"Is that all you have to say?" Harrell asked, now somewhat irritated.

"I guess so."

"But if we foreclose and pull out your new equipment, won't that be the end of Enfield Manufacturing?"

"Not really. If you call the loan, we'll have to file for Chapter Eleven under the bankruptcy act. Then we'll have 120 days to present a plan to the bankruptcy court. By the time we go through the whole process, I suppose we could buy ourselves a year to restructure and downsize the company. As for the new equipment, we're already seriously considering discontinuing the product line being run on that equipment and then selling the equipment."

Brent glanced at Richard and Alan, who were enjoying this performance immensely. They had never seen a banker squirming the way Harrell was now.

Harrell was back on the defensive as he said, "Mr. Powell, you have characterized a rather severe resolution of this problem. Don't you think we would all be better off if we worked out something more amicable than having this problem resolved in the bankruptcy court?"

"An amicable solution might be better for both your bank and those at Enfield. But speaking for myself, since I'm not receiving any compensation from Enfield and don't have any vested interest, bankruptcy might be the quickest and cleanest way to wrap things up so I can get about my other business."

Harrell looked defeated as he sank back in his chair, and said. "What would you recommend that we do?"

Brent remained silent for several seconds, allowing the tension to build. Finally he said, "I plan to be here approximately three months. I'll give you a written report every two weeks on the status of the company. If during this period our condition improves to the extent we can begin paying the interest on the loan and perhaps start reducing the principal, I'll let you know."

Paul Harrell stood up. "I can't give you much encouragement, but I'll talk to my loan committee and get back to you with our decision."

By the time Harrell had left the office, Alan and Richard were ecstatic. Alan laughed. "Did you see Harrell's face drop when you told him we were considering discontinuing the #4000 series and selling the equipment? I believe he thinks you were serious."

"I was. After looking at your operating statements over the weekend, my opinion is that we should consider discontinuing the series."

"But we can't do that!" Alan exclaimed angrily.

"Give me a break, Alan. This is my first day here, and you'll have ample time to express your views before a decision is made."

Later in the afternoon, Paul Harrell called Brent to inform him that the bank would agree to give Enfield Manufacturing another moratorium of up to 90 days on the principal and interest payments, with the understanding that Brent would supply the bank with a status report on the company every two weeks.

TWO

The Focal Point of Management

5

• •

How to Conduct Efficient and Effective Meetings

After the management group had convened in Brent's office at nine, Brent said, "Richard indicated that because of some of your problems, and because you've been so busy, you haven't been meeting regularly. This may seem natural, but I believe it's important for an organizational group to meet regularly no matter how much pressure you may be under."

"I really don't agree," Alan said bluntly. "I've found that most of our meetings have been a waste of time, and even though I stay well organized, a lack of time is my single biggest problem. Being interrupted by having to go to a lot of meetings only compounds my problem."

The group looked to see how Brent would react to being challenged. "Alan," he answered calmly, "I believe most managers would say that their biggest problem is a lack of time. However, I don't see this as the problem, but rather a symptom. The real problem is not handling their management jobs effectively."

Alan became defensive. "You have no way of knowing whether I'm effective or not."

"For all I know you are, but you said you were well organized, which only has to do with being efficient. It doesn't necessarily mean

35

that you're effective. Given a choice, I'd rather be effective than efficient."

Richard supported Brent's position by saying, "Alan, a good example of this was when we installed our first automated production line. Although the system was operating efficiently, it wasn't effective. Many of the products coming off the line were defective and had to be manually reworked at a significant cost."

Brent continued, "Alan, you also mentioned how busy you are. I've found that being busy is an enemy of effectiveness, and the old cliche 'I'm so busy I can't think' is very true in the case of too many managers."

Richard then tried to relieve the tension that was building between Brent and Alan by recalling an incident that had occurred shortly after he joined the company. "One day I was alone in my office wondering how I should deal with a particularly troublesome personnel problem. I was leaning back in my chair, staring out of the window, with my feet propped up on my desk. All of a sudden Stanley walked in and caught me by surprise. I was embarrassed, and when I apologized, Stanley asked if I was thinking about my work or just staring out of the window. When I told him I was thinking about my work, *he* apologized for interrupting me, and told me to put my feet up on the desk and get back to work."

Brent smiled and said, "Most managers could be more effective if they would allocate more time for creative thinking, which in your case was while you were staring out of the window with your feet on your desk.

"I recognized thinking as a component of my job after attending IBM's sales training program in Endicott, New York. Each morning I walked up five steps into the Department of Education building. A word had been chiseled into the stone on the riser of each step and embossed in gold:

Read
Listen
Discuss
Observe
Think

"I read those words every morning as I entered the building. Later, when I became a manager and reflected on these words, I realized that they describe the most effective use of a manager's time.

"Reading, listening, discussing, and observing are all communications into our minds. However, learning only takes place when we take the time to *think* about what we've read, listened to, discussed, and observed.

"You're in this room today, because somewhere along the line you've done some heavy-duty thinking. I'm not suggesting that any of you have lost this capacity, but rather that some of you have perhaps been diverted from the very important thinking component of your job.

"Many businesses fail, not because of a lack of money, but because of the lack of new ideas. This doesn't necessarily just apply to new products or services, but perhaps more importantly to coming up with ideas about how to improve our existing products or services in order to remain competitive.

"I believe that managers who assume the philosophy of, 'If it ain't broke, don't fix it,' are courting disaster. As a constant reminder of this, when I was the CEO of my own business, I had a clipping under the glass on my desk that read: 'Everything this company is now producing is going to be produced differently and better in the future, and if we don't do it, our competition will.'"

Alan appeared more amicable as he said, "Your point about creative thinking-time makes sense, and I'm trying to block out more time for it, but meetings are a different matter. I still believe that much of the time each of us spend in meetings could be better spent doing our own work."

"As Alan suggested," Brent continued, "meetings can be a great waste of time, and I share his aversion to those that are. Nevertheless, effective meetings can provide the best forum for good communications between managers and their people."

Barbara asked, "Would you call it a meeting when two people talk to each other in the hallway about business?"

"I would if you accept that a meeting is simply an act or process of coming together to communicate, and I believe conversations in hallways, break rooms, and other ad hoc sessions are perhaps the ones that are the most productive for implementing objectives. Even a telephone call could be considered a meeting. The important thing is to have a meeting of the minds among those who can make a contribution."

Brent then passed out copies of a meeting agenda. "I believe the key to effective regular meetings is to develop an agenda that provides for flexibility. The jobs of managers in all organizations are more alike than they are different. Therefore, the subjects covered in meetings at all levels of management tend to be more alike than different. As a result, I believe you will find that this generic agenda can be fine-tuned to meet our needs, as well as the needs of almost any organizational meeting."

● ● ● ● ● ● ● ● ● ● ● ● ● ● ●

A Generic Meeting Agenda

I. Status of Existing Objectives
    A. Compared to our plans, what is our status in the achieving of our existing objectives?
    B. To what extent are our assumptions still valid?
        1. What is our current assessment of the risk involved?
    C. What additional resources will be required to achieve our objectives? How should these resources be organized?
    D. Who will be responsible for continuing to pursue the various components of our objectives?
        1. Have we obtained their commitments to assume these responsibilities?
        2. Is it clear how much authority they will have over our resources in order to discharge their responsibilities?
    E. When should our objectives be achieved?
    F. What recommendations do we have for altering or aborting our objectives and/or our plans for achieving them?
    G. Are there any changes that we should make in the priority sequence of achieving our objectives?
II. Discussion of Proposed Objectives
    A. Description of the objectives
    B. What are the recommended plans for achieving the proposed objectives?
    C. What are the assumptions?
        1. What is our assessment of the risk involved?
    D. What available resources will our plans require, and how should these resources be organized?
    E. Who would be responsible for pursuing the various components of the proposed objectives?
        1. How can we obtain their commitments to achieve these responsibilities?

      2. How much authority should they have over our re-
sources in order to discharge these responsibilities?
  F. How can we monitor and control the achievement of the
proposed objectives?
      1. To whom should our progress be reported?
      2. Where should we establish check points to measure our
progress compared with where we planned to be at those
points?
      3. What action should we take, if any, if we are off schedule
at these check points?
  G. When should the proposed objectives be achieved?
  H. Where should the proposed objectives fall within the priority sequence of our present objectives?

III. Staffing
  A. Are there any recommended changes in personnel respon-
sibilities?
  B. Are there any recommended promotions?
  C. Are there any recommended additions?
  D. Are there any personnel problems that should be brought
before this group?
  E. Are we highly vulnerable to losing anyone in our group?
If so,
      1. Should we consider cross-training to deal with this?
      2. Should we consider reorganizing responsibilities?
  F. What is being done, and what are our plans, for the contin-
ued training and further development of our associates?
  G. Are there any recommendations for terminating any em-
ployees?

IV. Communications
  A. What needs to be and/or should be communicated?
      1. Within our management group
      2. To those outside the group
        a. Within the organization
        b. Outside the organization

"Although the chairman can always extend the meeting," Brent
added, "a specific amount of time should be allocated. With a time
limitation, the meeting will move more briskly, and there'll be a tendency for participants to be more attentive and stick to the agenda.

● ● ● ● ● ● ● ● ● ● ● ● ● ● ● ● ●

An Effective Planning Process

Brent said, "The managerial function of planning is as important, if not more important, than establishing objectives. During the planning process you determine if you have an achievable objective, a viable plan, and develop a conviction about achieving the objective.

"When you have established the right objectives, effective strategic planning enables you to achieve them with a sufficient amount of your resources, which are: your people, money, time, and information, as well as your physical resources.

"The other managerial functions of organizing, staffing, communicating, developing, and monitoring and controlling are tactical in nature and are used primarily to implement planning. Therefore, if you establish the right objectives, how well you develop your plans usually determines the degree of success.

"This is why participation in the planning process is as important as participation in establishing the right objectives."

Richard asked, "Brent, could we take a hypothetical objective and follow the sequence of the planning steps to achieve it?"

"All right. Let's say that this year we estimate our sales will be $24 million, and for next year we establish an objective of $30 million.

"In the planning process, I've found it very effective to address these eight major planning questions in formulating almost any plan:

Eight Major Planning Questions

1. *Where are we now?*

   Our sales are now approximately $2 million a month, or $24 million a year.

2. *Where will we be at the end of our next fiscal year if we follow our present path?*

   Based on our current momentum, our sales will remain at $24 million.

3. *Where do we want to be?*

   We want to increase our sales to $30 million. The difference between our results if we follow our present path and those if we successfully implement our plan is known as the *planning gap*.

4. *What resources will be required to achieve the objective, and how will this impact the achieving of our other objectives?*

   The answer to this important question will indicate whether or not we can afford to implement the plan. If we can't, we'll either have to modify or abort our objective. In our example, increasing our sales volume from $24 million to $30 million might require additional salespeople at a cost of $500,000 and additional equipment at a cost of $4 million. The added working capital required to cover the increase in accounts receivable generated by the additional sales will be $1,000,000.

5. *When will we achieve our objective?*

   The biggest problem I've encountered in planning is not allowing for the high cost of time. Not achieving an objective on time is very often the cause of the failure. You should have a target date for completion and a timetable for where you *expect to be* at various times during the process. If you're not meeting your schedule, reevaluate your plans and your resources immediately to make sure the objective is still feasible.

6. *Who is going to carry out the plan?*

   Obtain firm commitments from those who will have specific responsibilities. If there is any question about who has these responsibilities, it is extremely doubtful that they'll be handled.

7. *What will the implementation of our plans require in the way of human, financial, time, information, and physical resources?*

   Being realistic about costs is an important consideration. Always estimate costs on a worst case basis by allowing for any contingencies that might occur. Then, ask the last and most important question:

8. *Is the overall plan practical?*

   Can we realistically accomplish the objective, or will we have to modify or abort it?

   "Before we leave the subject of planning, there's an ironic aspect I'd like to mention.

   "The process of planning is often more important than the plan itself. By addressing these eight questions you can usually determine if the objective is practical. If it is, the plan itself is like a procedure manual for achieving the objective.

"Until things are running more smoothly, I'd like to meet with you for 45 minutes on Monday mornings at nine and on Wednesday and Friday afternoons at four. This totals two hours and 15 minutes and represents no more than 5 or 6 percent of a 40-hour work week. I believe we'll find this to be a good investment of our time."

"I still don't see what we are going to find to talk about in all of these meetings," Alan argued.

"In addition to following the generic agenda we'll discuss how to think about management the right way and how we can manage ourselves, our people, and our other managerial resources. In these sessions we can also cover any of your specific personnel problems.

"Between these scheduled meetings, any of us can get together to discuss matters requiring immediate attention or those that wouldn't be of particular interest to the rest of the group."

A few minutes later, the meeting adjourned. Brent walked to the window and looked at the distant hills. He was beginning to feel confident that he would be able to turn Enfield around with the present management staff if he could overcome the resentment from Alan Braswell and Barbara Lansing toward him.

He decided that on Monday he would tell them about the two most important management lessons he had ever learned.

· ·

THREE

The Secret of Becoming a Better Manager

• •

What Is Management, and When Are You Managing?

Brent opened the meeting. "Today I'd like to discuss how managers can become more effective by developing a better understanding of the management process."

Alan was visibly irritated. "Isn't it a little late in the game for this group to start learning what management is all about? In my opinion, unless you're a natural born manager like Stanley Wilson, you either learn how to manage on the job or you learn it in school. I worked hard to get an M.B.A. at Wharton, and now you want us to start all over learning how to manage."

Brent was concerned about the tension between himself and Alan. He would not allow Alan to intimidate him, yet he didn't want to inhibit or embarrass Alan by being critical of him in front of his peers. So he smiled deliberately and said, "It's funny you should refer to Stanley as a natural-born manager. I made the mistake of characterizing him that way once when we were talking. I meant it as a compliment, but my remark irritated him. He let me know that he was not a natural-born manager but had worked hard to become a good manager. He felt that very few people are born with an aptitude for doing what is *unnatural,* but necessary, in order to become an effective manager.

"Stanley took the position that you can learn to become a good manager, but you learn by managing, not by going to school. He was in favor of education as a good background but believed that too much schooling can so precondition a person that it becomes more difficult to learn management as a profession. He said that you learn to play the game only by playing, but how well and how quickly you learn the fundamentals determine how well you will play."

Brent lifted the glass top of the work table and removed a slip of paper. "Stanley often referred to this quotation from John O'Toole's book, *The Trouble with Advertising.*"

Brent read aloud, "Every human activity, whether fruitful or frivolous, can be reduced to fundamental steps so that those who do it well and almost instinctively can teach it to those who don't. The latter group may never attain the perfection of the former; then again, they may. But it all begins with fundamentals."

Barbara said, "You referred to management as a profession. Several friends and I once had a discussion about whether management really is a profession, and we finally came to the conclusion that it isn't."

"I don't agree." Brent countered. "The biggest mistake I ever made as a manager was not recognizing management as a profession. A profession is an organized body of knowledge, and I looked at management as nothing more than common sense, dealing primarily with practicing good human relations. I'd been very successful in sales, and sales came naturally for me. I assumed that being successful in management would involve nothing more than following the same successful sales practices."

"What were some of those practices?" Barbara asked.

"Being very much 'hands-on,' keeping up with a lot of details, being high profile, and spending a lot of time face to face with prospects and customers, persuading them to follow me down a predetermined path where I wanted them to go.

"One definition of leadership is that it's an ingredient of personality that causes others to follow. Based on my sales record, I apparently had that ingredient.

"After I became a manager, I continued to practice this hands-on style, and it almost destroyed me before I learned some effective management practices that were unnatural for me. I found later that they are unnatural for most managers.

"Effective management is often unnatural for us because it's contrary to human nature. It's natural for us to produce results ourselves. It's *unnatural* for us to decide to produce results through others, especially if we're better qualified to produce them. It's *un-*

natural to work at giving others credit for the good results we've orchestrated, and take the blame for the bad results which may not have been our fault, but were our responsibilities.

"It also seems unnatural to me that the best way for us to leverage our human resources is to further develop our own management skills. The best way to learn anything is to teach it, and the best way to teach management is by our own example as role models.

"I learned from Stanley's example that if I wanted to get more leverage out of those who answer to me, I should focus my efforts on further developing myself.

● ●

Two Vital Lessons for Becoming More Effective

"Now I'd like to tell you about an incident that changed my life, and the end of the story took place in this very room."

Brent described his chance meeting with Stanley Wilson on the commuter train, and then continued, "Two weeks after we met, I called Stanley, not knowing if he would even remember me. However, he seemed pleased to hear from me and invited me to visit him here at Enfield.

"On that first visit, I sat across this table from him in that same chair Gordon is sitting in. We talked for a few minutes, and then Stanley asked me what he could do for me.

"I reminded him that on the train he had said I could be an effective manager when I learned that management is an unnatural act and then he quoted: 'When the great leader's work is done, the people say, "We did it ourselves."'

"I told Stanley he had convinced me that good management is an *unnatural* process, but my frustration was that I didn't know where to begin learning what I needed to know.

"Stanley then stood and walked to that window, and he looked out at the hills. Later I found he often did this when he was deep in thought or in a serious discussion. Then he turned and looked at me for a few seconds as though he had something to say, but wasn't sure he should say it.

"Finally he said, 'Young man, I'm going to tell you about two management lessons that can be used as the framework for becoming an effective manager. Most managers never learn these lessons, and they are so simple there's a good chance you will ignore them, as have others. That's why there aren't more good managers. The first lesson is to develop an understanding of what management *really* is, and the second lesson is to learn to recognize when you're managing and when you're not.'

"When Stanley told me this, I was disappointed, because I'd expected something more profound, and you may have the same reaction. Nevertheless, these were the most important management lessons I ever learned."

Brent seemed a little embarrassed, as if he had overdramatized this session with Stanley and had expressed something more personal than he had intended, so he quickly asked, "Who would volunteer a description of management?"

Gordon said, "The classic one seems to be that management is getting things done through people."

Brent responded, "That is the classic definition, but I believe it is misleading. Consider this: the objective of management is not just getting things done, the challenge is to get the *right* things done.

"For example, an Egyptian Pharaoh had an objective of wanting a burial site, so he used a force of 100,000 slaves over a period of 20 years to build a pyramid 40 stories high, with a base the size of eight football fields. The Pharaoh was 'getting things done through people,' although it is arguable that it was the right thing, when you consider that in less than a day, one grave digger with a shovel could have provided a place for the Pharaoh to be buried.

"As for getting things done 'through people,' people represent only one of the managerial resources, so to say that management is getting things done through people is like saying that the game of football is only kicking field goals. That's just a part of the game.

"I have adopted Stanley's description of management," Brent continued, as he passed out copies of the following:

> Management is a mental process
> of establishing, and then indirectly achieving, the right objectives
> in the right priority sequence
> with a sufficient amount of resources.

"The whole process is decision based. We decide what we believe are the right objectives, and then we make decisions about how to achieve them. Managers and organizations succeed or fail based on the quality of these decisions.

● ●

Recognizing Management as a Bifocal Process

"The two strategic management functions of establishing new objectives and planning how to achieve these objectives have to do with the work of tomorrow. Achieving existing objectives has to do with the work of today. Therefore, we could say that management is a 'bifocal' process. Think of bifocal eyeglasses. Their purpose is to assist us in seeing what is up close as well as what is in the distance. Managers have to deal simultaneously with the work of today, which is up close, and the work of tomorrow, which is in the distance.

"Stanley used to say that although the most important part of managers' work is dealing with what will happen tomorrow, the most demanding part of their job is dealing with what's happening today. Those attention-getting details that come up daily often make it difficult for managers to keep their noses to the grindstones of today while keeping their eyes on the hills of tomorrow.

"Stanley said he was glad to be able to look out of the window and see the hills in the distance because it was a constant reminder of where his most important focus should be.

"Whereas the two strategic management functions that deal primarily with tomorrow's work are establishing objectives and planning how to achieve those objectives, the other five management functions are more tactical in nature and have to do with both tomorrow and today:

- Organizing your resources
- Staffing
- Communicating
- Monitoring and controlling the achievement of objectives
- Further developing your associates

"I break down the managerial resources into five categories. There are *people*: both inside and outside the organization, as well as the managers themselves, when they're not managing.

"Then there is *money*: the money we generate internally, and what we have available from outside creditors, such as banks. We also have the equivalent of interest-free loans from vendors from the time we receive their materials and services until we pay for them.

"*Physical assets* are the third resource: our plant, equipment, and inventory.

"The fourth resource is *time*: your own time when you aren't managing, and the time of others. Time is also a resource as the measurement of the time frame available to achieve an objective.

"And last there is *information*. Until a few years ago, managers were starved for more information. Now the problem is just the opposite—we suffer from information overload."

Richard commented, "In our meeting on Friday, you said that the jobs of managers in all organizations are more alike than they're different. This discussion supports that view. Think about it. Managers in most organizations establish objectives and then go about achieving them, using the same types of resources. The managers perform the same functions and have many of the same challenges in dealing with human relations.

"Managers should feel secure in knowing that management skills are transportable, and if any of you decide to leave Enfield you can take these skills with you."

Mike smiled. "Richard, are you trying to get rid of us?"

"Not at all, Mike. I'm simply trying to point out the value of continuing to develop your management skills, and that your real job security comes from these skills you possess; and it's not dependent on Enfield or any other organization if you're an effective manager."

● ●

How to Recognize When You Are Managing and When You Are Not

"The second vital management lesson I learned from Stanley during our first meeting," Brent said "is that another *unnatural* aspect of management is that although we're ultimately judged on our results, when we're managing we aren't producing results directly. We're only managing when we're producing results indirectly through our managerial resources."

Barbara interrupted. "To say that when we're managing we aren't producing results directly sounds a little ridiculous."

"In what respect?"

"When I personally call on some of our larger accounts and make sales, I'm certainly producing results."

Brent said, "Yes, (but) you aren't managing. You're performing the function of a salesperson." He then set a trap. "Why do you make sales calls?"

Barbara fell into the trap without hesitation. "Because I feel I'm better qualified than any of my people."

"Then why don't you get rid of your salespeople and make all the calls yourself?"

Barbara did not offer a reply, and she knew one was not expected. She had needled Brent again, and he had put her down.

Brent said to Barbara, "Asking yourself who is best qualified to make sales calls is natural. But I suggest that as a sales manager you should do what is *unnatural* and ask, 'Who *should* make the calls?' It should rarely be you, except to observe your salespeople or to coach them in their skills.

"Barbara, you and I both came from sales backgrounds. When I started my company, I hated sitting behind a desk. It was more natural for me to be out of my office selling more business, because I felt that's where the action was, and I naively assumed that selling was a part of my management job. Later I found that being a good salesperson and a lousy manager is a dangerous combination."

● ●

A Good Manager Can Manage Anything (with Sufficient Resources)

Alan asked, "When you gave us your description of management, why did you emphasize achieving objectives with a *sufficient* amount of resources?"

"Because of the dramatic and very important difference between what is *sufficient* and what is *enough*. *Sufficient* suggests a close meeting of a need. Even bad managers can achieve difficult objectives if they have enough resources. However, many organizations with enough resources often dissipate them to the extent that they are no longer sufficient. Then, they usually file for bankruptcy.

"Although many managers would disagree, I believe good managers can manage anything within reason *if* they have sufficient resources. Without sufficient resources managers can't achieve their objectives, no matter how good they are."

"How about Lee Iacocca when Chrysler was in trouble?" Gordon asked.

"How about him?" Brent responded. "As a good manager, Iacocca had a clear objective of obtaining sufficient resources. He might not have had as many resources as he would have liked, but they were nevertheless sufficient."

"Yes, but if the government hadn't loaned Chrysler a sufficient amount of money to continue to operate, the company wouldn't have made it," Gordon argued.

"You're right, but remember that the managerial resource of money includes that from creditors, which was the United States government in the case of Chrysler."

"How do you decide what constitutes sufficient resources?" Barbara asked.

"That's part of the *art* of management. What's sufficient for one manager may not be for another, even when they're both good managers. As a general rule, you might say the better the manager, the fewer the resources required to be sufficient."

"Wouldn't that always be so?"

"Not necessarily. Some managers' greatest talent lies in achieving maximum leverage out of a minimum amount of resources, including those that are borrowed, as with Iacocca. Other managers get good results but require greater resources.

"Perhaps the most dramatic examples are those managers in the military during warfare, who are better known as combat generals. In the military they use the expression '*economy of forces*,' which is the equivalent of sufficient resources for managers in nonmilitary types of organizations. For instance, Union Army General Ulysses S. Grant was well known for his high rate of casualties compared to that of other combat generals during the Civil War."

"I can see how sufficient resources differ from manager to manager," Barbara said, "but you still haven't answered my question about what is sufficient."

"Barbara, I don't mean to hedge, but managers can't really quantify what is sufficient, they can only estimate. That's why when we discussed the process of planning, I urged you to always estimate the cost of your resources on a worst-case basis with a reasonable margin for contingencies. By doing so, if you don't believe you will have sufficient resources, you have the opportunity to alter or abort the objectives before embarking on a plan to achieve them.

"Even after embarking on the plan, you should continue to overestimate, within reason, the resources required to complete the plan.

Then you can alter the plan as necessary to conform to the amount of resources you have or are willing to commit."

● ●

Forget Your Optimism When Making Projections

"But isn't the management job simplified by having computers make some of the decisions?" Gordon asked.

"Computers don't make management decisions—only managers make them. Computers often only complicate the process by turning out so much information that the manager's greatest challenge is to determine what is relevant."

"It sounds like you have a bias against computers," Alan observed.

"Alan, I was in the computer services business for several years, and my bias is not against computers but rather against managers who substitute computers for the exercise of their own good judgment.

"Managers become menaces when they believe their projections are preordained to happen just because they come out of the computer in the form of neat little printouts.

"The computer has made it extremely simple for managers to obtain printouts of financial projections on new or proposed projects. So what happens? Take the #4000 series. I looked at the financial projection on the first computer printouts. They showed conservative sales and cost figures, and the projection showed a loss. The next computer printout showed more optimistic estimates of sales and cost, and the projection then showed a profit, so Scott went with that projection."

"They weren't my projections," Gordon argued. "I just ran the numbers that Alan gave to Scott."

"Hell, Gordon," Alan bristled, "I gave Scott a range of projected costs, and he gave you the ones on the low side. If you look at the actual costs, you'll find my projections on the high side were correct."

"So much for the costs side," Brent continued. "Even on the sales side, the actual sales of the #4000 series don't bear any resemblance to what was projected."

"Those sales projections came from Scott, not from me," Barbara protested.

"Wait a minute," Brent interrupted. "I'm not trying to start a family squabble here. My point is that making unrealistic financial projections has been a managerial problem that existed before anyone ever heard of a computer, and the ease of obtaining computerized financial projections has only compounded the problem.

"As *unnatural* as it is for most of us in management, we should opt for conservatism, and within reason, overestimate costs and underestimate sales.

"I'm sorry if I'm touching some raw nerves, but here's something else that was interesting. Some of the projections I found on the #4000 series were dated just prior to the installation of the new equipment. A few were dated just after the equipment was installed. Then, they stopped abruptly about the time it became obvious the #4000 series was losing money.

"This might be a symptom of what I refer to as the 'ostrich syndrome' among managers: making projections as long as they remain optimistic but burying their heads in the sand and ceasing to make projections when things start turning sour. When this is the case, managers are beginning to confuse stubbornness with persistence.

●●●●●●●●●●●●●●●●●●●●●●●●●●●●●●●●●●

How to Avoid Confusing Stubbornness with Persistence

"When we commit to what we believe are worthwhile objectives, and then during the implementation process we discover that we're not achieving these objectives as planned, we should take the unnatural approach of making even more projections than we do when things are going well.

"By doing so, there's less danger that we'll confuse stubbornness with persistence and be guilty of pursuing objectives beyond the point when they should have been altered or aborted."

Mike looked disturbed. "You just described what I did on a project last year. I spent several weeks trying to work out a way to use a smaller motor to improve the efficiency of our #2000 series. I finally gave up. In looking back, I realized I was being stubborn and just wasting my time."

Brent laughed and quoted W. C. Fields, "'If at first you don't succeed, try again. . . . Then give up. . . . There's no sense in being a damn fool about it.' Mike, there's a fine line between stubbornness and persistence. Persistence is only an activity and doesn't mean a thing if it doesn't produce results."

Barbara added, "My sales experience has taught me a lot about stubbornness. Since sales performance is clearly measurable, the price of being stubborn is painfully obvious.

"Our primary objective in sales is to convert prospects into customers. We prioritize the prospects in sequence of importance to us, and then we persistently try to convert them into customers. However, when our persistence develops into stubbornness, we make fewer sales."

Brent responded, "Salespeople and managers who stubbornly pursue objectives beyond the point when they should be abandoned are hurting themselves and the organization. What appeared to be the right objectives have become the wrong objectives. This is why I emphasized pursuing the right objectives in my description of management.

"When our egos are involved, we tend to confuse stubbornness with persistence, but we can learn to recognize the difference by prioritizing our objectives and then continuously keeping them updated. We should be our own worst critics by always questioning if the pursuit of any of our objectives has turned counterproductive, because in the competitive marketplace there's very little margin for being martyrs in the pursuit of lost causes.

"Don't get me wrong. I'm a great believer in persistence, and I subscribe to the message in that quote over there on the wall."

Brent read:

NOTHING CAN TAKE THE PLACE OF PERSISTENCE
Nothing in the world can take
the place of persistence...
Talent will not; nothing is more
common than unsuccessful
men with talent...
Genius will not; unrewarded
genius is almost a proverb.
Education will not; the world
is full of educated derelicts.
Persistence and determination
alone are omnipotent. The
slogan "press on" has solved,
and will always solve, the
problems of the human race.

● ●

When Your Managerial Authority Is Challenged

Brent was doing paperwork in his office when Mike phoned.

"Brent," he said, "I need to talk to you and find out just who the hell I'm supposed to report to."

"Take it easy, Mike. I'll be right down."

When Brent arrived, Mike was visibly upset as he said, "Richard is telling me to do one thing, Scott Wilson is telling me to do just the opposite, and I'm damned tired of it."

"But Scott isn't here."

"Yeah, but he still has a telephone. He calls every day asking questions about the plant and about what I'm producing on the line. Then he always tells me to do something different.

"I told Scott that by changing my priorities, I'm going against what Richard and I agreed to, but Scott says he's still president of Enfield and what he says goes. So far I've been able to keep both Richard and Scott satisfied, but it's taking a lot of overtime, and I'm about to come apart at the seams. When Richard sees the overtime report next week, he'll give me hell."

"What has Scott been telling you to do that's contrary to what you and Richard have agreed on?"

"Scott always wants to give the highest priority to the larger accounts who buy the #4000 series. He treats our older, smaller accounts like stepchildren. They don't like it, and I don't either."

"Have you told Richard about your calls from Scott?"

"No, Scott asked me not to tell Richard that he's been calling me, but he didn't say anything about not telling you. He probably figured I wouldn't go over Richard's head, and I wouldn't have, except that I'm at the end of my rope."

"Mike, this may sound complicated, but like many management problems, it has a fairly simple solution.

"I promise you that we are going to keep the lines of communication open at Enfield. You and I can talk, you and Scott can talk, or you and anyone else can talk, but as long as you answer to Richard, he's the only one who has the authority to redirect your efforts. This includes Scott, me, or anyone else who might try to come between you and Richard."

"But what do I tell Scott?"

"You can quote me verbatim. If Scott has a problem with what I said, tell him to call me."

"Thanks, Brent. I appreciate that, but there will be some fireworks the next time Scott calls."

"Don't worry about it. Let me deal with the problem, because I don't want you to be caught in the middle."

Shortly after Brent returned to his office, Richard called, and the anger in his voice was out of character.

"Brent, I just received a call from Scott that we need to discuss."

"Okay, how about now?"

"I'll be there immediately."

"I can guess what this is about," Brent said to himself as he hung up the phone.

"Have a seat, Richard," Brent said when Richard appeared at his door a few moments later, but Richard remained standing.

"I'd like to know what's going on," he demanded. "I just learned that Scott and Mike are talking to each other, you and Mike are talking to each other, and now Scott just informed me that he will fire me if I don't follow his production priorities. I'm not intimidated by Scott, and I won't miss any meals if he fires me. However, if he does, I don't believe it will help matters at Enfield, particularly since you've been here less than two weeks."

"Calm down, Richard. Why don't you sit down, and let's talk about it?"

Richard then took a seat as Brent continued. "My advice is that you listen to Scott when he calls, then do exactly what *you* think is best.

As long as I'm here and you are the executive vice-president, no one is going to preempt the final authority you have over production."

"Yeah," Richard said, "but when Scott comes back you can bet that he'll take Mike and me to task for 'blowing the whistle' on him by going to you."

"I don't believe you'll have to worry about that because based on what Helen told me, Scott won't be coming back."

Richard looked shocked. "Do you mean he may not recover from his heart attack?"

"No, it isn't that. Helen and Scott's sisters recognize his managerial deficiencies and the harm he's done to the company, and they don't want him back."

"Are you going to take over as president?"

"I don't think so, Richard, I have other things I want to do."

"Well, it won't be me. I wouldn't have the job, but you already know that."

"You've made that very clear. But now that the subject has come up, who do you think should replace Scott?"

Richard responded, "In my opinion, we don't have anyone in the company who's appropriate for the position, so we'll have to look elsewhere."

"I'm inclined to agree. Do you have anyone in mind?"

"No, but I can contact some headhunters, and they can put out their feelers."

"Let's hold off on that until we know for sure what Helen decides to do about Scott. In the meantime, try to keep this quiet so the rumor mill doesn't get cranked up any more than it already has."

Because of the incident with Scott, Brent decided to discuss the issue of managerial authority in the afternoon meeting.

● ●
Managerial Authority: Like an Iron Fist in a Velvet Glove

Brent opened the meeting by saying, "All of you are aware of a situation that occurred this morning involving Mike, Richard, and me, in which the individual authority of each of us was challenged by Scott Wilson. We did what effective managers should do. . . . We *reacted* strongly in defending our authority.

"I emphasized the word *reacted,* because I have found that managerial authority is most effective when used like 'an iron fist in a velvet glove,' and only displayed when it is challenged.

"Managerial authority can become counterproductive when managers fall into three traps. First, when they display too much authority; second, when they display too little authority; and third, when they fail to always defend or display their authority when it is challenged.

"Richard and I defended our positions during the incident with Scott, because we didn't believe he was justified in challenging our authority. We were both ready to leave the business rather than let Scott bluff us into relinquishing our positions.

"Displaying too much authority is often a problem with hands-on managers, as it was with me early in my management career when I kept a high profile and managed with a strong hand. I displayed my position of authority as obviously as it is displayed in the military on the sleeves and shoulders of uniforms for all to see. The result was that most of my associates were intimidated or were afraid of me.

"When people fear you, they have a negative attitude toward your managerial authority as a result. Lao-tse referred to the negative aspect of fear in the rest of the passage from which this quote was taken." Brent pointed again to the framed plaque over the rolltop desk and recited from memory:

As for the best leaders, the people do not notice their existence. The next best, the people honor and praise. The next, *the people fear,* and the next, the people hate. . . . When the great leader's work is done, the people say, "We did it ourselves!"

"At the other extreme, some managers display too little authority. After I became a hands-off manager and began keeping a lower profile, I discovered that a hands-off style was often an invitation for people to challenge my authority and treat me more like one of the gang."

Barbara commented, "I had the same problem, but for a different reason. When I was promoted to sales manager, some of the people who had been my peers were now answering to me as their manager. At first I exercised too little authority, but then I discovered that some of my sales people were taking advantage of our previous relationship."

Brent said, "It is an exercise in futility for you, as a manager, to ever attempt to be one of the gang. Your people will always view you differently, even if they are your friends, because in your position of authority, you can make important decisions that will affect their careers."

Gordon said to Brent, "The first day we met, you asked me to call you 'Brent.' That made me feel more at ease with you, but I wonder if this kind of informality ever detracts from the respect people have for their managers' authority?"

"Gordon, managers can be given status by virtue of their titles, but they have to *earn* respect. You can't force-feed respect into people by requiring them to address you as 'Mister.' "

Richard added, "I believe our role as managers can be compared with the role parents assume with regard to their children. Our associates may resent or fear us, and our children may resent or fear us as parents, and perhaps even be angry with us at times. "However, if we're effective managers and parents, they will respect our authority and turn to us when they're in trouble or need help."

A few minutes after the meeting was over, Helen called, and she sounded concerned. "Brent, I went into New York for the day, and when I returned Scott called me. He's furious, because Mike refused to follow some instructions that he had given him yesterday. Mike told Scott the orders were contrary to what Richard wanted him to do, and that he answered to Richard.

"To make matters worse, Scott then called Richard, who also refused to do what he wanted done. Scott told Richard he was fired, and Richard's response was that he answered to you, not to Scott.

"Scott called back after that and told me he wants you out of the business immediately. He said he could direct the activities of the company from home until he's able to return to work."

There was a long pause before Brent quietly said, "Well, Helen, the ball is in your court. If you want me out, I can be out of this office in less than 15 minutes."

"That's the last thing I want. I told Scott that his sisters and I want you to stay, and that we're convinced it's for his own good. I explained that we loved him and didn't want to see the business destroy him, so we didn't think he should return to Enfield. With that, he hung up on me.

"Brent, I want you to please reconsider taking over as president of Enfield. You can name your own price."

"Helen, I appreciate the vote of confidence, but I'm not the one for the job. At this point, I don't believe my heart would be in it.

However, don't worry about a suitable candidate; Richard and I will begin looking for someone."

"Whatever you say, Brent. We're very grateful for what you're doing, and we trust your judgment."

"Thanks, Helen. I'll get back in touch with you."

Brent hung up the phone and stared out of the window. He hoped he was handling Enfield the way Stanley would have wanted.

FOUR

The Three Most Common Managerial Pitfalls and How to Avoid Them

Friday, February 15

• •

How to Avoid Being Overcommitted

Gordon had been looking forward to today's meeting, so that he would have an opportunity to bring up a problem he was having.

When Brent asked if anyone had any problems they would like to discuss, Gordon quickly responded. "I'm pretty good at establishing and prioritizing my objectives, and I can delegate fairly well. However, no matter how hard and efficiently I work, I just don't have the time to meet all of my commitments. Do you have any advice for solving this problem?"

"As I said in our first meeting together, when managers claim they don't have enough time this is only a symptom of a problem. If you were able to free up additional time, you would just overcommit yourself even more.

"I wish I could sugarcoat it for you, Gordon, but your problem is that you aren't handling your management job effectively, as evidenced by the fact you are overcommitted.

"The poet Robert Browning wrote, 'A man's reach should exceed his grasp, or what's a heaven for?' Browning's advice might be great for seeking the spiritual values he was writing about, but I believe this is terrible advice for managers. When the reach of managers exceeds their grasp, they're often not able to meet their commitments, and apparently the reach of your commitments is exceeding your grasp. I can relate to this because I've experienced the same problem, and it's an occupational hazard shared by many managers.

65

"The reach of managers should be *less than* their grasp. They should *undercommit* themselves, and then only to the very few objectives that are highest on their list of priorities and provide the greatest payoff in results."

"What are the major reasons why managers become overcommitted?" Barbara asked.

"At times it is because they succumb to pressures from their own managers, and even from those who answer to them to overcommit to more than they can effectively do.

"I became overcommitted because in addition to being a workaholic, I was something of an egomaniac. I didn't believe anyone else was capable of doing what I could do and I had this crazy notion that I was irreplaceable.

"I started my business without any previous management experience and tried to compensate by putting in long hours. That worked as long as the company was very small, but as we grew, I overcommitted myself and the company to unrealistic deadlines.

"The larger we grew, the further behind we fell on our commitments to customers. More of our problems were becoming emergencies, and more of our emergencies were becoming crises. I was too busy to do any intelligent planning and was just 'greasing the squeaky wheels.'

"I wasn't meeting regularly with my staff, and I was making all of the important management decisions without their participation. They had no way of knowing what was going on in the company because we weren't spending any quality time together, and I wasn't making any attempt to keep them informed.

"I was also working harder and putting in longer hours than anyone else. Instead of delegating responsibilities, I was telling people what to do, then second guessing them and interfering with their work. People were constantly bouncing into my office, asking questions and getting my approval on what they should do next. This left me even less time to do my own work. To add to my problems, personnel turnover was high and morale was low, especially among our best employees.

"My personal life was also suffering because I wasn't spending enough time with my family. In addition, my business problems were always on my mind, and this caused me to be very moody.

"By the end of my second year in business, I was burned out, ready to make a career change, and strongly considering going back into sales with another organization. Up to that point, I had taken vacations for only a day or two at a time, but now I felt the need to spend an extended period of time away from the business to think about my future plans. That is how, quite by accident, I learned a great management lesson.

"One morning, I met with my management group and told them I was going to be away for a month. I expected a strong reaction, but they accepted this very matter-of-factly. We got in agreement about who would handle my responsibilities during my absence.

"The next day I left on a trip with my family, assuming that when I returned the business would be in shambles. This wasn't of great concern to me, because I was already strongly inclined to make a career change.

"A month later, when I returned to my office, I was shocked. The company seemed to be running more smoothly than it was when I left. My responsibilities were being handled among several people, and since I hadn't been there to continue overcommitting myself, that pressure had also gone away.

"Before I went on vacation, I'd also caused many of our company's problems by overcommitting to our customers. Even though the well-known saying suggests that 'the customer is always right,' I learned that the customer is not always *reasonable*.

"When I returned to the office, I found that my people had discontinued my bad habit of agreeing to unreasonable delivery schedules, and we hadn't lost any customers. On the contrary, our customers were happier because we had begun meeting our more reasonable delivery schedules. However, now that I was back, my natural impulse was to again make myself the focal point of the company.

"Fortunately, two days later I went into New York for the day and happened to meet Stanley Wilson. This was when I heard his management creed for the first time: 'When the great leader's work is done, the people say, "We did it ourselves." '

"I began to realize that if my company could run smoothly during my absence, it could run just as smoothly when I was there. So I decided to do what was *unnatural* for me by encouraging my people to continue managing themselves.

"I soon began a new discipline of continuously establishing, reviewing, and updating my priorities, and then maintaining a laser beam–like focus on them. Although I get sidetracked at times by necessary distractions, after dealing with them I return to my priorities.

"I also changed the way I delegated responsibility. I used to ask myself, 'Who can best assume this responsibility?' and it was usually me. I decided this question was irrelevant, so I began asking, 'Who *should* handle this responsibility?' and it usually *wasn't* me. Many managers have difficulty at first in delegating responsibility, but I was strongly motivated by my own desperation.

"Even if you're a high-achieving workaholic, as many of us in management are, this approach provides the discipline that will enable you to avoid being an overachiever, and you'll be more effective. The reason is that you'll be able to program yourself to put your major focus on your objectives.

"On one hand, high achievers recognize their limitations and pace themselves accordingly. They *overplan,* but *undercommit*. This provides a backlog of projects to accomplish without agreeing to do more than they reasonably can do.

"On the other hand, although overachievers produce an above average amount of results, these results are often not of high quality, because overachievers are characteristically spread very thin. Even when their results are of sufficient quality, overachievers usually come under criticism for producing the results later than were promised.

"Discovering the dramatic difference between overcommitting and overplanning led me to a simple management style, which has worked effectively for me, and I suggest that you consider adopting it if you're overcommitting.

How to Avoid Being Overcommitted

1. Make a list of all of your objectives within reason that you would like to achieve.

2. Prioritize these objectives based on their urgency, payoff, and importance to you.

3. Continuously update this list.

4. Always plan to achieve more of these objectives than you believe is possible, thereby providing a backlog of projects.

5. Commit yourself to less than you can do or are willing to do, and only commit to those objectives that are highest in your sequence of priorities.

"There are two very logical reasons why managers should take this approach. The first is that most of us have more that we would like to do than we possibly can do. The second is that we achieve most of our results from a fairly small fraction of our activity. Pareto's Law, often referred to as the 80/20 rule, even suggests that we get 80 percent of our results from only 20 percent of our activity.

"Obviously, you will still encounter problems but fewer of them will become crises, and the big payoff is that you will begin to feel less stress and enjoy your work more."

"You make it sound too easy," Alan interrupted.

"It is easy when you find yourself, as I did, in so much trouble that there's no other choice."

9

• •

How Managers Can Obtain Assistance and Objectivity in Performing Their Own Work

Brent turned to Gordon. "Earlier, you said that you delegated fairly well, and the first day we met together Alan took me to task for proposing so many meetings when he's already too busy to do all of his work. You both may be like a lot of other managers who get into trouble by overcommitting and then find themselves in even more trouble by being too good at delegating."

Alan looked puzzled. "That doesn't make any sense."

"It might if you think about it this way. Perhaps you and Gordon have delegated so well in giving your people their own work to do that they don't have time to help you with yours."

"So what can we do?" Alan asked.

"Select a number two person."

• •
A Number Two Person for Managers

"A number two person?" Alan exclaimed. "On one hand, we're having profit problems and you're telling us to cut back on personnel. On the other hand, you're talking about hiring more people."

"I'm not suggesting that you hire more people but rather that *good* you give to one or more of those you already have the additional *point* responsibility of helping you with your responsibilities.

"Although the responsibilities will still be yours and you will be accountable for the results, a number two person can serve as an extension of yourself. He or she can play the role of an alter ego, a confidant, expediter, and buffer between you and those intruders who would attempt to get on your turf."

Gordon asked, "How many people should a manager have answering to him or her before someone is needed in this position?"

"Even those managers who have only one person answering to them should use that person to fill this role part of the time."

Mike asked, "Does having a number two person increase the number of people a manager can effectively manage?"

"Yes. Management books describe the so-called *span of control*, and some of them state that five people is the ideal number that one person can manage. I don't agree that there is an ideal number, but a number two person can enable you to expand the number of people you can manage effectively."

Barbara asked, "Would you say that the more people you have answering to you, the more responsibilities you can delegate, and the less the need for a number two person?"

"Not necessarily. By delegating properly, you give people their own work to do. No matter how many people you have answering to you, they may have so many responsibilities of their own that they can't help you with yours unless helping you is one of their responsibilities."

"How could I have a number two person?" Barbara asked. "My people are on commission. If I used Susan, for example, in this capacity, she would lose sales while she was out of her territory."

"You could consider increasing her base pay to offset her loss of commissions," Brent replied. "There is the risk of losing a few sales, but the potential reward would be the additional leverage on your own time and being able to show a net overall increase in your total sales."

Barbara responded, "Assuming I did use Susan in this position, what characteristics do you feel she should have?"

"You should be able to trust her to either do what you ask or tell you ahead of time when she can't, and not to second guess you or do something different from what you had agreed on.

"You should be comfortable with her. This overlaps with trust but goes beyond that. You need to be on the same wavelength and be able to communicate, both verbally and nonverbally. She should be able to read you and anticipate how you will react to almost any situation without having to speculate about your feelings. This minimizes misunderstandings and communications misfires.

"She also shouldn't be intimidated by you, be hesitant to disagree, or take any of your disagreements personally.

"She will speak and act for you at times, and you'll be judged by her actions. Therefore, you never want to feel that she is an embarrassment or that you must apologize for her. She should be satisfied in her position and not assume that she's the heir apparent to your job. If your job becomes available, she must accept the fact that someone else might replace you.

"In my company, my number two person was Nolan Mallory. When I asked him to assume that role, I made it clear that I had no plans to retire, and he shouldn't have any illusions about taking my place. The truth is, I doubted his ability to succeed me as CEO, but I discovered later that this attitude is a mental block for most CEOs, especially if they founded the company, and had been in the same position for many years, as I had.

"Much later, after I accepted that I *was* replaceable and had decided to leave the company, I approached Nolan about replacing me. He was reluctant at first because he didn't feel qualified, but I saw a good fit between Nolan's qualifications and what I knew was required of a CEO."

● ● ● ● ● ● ● ● ● ● ● ● ● ● ● ● ● ●
Sounding Boards for Managers

Gordon commented, "You characterized a number two person as a confidant. Does this mean looking to him or her as a sounding board?"

"Not necessarily. As much as I admired Nolan and valued his judgment, he answered to me, and we were both inside the organization. When I want objectivity, I look to those who are outside of the organization. Stanley and I served in this role for each other. Those you respect in civic and trade organizations, and even those who are friendly competitors, are also great sources for obtaining objectivity, valuable information, and assistance."

Barbara said, "It sounds like you're just talking about networking."

Brent smiled, "You're exactly right, Barbara, and it's amusing how so many people think of networking as somewhat of a new communications medium, when in fact it is among the oldest. We have just recently legitimatized the concept by giving it a name.

"Before there was radio, television, and print media, networking was the only widespread communications medium available. In recent years, as we have experienced an information explosion, networking has become a marvelous medium for short-circuiting laborious research by contacting those with experience on matters of interest to us. This can speed up our learning process and enable us to get to the heart of the matter more efficiently.

"In order to be effective and lasting, networking must be mutually beneficial for everyone in your network. Those 'sponges' who are always looking for help without giving anything in return are self-eliminating problems. You just quietly drop them from your network.

"I have found that the key to effective networking is to focus on trying to help your colleagues in the network without any expectation of what you might receive in return. 'What goes around comes around,' and the day inevitably arrives when you'll have an opportunity to call in your markers."

● ● ● ● ● ● ● ● ● ● ● ● ● ● ● ● ●
Devil's Advocates for Managers

Gordon commented, "It seems as though accountants, attorneys, and boards of directors would be the best sounding boards because they are outsiders yet still are close to the organization."

"Gordon, as I see it, the problem is that they're too close, and they all see the organization from a limited perspective, based on their respective interests and expertise. However, because of their vested interest in the organization, I believe they have real value as *devil's advocates,* but you have to allow for their lack of objectivity."

Alan observed, "I can see where it's difficult for accountants and attorneys to really be objective, because they're paid a fee by the organization. However, it appears to me that the boards of directors could provide objectivity because of their responsibility to protect the stockholders."

"Alan," Brent said, "their responsibility to protect the stockholders is precisely what clouds their objectivity, often to the point of paranoia.

"Board members' responsibilities are usually small, part-time jobs compared with their other interests, and they spend very little time inside the organization. Most of what they know about the organization is communicated to them either by financial statements or by the CEOs. The financial statements only reflect what has already happened. Since the CEOs technically answer to their boards, they present the financials to their boards with their own biased interpretations in favor of their positions and with the benefit of hindsight in explaining away any unpleasant surprises.

"This is not to imply that the CEOs are lying or are deliberately being deceitful. CEOs try to deal with their jobs as optimistically as possible, and they tend to report plans to their boards accordingly. As a result, the boards' perception too often becomes the reflection of the CEOs' biased, distilled, and sanitized interpretation of reality."

Mike asked, "Assuming directors know this, what can they do?"

"Most enlightened directors understand that the information they receive is distorted. Furthermore, they tend to be very conservative because of their legal liability for the actions of the organization and their fiduciary and moral obligations to the stockholders.

"To summarize, we talked about the thinking component of a manager's job earlier, and I told you the story about the five words—read, listen, discuss, observe, and think—that were chiseled into the riser of the stone steps leading into an IBM building. I also expressed my belief that this describes the most effective use of a manager's time.

"Managers are challenged to seek out assistance from all of the sources we have mentioned, but, in the final analysis, managers have to think through what is relevant to their particular needs, and make their own decisions."

10

● ●

How to Avoid
Becoming Irreplaceable

As he had almost every morning, Brent walked around the plant floor, observing, asking questions, and looking for anything that might require his attention. He always referred to this as MPA: "Management by Poking Around." He felt that the well-known expression, "Management by Walking Around," could suggest aimless wandering without a purpose.

Mike was in his office. When he saw Brent through his window, Mike called to him. "Brent, may I see you for a minute?" After Brent walked into Mike's office and sat down, Mike said, "Stanley used to tell us that when someone brings a problem to a manager, an effective manager should insist on a recommended solution. I have a personnel problem, but I really don't have a recommendation for solving it."

"Okay, tell me about it."

"On Friday, you said one of the reasons you once were over-committed is you felt you were irreplaceable. My maintenance supervisor, Bud Randall, is irreplaceable, and he knows it. He causes me a lot of grief because he isn't a team player, and I'm convinced he even works at keeping me vulnerable to him."

"Mike, one of the most severe criticisms that can be made of a manager is that he is irreplaceable or that he tolerates irreplaceability among any of his people. Good managers will take whatever steps are necessary to ensure that the job of every manager and direct producer is structured so that no one approaches becoming irreplaceable."

75

"Normally I would agree, but Randall is an exception. He's the only one who can troubleshoot the large punch press when it goes down."

"If Randall drops dead tonight, will we have to close the business?"

"Well, no, but...."

"But nothing. By your own admission, he's not irreplaceable if we can stay in business without him. Your challenge is to rehabilitate him, if possible. Otherwise, you should replace him."

"How?"

"I'll answer your question, but first let's put the problem in perspective by getting the idea out of your head that Randall is irreplaceable. Then let Randall know how you feel. You're a tough guy. Let him know you won't be intimidated by him, no matter how vulnerable you now are to him. Has the machine ever gone down when Randall wasn't here?"

"Yes, twice."

"What did you do?"

"Once, when he was out sick, I repaired it myself, but it took almost all night. Randall could have fixed the damned machine in ten minutes. Another time, he'd taken the day off to go fishing. I couldn't get in touch with him, and I had to call in a factory maintenance person. That cost us a lot of money and a big delay in production."

Brent said, "Holiday Inn used to have a slogan, 'The best surprise is no surprise.' The same is true in management. You don't like being surprised to find that the press is down, Randall is gone, and you're the one who has to stay up most of the night to fix it.

"That's why irreplaceables are a serious organizational problem. In mechanical systems, all of the components should be replaceable. By the same token, all of the components of an effective organizational system should be replaceable—including Mr. Randall.

"If Randall works at making you vulnerable to him on the assumption that it gives him more job security, he's kidding himself. People actually make themselves more valuable, and therefore more secure, by working at *not* being irreplaceable."

"What do you mean by that?" Mike asked.

"When people are *replaceable*, those answering to them are not overly dependent on them, and the organization isn't vulnerable to these people. If Randall had trained someone else to troubleshoot the punch press, it wouldn't have caused a problem when he was out.

"However, Randall did cause you a problem, and if I were in your place, I would let Randall know in a hurry that if people who answer to me continue to cause me problems, they have very little, if any, job security.

"Managers like Randall represent barriers to the progress of the people who answer to them. Their people can't grow in their jobs or be promoted because their managers won't let them. This often results in an organization's best people becoming frustrated and leaving.

"An irreplaceable like Randall is a nuisance when he's away from his work because his problems usually become emergencies, and his emergencies become crises because no one has been trained to handle his responsibilities. Therefore, they invariably have to be assumed by someone higher in the organization, probably you, instead of by a peer or someone lower, which should be the case.

"Mike, I'll bet you a case of beer that Randall always takes his vacations a day or two at a time."

"No bet, he's never off for more than a day or two."

"If I were you, I would tell Randall, and any other people who think they're irreplaceable, that in the future they're going to take their vacations for periods of at least a week or more. Give them enough notice so that they'll be able to think through the consequences of being away and have them prepare a plan for having their responsibilities covered while they're gone. But make it clear that this plan shouldn't include an assumption that you'll handle their responsibilities, because they should be handled by people at their same, or at a lower, level."

"When you make these irreplaceables take vacations, don't the skeletons come out of the closets, and the irreplaceables' problems turn into crises?" Mike asked.

"At times, but that's a cheap price to pay for the opportunity to eliminate the irreplaceability of any of your people. It's much better to face the problem while these people are on the payroll than to risk losing them unexpectedly while they're still irreplaceable.

"Higher management will probably have to become involved the first time they're away, but this provides an opportunity to become familiar with their jobs and take corrective action.

"The vacationers should return to find changed descriptions of their job responsibilities, including disciplines and controls that will reduce the possibility of their continuing to be or becoming irreplaceable. It should also be made clear to them why the organization can't afford to have anyone who is irreplaceable."

"You're right. I'm going to have it out with Randall. If he quits, I can use a factory maintenance person to service the machine until I can send a couple of my people to the factory for training. It'll probably shake Randall up when I talk to him, but I doubt that he'll quit." Then Mike asked, "During the period you were so overcommitted, why were you also irreplaceable?"

"For the same three reasons most managers become irreplaceable, because of their:

- Irreplaceable, hands-on, nonmanagement skills; or
- *Unwillingness* to adequately delegate responsibilities; or
- Being *unable* to delegate adequately because of a lack of talented people who *can* assume more responsibilities.

"Therefore, as an irreplaceable manager I had one of three choices:

- Delegate more responsibilities to my present staff;
- Attract additional talent so I could delegate even more responsibilities; or
- Continue to be a hands-on manager, stifle the further growth of my group, and increase the risk of failure in the future.

"Stanley made me realize the *unnatural* paradox that managers don't become irreplaceable because of their management skills, but rather because of their *nonmanagement* skills.

"He also taught me that the value added to an organization by management is in

- Establishing objectives,
- Planning to achieve these objectives,
- Orchestrating the use of resources, and
- Giving guidance in achieving the objectives.

"These are *not* irreplaceable functions," Brent added.

Mike asked, "What are some of the warning signals to managers that they are, or are becoming, irreplaceable?"

"Well, Mike, they could start by asking themselves these questions:

good point

Nine Warning Signals of Irreplaceability

1. Do I either take vacations one or two days at a time or not at all?

2. Do I phone in constantly while I'm away and try to perform my job by long distance?

3. Do I spend too much time trying to *monitor* and *control* the activities of my people?

4. Is there a constant parade of people coming to me with questions and problems but no recommended answers and solutions?

5. Am I too busy to spend any quality time with my people except before or after office hours?

6. Is there poor morale and a sense of frustration among the people who answer to me?

7. Are my people not being promoted within the organization or are they leaving to take higher positions in other organizations?

8. When I'm away, do problems turn into emergencies and emergencies into crises?

9. During my absence, does someone higher up in the organization have to handle my responsibilities?

"Mike, I hope that you'll learn from my experience, and not learn the hard way as I did, how to avoid becoming irreplaceable yourself and how to prevent any of your people from becoming so."

● ●

How to Keep
the Intruders
off Your Turf

think about

yes

Brent opened the meeting. "Today, I would like to discuss what I believe is the single biggest obstacle to the effectiveness of managers, that is, the intruders on their turf.

"As a manager, my most productive time has been spent with the people who answer to me. Strangely enough, some of my least productive time has been spent with the same people, dealing with matters I neither wanted to be, nor should have been, involved with.

"These people were then intruders on my turf, uninvited, unwelcome, and unwanted. Nevertheless, my challenge was never to give my associates the feeling that they were intruding, for fear they might not come to me when necessary.

"Intruders would bring me their problems, without recommending solutions. I made myself available to anyone who wanted to see me because I felt I *owed* my people big chunks of my time, and all of my time seemed to belong to everyone but me. Later I realized I was blaming my people for a problem I had created myself.

y

"The problem was compounded by my own ego, my knowledge of the business, and my natural inclination to want to have all the answers. However, this discouraged my staff from thinking for themselves.

"I was showing and telling them what to do, instead of observing and asking questions. By doing so, I was in effect, volunteering to assume their responsibilities. As my associates became more dependent on me, I began feeling uneasy any time I was away from the office.

"When we discussed overcommitting, I indicated that I was once too overcommitted to spend enough time with my people. By learning how to make myself more available, I created the problem of spending too much time with them, until finally I didn't have enough time to do my own work.

"I tried to create additional time by working at night and on weekends when I was alone, but as my company grew, I finally reached the point where I couldn't get my own work done no matter how many hours I put in. It was only then that I decided I would no longer be a primary resource for those who answered to me unless it was my choice, not theirs.

"Instead of continuing to try to find ways of creating additional time, I began focusing on the real source of my problem: the intruders on my turf. Through a process of trial and error, I also found that I could effectively deal with intruders, both inside and outside of my organization, by

- Staying well organized
- Focusing on continuously updated priorities
- Practicing techniques to keep intruders off my turf

"Staying well organized with daily plans and priorities creates a natural resistance to intruders. When anything unexpected arises, ask yourself if responding is more important than what you had planned to do. If not, either refuse to do it or give it a lower priority. Whenever you begin a day uncertain about your plans and priorities, you're fair game for any intrusion that comes along.

"By focusing on your continuously updated priorities, if they're changed, it will be your choice, not that of intruders who would impose their priorities on you."

● ● ● ● ● ● ● ● ● ● ● ● ● ● ● ● ● ●
A Lesson in Focusing on Objectives

Mike laughed and said, "This reminds me of the discussion you and I had last week when you were out in the plant and I came storming in after I'd just had my annual physical exam. I was raising hell because the doctor kept me waiting for an hour beyond my appointment time and I was complaining that doctors are bad businessmen and lousy managers for not keeping their appointments. Then you said we could learn a good lesson from doctors about being effective, and I thought you were nuts."

"Yeah," Brent responded, "I told you that because of the nature of their work, doctors find it much easier to focus on their priorities than managers do. When doctors practice medicine, they do what's *natural* for them by producing results directly in their one-on-one relationships with their patients, who are usually their top priorities. If they're halfway through emergency operations and it's time for their next appointment, they don't leave their patients in the operating rooms and rush back to their offices to give physical examinations.

"Unlike doctors, managers produce results indirectly through their resources, which is *unnatural*. This is why managers can rarely deal with just one priority at a time and be as sharply focused as doctors are with their patients. However, there are techniques managers can use to help keep their various priorities in the proper sequence."

Brent then distributed copies of this list.

Six Common Intruders and How to Deal with Them

1. *People who want to see you may be intruders.*

   Ask why they want to meet. If they are members of your organization and you determine that they are intruders, explain why it would be counterproductive for you to get together, and then direct them to the appropriate parties.

   If the intruders are those from outside the organization, you can refuse to see them and perhaps suggest that they go elsewhere.

2. *People who bring you matters that are their responsibilities and for which they have not developed recommendations.*

   Providing *guidance* instead of *directing* people is the key to inspirational management. A very effective way of keeping intruders off your turf is to always ask this magic question in providing guidance: "What do *you* recommend?"—with a great deal of emphasis on *you*. Then refuse to offer any advice until they do their homework and come back with *their* recommendations. This is often the last you will hear about the problems, and this is excellent management development because the intruders will have found solutions to their own problems, and they will discover that their managers do not have to be involved.

You do your people a disservice if you do not discipline them to think through their own recommendations about how to handle their responsibilities. As the ancient Chinese proverb puts it: "If you give a man a fish, you feed him for a day. If you teach him how to fish, he can feed himself for a lifetime."

3. *People who come to you when others should be involved but are not available.*

Unless it is an emergency, postpone the discussion until all the interested parties can be present.

4. *People who have gone over their managers' heads and contacted you.*

Suggest that they talk to their managers first or agree to have their managers present when you get together. If they are not willing to do this, you should agree to see them in order to maintain an effective open-door policy.

5. *People who bring you matters that should be more appropriately handled in a regular meeting.*

Ask the intruders to bring the matters up at the next meeting.

6. *People who stroll into your office unannounced.*

Here are a couple of ways of handling these intruders:

- If you are working on something and don't want to be interrupted, ask if the matter can wait until you reach a good stopping place.
- Close your office door as a signal that you do not want to be interrupted.

7. *Intruders who attempt to use you as an involuntary resource.*

There are intruders who will attempt to shift some of their responsibilities to you and use you as an involuntary resource. Help them within reason, but if they begin taking advantage, keep track of what you do for them and expect to be repaid in kind at a later date.

"In addition to these techniques," Brent continued, "after I decided to become a hands-off manager, I dramatized my new style by moving my office to a more remote location in the company, and the symbolism of this proved to be very effective.

"I also found that I had fewer intrusions than I did when I was a hands-on manager and *wanted* my office to be the focal point of the inside of my company, so I could stay in close touch with the activities of my people."

Mike asked, "I've noticed that every time I want to see you, you always tell me that you will come to my office. Do you do that to keep me 'off your turf'?"

Brent smiled as he answered. "That's one of the reasons, Mike, because if the session becomes counterproductive, I can easily end it by indicating that I have another commitment.

"However, the main reason I go to your office is to convey my attitude that I want to support you. When I used to have people come to my office, it conveyed the impression that I was leading the pack, and they were supporting me. This attitude is consistent with Lao-tse's advice about leading people by getting behind them."

Brent passed out copies of another list, adding, "When you *do* agree to meet with others, there is often the risk that the sessions will become counterproductive, so you might consider this."

How to Make Sessions with Associates More Productive

1. If you are dealing with problems or decisions that are the intruders' responsibilities, ask them to be prepared to present their recommendations and proposed plans.

2. Ask them to be prepared on any other subjects that need to be discussed. This usually reduces the number of future sessions.

3. Provide an escape hatch for yourself by asking how much time you should allow for the meeting. Parkinson's Law suggests that work tends to be accomplished within the time available for its completion, and meetings are usually completed within the time allotted for them. This still leaves you the option of extending the time as long as the session is productive.

4. Look at your watch. When a session begins to drag, an obvious glance at your watch is usually all that is necessary to speed up the pace and get back on track.

● ●

You May Be the Biggest Obstacle to Your Own Effectiveness

Richard commented, "By learning to identify and deal with intruders, I've become acutely aware that this can be a two-way street. As a manager, I represent the greatest potential intrusion on my people if I indiscriminately interrupt them. Furthermore, since my results are achieved through them, interrupting them can have a negative impact on my own effectiveness."

Barbara asked, "Is this why you always ask if I have time to talk when you contact me?"

"I try to do unto you as I would have you do unto me. If you will tell me when I'm intruding on you, I can either explain why it's necessary that we meet then, or ask if we can meet at a mutually convenient time. If you don't tell me, you're not being fair to either of us."

Gordon asked, "What if people tell their managers they're intruding and the managers become offended?"

"Then the managers are only hurting themselves," Richard answered. "However, when this does occur, those answering to the managers should try to discuss the problem rationally with their managers. If this doesn't work and the managers continue to be offended, they should consider taking the steps necessary to answer to different managers. As drastic as it may sound, this includes the possibility of leaving the organization because these managers are menaces to those who answer to them."

● ●
Dealing with the Intrusion of the Work of Today

Richard continued. "We talked about the bifocal aspect of the managerial job: dealing with tomorrow and today simultaneously. I believe the greatest intrusion to managerial effectiveness is the pull of today that Brent referred to. This includes all those immediate but unexpected matters you can't prioritize ahead of time that continue to come up on a daily basis.

"I learned how to solve this problem the hard way soon after I joined Enfield. Stanley came into my office one afternoon to ask about a report I had promised to prepare for him by that morning. I hadn't completed the report because something unexpected had come up that I considered to be more important.

"This resulted in my first discussion with Stanley concerning his management philosophy about priorities. He pointed out that when the right things are done in the wrong sequence, they're no longer the right things.

"This made me angry, and I told him that what had come up was clearly more important than his report. He said that was beside the point and that he was upset because I had decided to assign a lower priority to my commitment to him without first discussing it with him.

"This was one of those extremely rare occasions when he appeared to be angry, and I discovered later this was only for effect. He wanted to get my attention, and he did. He made it clear that he wasn't paid to follow me around making sure I was doing what I had agreed to do. Later I realized he was right, and I apologized."

Brent smiled. "I learned that lesson the hard way at IBM. Every Monday morning we each turned in a working plan for the week along with a report of what we had actually done the previous week. If what I'd planned to do and what I actually did were out of sync, particularly if I wasn't meeting my sales quota, my manager would call me into his corner office to explain why I wasn't able to stay on track. These sessions aren't among my most pleasant memories, but it was great management development training."

● ●
Dealing with the Intrusion of the Telephone

Mike spoke up. "The biggest intrusion I have on a daily basis is my telephone. I don't have anyone to screen my phone calls, and I'm constantly being interrupted. How can I deal with this?"

"I don't screen my phone calls," Brent responded, "and have never found it necessary. Obviously, some managers are in positions where they must screen phone calls. The president of the United States, for example.

"Even though not screening calls leaves me open to potential intruders, I don't want someone else deciding which calls I should take."

Alan commented, with a slight tone of irritation, "I've noticed that you have even taken phone calls when some of us are in your office."

"You're right, but you might have observed that in most instances I do get the caller off the phone immediately by asking if I might return the call in a few minutes."

Richard supported Brent's position. "When people are in my office and I get the caller off the phone immediately, it should be a signal to them that I place more importance on them at that time than I do on the caller."

Gordon asked, "If you don't have time to talk, why don't you just block phone calls?"

"Whether or not I have time to talk depends on the individual and the circumstances. I take those calls which in my judgment should take precedence over what I might be discussing with some of you at the time. This could be the case when I receive calls from some of our customers, members of the Wilson family, or perhaps even personal family emergencies.

"When I have people in my office and in my judgment I should not get the callers off the line immediately, I apologize to you for the interruption and ask you to excuse me and let me get back to you afterward."

Barbara commented, "I've learned from my sales experience that it's illogical to assume that just because people answer their phones, that they have time to talk to you. Therefore, I *always* begin phone conversations by asking if they do have the time."

Alan asked Brent, "When do you block phone calls?"

"When I'm in a formal meeting, have several people in my office, or when I'm discussing a serious matter with even one person. I also block calls when I'm alone and need an uninterrupted period of creative thinking time. Then I ask the receptionist to take messages because I will be unavailable for a while."

"Do you always return calls?" Alan asked skeptically.

"I do, unless they're from people who would obviously waste my time or from salespeople, unless I know them or feel it would be to my advantage to do so."

"What do you have against salespeople?" Barbara asked sarcastically.

"Nothing. I'm one myself, but unless salespeople have a justification for doing so I believe it is unprofessional for them to phone prospects and leave messages for the prospects to return their calls."

Brent then said, "Let me summarize the benefits of keeping intruders off your turf.

Benefits of Keeping Intruders Off Your Turf

1. Creates more time to maximize the focus on your own priorities and minimizes the intrusions that will prevent you from pursuing them.

2. Creates more discretionary, quality time to spend with your people and enables you to be more highly visible where and when you're needed.

3. Forces your people to be less dependent on you and to handle more of their own responsibilities. This reduces the amount of stress on you and the danger of you becoming irreplaceable.

4. Results in excellent management development because responsibilities will be handled and decisions will be made at the lowest appropriate level.

"Right now my top priority is to let you people get back to work, so we'll adjourn."

······································

How to Maintain Open and Effective Communications

12

• •

An Open-Door Policy That Works

Brent was in his office when he received a call from Mary Hastings, the receptionist. "Brent, I'm on my afternoon break and I wondered if I could talk to you in your office for a minute?"

"Sure, Mary, come on down."

"What's that all about?" Brent wondered aloud as he hung up the phone.

Mary appeared nervous as she entered Brent's office and took a seat on one of the visitor's chairs. Brent sat on the sofa nearby. He had learned from his sales experience that when having a conversation with someone, a physical barrier, such as a table or a desk, can become a mental barrier to open communications.

"What can I do for you, Mary?"

"I'm not sure. I have a problem . . . or rather, I know someone in this company who has a problem."

"Who is it?"

"You wouldn't know him. He's my uncle. He works in the plant."

"Why didn't he call me?"

"He was afraid to. In fact, he was very reluctant to have me talk to you, even after I told him we could trust you."

"Then why don't you tell me what the problem is, and we'll go from there?"

Mary paused several seconds, then took a deep breath.

Brent smiled and said, "Take it easy, Mary. It can't be that bad."

"Well, my uncle is Ned Connors. He's the third-shift supervisor. The problem has something to do with Mike Cline, but I don't know all the details. Ned would have to explain it to you himself."

"But you said he was afraid to talk with me."

"He is unless he has your assurance that he won't be fired."

"Mary, he might get fired for something else, but as long as I'm here, I assure you it will not be because he came to me.

"Has he talked with Mike?"

"No, because Ned said Larry Crawford was fired for going over Mike's head to Scott Wilson with a grievance."

"Mary, why don't you tell Ned to call me? I'll keep the conversation in complete confidence. We can even meet away from the plant if it will make him feel more comfortable."

As Mary left, Brent began to wonder if there was more of a problem here than he had at first suspected, and he remembered how Stanley had always kept the lines of communications open at Enfield. He wouldn't have liked the sound of the Ned Connors problem.

Later that afternoon, Ned called, and after Brent satisfied him that his job would not be in jeopardy for going over Mike's head, Ned and Brent decided to meet early the next morning at the Holiday Inn, just after the third shift closed down.

The next morning, as Brent entered the Holiday Inn coffee shop, he identified Ned Connors by the green jacket Ned said he would be wearing.

Brent casually attempted to put Ned more at ease, then got to the point. "Mary tells me you have a problem but that you haven't talked to Mike Cline about it. Do you mind telling me why not?"

"Because Larry Crawford was fired for going over Mike's head to Scott Wilson, and I can't take a chance on the same thing happening to me."

"What's the problem?"

"Mike is putting too many demands on us in the plant. We can't meet his unrealistic schedules, and everyone is under a lot of pressure. We're working a lot of overtime, morale is going down, and I'm fed up."

"If you don't want to talk to Mike by yourself, would you talk with him if I were there?"

"No, I wouldn't want to do that."

Brent felt on the defensive. At his former company, it was unusual for his employees to be unwilling to have their managers involved in discussions about grievances as long as Brent was also present. This might be an indication that Mike was discouraging his people from invoking the open-door policy and going over his head.

Ned was becoming upset, so with the assurance that their conversation would be held in confidence, Brent gave him a chance to let off some steam by encouraging him to elaborate on the problems that were bothering him. Brent had found that disgruntled employees often neither expect nor want him to take any specific action. They just want an opportunity to go on record with their positions, and that was often the end of the matter. In this case, Ned wanted to press on.

Brent then tried his next tactic, "If any of your coworkers or the other shift supervisors feel the same way, do you mind if I speak with them?"

"There are some others who feel the same way, but if you talked to them, it might get back to Mike."

That posed a problem. Without talking with the others, Brent could not determine whether the dissatisfaction was shared by them or was just a problem between Ned and Mike.

"Since you don't want me to talk to Mike, or anyone else, my hands are tied. It wouldn't be fair to Mike if I tried to settle your complaint without hearing his side. I must assume he's innocent until proven guilty, and because he's your manager, I owe him the benefit of any doubt.

"If you don't want to be involved in a discussion with Mike, one alternative is for me to discuss your grievance with him. This could be risky for you, because I can't control personal feelings and Mike may not take your criticism lightly.

"I would let him know that the company won't tolerate any display of hard feelings or revenge because you came to me with a complaint. However, as your manager, he would still be in a position where he could make things uncomfortable for you, or even discriminate against you in a way that could not be easily detected or proven.

"Ned, you should also keep in mind that fact-finding investigations can often make those with the grievances look bad when it is found that the grievances were unfounded."

Ned was opposed to Brent talking directly to Mike because of these possible repercussions, so finally Brent asked, "Just what do you want me to do?"

"I don't know, but I can't keep putting up with things the way they are."

Brent felt that Ned wasn't being realistic by presenting a problem without allowing him any flexibility for solving it, so he decided to take a more dramatic approach.

"Would you like for me to fire Mike Cline?"

"No . . . not really," was Ned's startled response.

"In that case, is there another job in the company you feel qualified to handle where you wouldn't be answering to Mike?"

"I . . . I don't think so," Ned stammered.

"Well, since you don't want me to fire Mike, and there doesn't seem to be any other place for you at Enfield, have you considered looking for a position with another company?"

The shocked look on Ned's face told Brent that he was beginning to realize if someone had to leave the company, it probably would not be Mike Cline. His choices were to resolve the complaint by meeting with Mike, back off and learn to get along with Mike, or leave the organization.

Ned was silent for a few moments, then said, "I don't want to leave Enfield, so I guess I should talk to Mike—but only if you're there."

They decided to meet the next morning, and Ned agreed that Brent should discuss Ned's grievance with Mike before they all met. When Brent returned to Enfield, he went by Mike Cline's office and asked if he had time to talk.

"Sure, Brent, what's up?"

"Mike, I have a ticklish situation I'd like to discuss with you. One of your people contacted me about a problem that concerns you."

"That's fine with me," Mike casually responded, "but why didn't he just come to me?"

"He didn't think you would do anything about it. In fact, he was even afraid to go over your head for fear you would fire him."

"That's ridiculous. I'd never fire anyone for going over my head. Why would he think that?"

"He said you fired Larry Crawford for going over your head to Scott Wilson."

"Larry Crawford! That's crazy! I didn't fire Larry. Scott did. I was so damned mad that I even threatened to quit myself because Scott had interfered with my authority. I needed Larry, and firing him was the last thing I would've done."

"Then why would he have thought you fired Larry?"

"What the hell was I supposed to do? Risk losing the respect of my people by blaming Scott? That would've looked like a cop-out."

"I suppose you're right, Mike. It looks like you were caught in a no-win situation."

"You're damned right I was. Scott screwed up in dealing with Larry, and he knew it, but he let me take the blame. That might explain why my people haven't seemed to be very open with me lately. Now that I think about it, this started about the time Larry left the company."

Then Brent described his discussion with Ned Connors and asked, "Was I safe in assuring him that there wouldn't be any hard feelings or retribution on your part?"

"Of course. I'm probably more frustrated than Ned is, and I want to do anything I can to keep the lines of communications open with my people. What's Ned's complaint?"

"He's unhappy because he feels you're overcommitting production. He says this is creating overtime, everyone is under pressure, and you have unrealistic expectations of your people."

"He's mostly right. Production is overcommitted, but not by me. There are also unrealistic expectations, but they aren't mine. Scott and the sales department have been committing us to delivery schedules we can't possibly meet without a lot of overtime. They're fanatics about turning out production faster than the competition.

"When Stanley was here, our customers were satisfied with a six-week delivery schedule, and we geared our production accordingly. Back then, we had almost no overtime because we were set up to produce a fixed amount of volume every week instead of gearing our production to the volume of incoming orders the way we do now.

"After Scott took over, we started adjusting production to the volume of incoming orders. When the orders go up, we increase production and add more people. When the orders go down, we decrease production and lay people off.

"Since we aren't in a seasonal business, it makes more sense to me to stretch out our production schedule like we used to, let our volume of production stay fairly even, and let our backlog of production orders fluctuate between the equivalent of four to eight weeks of sales.

"If the backlog gets too high, we can gear up our production slightly until our backlog returns to normal. If the backlog gets too low, we can gear down our production accordingly."

"Did you ever run this by Scott?"

"Hell yeah, several times, but I finally gave up. He didn't want it that way, probably because that's the way his father did it. But as usual, I couldn't get a straight answer out of him.

"This may sound like a lame excuse, but this is the reason I quit having regular meetings with my people in the plant. I have been living in a vacuum since top management hasn't been meeting regularly, and I never know what's going on until I walk into this office and find a fistful of new production orders that the sales department always wants out of here in three to four weeks, in addition to everything else that's already in the pipeline."

At 8:30 the next morning, Brent met with Mike and Ned in Brent's office. Mike explained to Ned the reason the people in the plant had been under so much pressure and why it appeared that he was putting too many demands on them. He also told Ned that top management was now meeting regularly and that he would immediately resume having weekly meetings with the shift supervisors to keep them better informed.

The next day's management meeting had been called off because Alan and Gordon were going to be meeting with Enfield's auditors. However, Brent assured Mike and Ned that at the management meeting on Monday he would address the issue of the sales department overcommitting the plant and take steps to correct the problem. Ned was very pleased and expressed his appreciation for the interest that both Brent and Mike had displayed.

● ●

How to Keep the Communications Pipeline Open

"Since we met last Wednesday," Brent told the management group when they had assembled for their regular meeting, "I've been involved in two issues that relate to communications within the company. The first had to do with Enfield's open–door policy; the second with keeping your people better informed.

"I'm familiar with what the open–door policy was when Stanley was here, but I'm not familiar with how it might have changed since then. Today let's come to an agreement about what our policy should be."

Alan spoke up first. "In all honesty, I'm opposed to the policy because it's irritating to me when my people go over my head when they could have come straight to me."

"It's natural to feel that way," Brent said, "but I suggest that managers should do what is *unnatural* and encourage people to go over their heads if they feel it's justified. Even when managers feel insecure about their own jobs, when the policy is invoked, it will probably help them feel more secure, because it usually results in the managers' authority being reconfirmed and reinforced.

"When the policy is properly administered, it displays that higher management is responsive to the concerns of those in the lower ranks. It also provides an early warning system when trouble is brewing in the lower ranks and reduces the chances that problems are being covered up or distorted in the process of going up through channels. Lower-level managers will also know that if they aren't fair, their people have recourse by going to higher authority.

"An open-door policy also gives those in the company the feeling they have allies at the top. Even if grievances aren't resolved in their favor, they know they'll have a fair hearing without putting their jobs on the line.

"Nevertheless, we can't afford to undermine the effectiveness and morale of our managers by encouraging people to go over their managers' heads needlessly."

Richard said, "I've found that most complaints are pretty routine, and when employees have problems with fellow workers, they usually take them to their own manager. When people come to me first instead of their own managers, it's usually those who have been here for years and feel more at ease talking to me. Even then, I can usually convince them to take their complaints back to their managers or at least agree to include the managers in our discussions."

Brent commented, "Grievances taken to higher authority can often be simply resolved by clarifying or changing policies and procedures, responsibilities, and lines of authority. This can usually be done in regular staff meetings without ever disclosing that these changes were initiated by those who went over their managers' heads with grievances."

Alan said, "My previous employer claimed to have an open-door policy, but it was usually an open door to unemployment."

"That's a good point," Brent responded. "Trust is the real key to making the open-door policy effective. When people don't know where else to turn, they have to be able to trust that they can go to someone at a higher level without fear of being labeled 'whistle blowers,' being ostracized, or perhaps being fired. The first time you violate this trust, you might as well forget the policy.

"In the case of managers who answer to you, they must be able to trust that if people go over their heads, you won't undermine their authority and that you'll give them a fair hearing, whatever the grievances against them."

At this point, Brent and Mike reviewed the details of the Ned Connors incident. "The situation we had yesterday with Ned," Brent observed, "was a result of information not being filtered down from the top. Since the management group hasn't been meeting regularly, Mike couldn't keep his people informed about what was going on because he didn't know himself.

"One of the best ways for managers to gain trust, simplify the management job, and make their people feel important is to keep them informed about how their work relates to the objectives of the organization.

"I've also found that uncertainty within an organization is a great cause of stress and that people want to be kept informed, even if it doesn't directly affect their own responsibilities. When people don't know what's going on, they'll guess. They'll usually guess wrong and negatively. If you only tell your associates the good news, when they're not hearing any news they'll assume that things must be going badly, and they're usually right. I've discovered that your best people will work harder when things aren't going well, assuming you keep them informed and give them the feeling of having a personal stake in the welfare of the group.

"After our first meeting, I also learned from Barbara that you haven't been receiving copies of the financial statements. However, as long as I'm here, you'll have them because I want you to have access to all of the information about Enfield that you feel you want or need.

"As a naive, young manager, I didn't want my people to know when my company was doing well for fear they might demand more money. When we weren't doing well, I didn't want them to know for fear they might get discouraged and quit.

"It's only natural to distrust the unknown. Since I kept my associates in the dark, they didn't trust me, and they tried to keep me in the dark. This resulted in a counterproductive stand-off for everyone.

"My attitude was that anything that didn't directly affect their jobs was none of their business. Besides, I was very busy, and didn't think it was worth my time to keep them informed.

"In the early days after starting my first business, most of my associates and I were putting in very long hours. Even though I was working much harder and making much less money than I did at IBM, I started hearing insinuations from some of my people that they were doing all the work, while I was making most of the money. So I decided to have a meeting to clear up their misunderstanding.

"First, I asked them to write down how much profit they thought the company was making, and how much they thought my salary was. Their answers were amazing. Everyone guessed far too high on both questions. Then I passed out and reviewed copies of our financial statements. I described how much we needed in sales just to break even. Since our sales had been increasing rapidly, I also explained how much profit we would have to generate to cover the working capital required to finance the cost of the increased sales.

"My financial vice-president was the only one who realized that cash gets tighter as sales increase. It made an obvious impact on the group when I explained that after the money was spent for labor and materials to produce the additional sales, we had to invoice the customer and then wait an average of 30 more days before we were paid.

"Once everyone saw the whole picture, their questions made me realize that they were genuinely interested in the welfare of the company, even in those facets of the business that didn't directly affect their areas of responsibility. This caused me to decide to have regular meetings of our management staff, where I would answer questions and distribute and review our monthly financial statements. I continued to do this for as long as I was in the business, whether we were doing well or not.

"Soon after we started having regular meetings, my managers began losing their inhibitions about speaking up as they came to know me better. This also improved our one-on-one communications on a daily basis. I discovered that the more light I shed about the business, the more useful information I received in return. Gradually, many of the burdens of running the business began to shift from me to my staff, and they seemed to welcome the responsibility."

"Did you ever intentionally withhold information from your people?" Alan asked skeptically.

"Yes, because there have been a few times when I thought it was not in the best interest of the company to be completely open. In those rare instances when I was questioned about anything that I felt should be kept confidential, I told my people that even though I couldn't give them an answer at that point, I would as soon as possible. They might have been curious and indulged in speculation, but they knew I'd keep my word and tell them later."

Gordon asked, "Could you give us any guidelines on how much information our people *need* to have, or that we owe them?"

"When in doubt about what they need," Brent answered, "overcommunicate because what people *need* to know is irrelevant. Put yourself in their position and ask what *you* would be interested in knowing, then try to tell them not only what they need to know, but what you think they *want* to know, and honestly answer their questions about the business.

"As for what you *owe* them, by taking this approach, you'll give them more information than you ever would have considered was owed to them."

● ●

Priming the Pump of Upward Communications

"So far in this discussion, we've been talking about the benefits of keeping our people informed, one of which is that we receive more information from them in return.

"Unfortunately, organizational communications, like water, have a natural tendency to flow downward, and just as managers have the option of telling their people only what they want them to know, their people have the same option in choosing what they want to tell their managers. Therefore, managers are challenged to induce upward communications, and the most effective tool for doing this is asking the right questions and then listening attentively to the answers.

"Rudyard Kipling wrote: 'I keep six honest serving men (They taught me all I know). Their names are what and why and when and how and where and who.' These are powerful communications words, but they are often not used by managers because asking questions and listening to the answers are *unnatural* acts for them. They are prone to talk too much and listen too little.

"When you're talking, you aren't listening, but more importantly, you aren't learning. If you'll listen, you can learn and respond to your people in a way that they can also often learn.

"The famous Socratic method teaches by asking the right questions. Socrates responded to questions with questions of his own that challenged others to come up with their own answers."

14

••••••••••••••••••••••••••••••••••

How to Structure an Effective Communications Hierarchy

Alan commented, "You talk about priming the pump of upward communications, but even if top management is able to induce upward communications from the lower levels, it seems as though a lot can be lost in translation as the information travels up through each level in the managerial hierarchy to the top."

"You're right," Brent responded, "because using the management hierarchy as the conduit for the transmission of information is almost always inefficient. A management hierarchy is not the same as a communications hierarchy, and the failure to understand this difference is a major obstacle in effective organizational communications.

"Regardless of the number of hierarchical levels, a major objective of any organization should be to speed up communications and minimize the chances of anything being lost in translation by going through the fewest possible levels of communications hierarchy.

"Ideally, information should be gathered near the top of the management pyramid, because people at the lower levels have a more narrow organizational perspective than do those at the higher levels.

"When information is gathered nearer the bottom of the pyramid, people interpret and summarize information in light of their own distorted self-serving interests. Then, as information passes through each level of the hierarchy on its way to top management, it becomes distorted even more. By the time the information reaches the top, it has often lost its meaning and results in decisions being made based on invalid assumptions.

"Obviously, the more levels information has to go through, the greater the distortion. This is why information should be gathered as close to the top as possible. This enhances the chances that when top management makes decisions and establishes objectives, they are more likely to be made on assumptions that are valid."

Alan asked, "Even when information is gathered nearer the top, isn't there an equally good chance that communications will be distorted at each level on the way to the lower levels?"

"Yes. Therefore, the most effective kind of communications hierarchy is one in which information is gathered near the top, then interpreted and summarized, and *directly* transmitted to the lower levels without going through intermediate levels. Conversely, there should also be a mechanism for providing feedback from the bottom *directly* to the top with the same lack of distortion."

"Could you give us an example?" Gordon asked.

Stew Leonard's Communications Hierarchy

Brent answered, "I have a good friend right here in Connecticut, whose name is Stew Leonard. He owns Stew Leonard's Dairy Store in Norwalk, which is not really a dairy store, but is rather a very large food store that does over $100 million in annual sales in one location. However, Leonard's carries only 600 or so items. This is less than 5 percent of the items you would normally find in a supermarket, but these items represent the bulk of food store sales.

"Stew Leonard's has over 800 employees, and I don't know of an organization that has a more efficient and effective communications hierarchy. Top management at Stew Leonard's uses four major but simple ways of communicating directly with their customers and then passing information down to managers at the lower levels, and then receiving feedback.

1. A large suggestion box is prominently displayed at the front of the store, with a sign that has a picture of Leonard and a message "What do you like, what don't you like...I'd love to know." The goal is to encourage customers to submit their suggestions

about how the store can better serve them. Each day, up to 100 suggestions are collected from the box by Stew Leonard's executive assistant. They are then summarized and distributed to the managers at the lower levels for appropriate action before 11 A.M..

2. "Focus Groups" are held monthly. They are attended by Leonard's department managers and approximately 20 customers. The meetings usually begin with Leonard asking, "What don't you like about our store?"

3. Top management also spends a considerable amount of time 'Managing by Poking Around'; walking around the store, observing, asking questions, and talking with customers and employees.

4. Approximately 30 managers, representing every level of management, meet weekly. These meetings provide the opportunity for managers at all levels of the management hierarchy to communicate directly with each other. A portion of each meeting is devoted to the various managers reporting on the action they have taken about suggestions from the suggestion box, the focus groups, and what has been observed by 'poking around.'"

Brent then turned to Gordon. "What I've just described appears to be a very effective communications hierarchy, but can you suggest a potential problem that this type of structure might create?"

"Would it be the possibility of some managers usurping the authority of other managers?"

"Exactly. Now what policy could enhance the chances that this wouldn't happen?"

"One that states that no one can usurp another person's authority."

"That's good, but we could make the policy more specific by saying that everyone in the organization can communicate freely among themselves as long as these communications do not redirect the efforts of anyone who answers to another manager, or in any other way undermines the authority of another manager."

"That sounds reasonable," Gordon said.

Richard added, "It's inexcusable for anyone, particularly a manager, to say or do anything that reflects unfavorably on another person's manager. This is disruptive, bad for morale, and makes the person doing the criticizing look unprofessional.

"For example, if I have a criticism of one of Barbara's salespeople, I should discuss it with Barbara and let her handle it. Since she's accountable for the salespeople, for me to criticize any of them directly would usurp her authority.

"In addition, if I'm critical of you to one of your people, it undermines your authority. In both instances, this makes me look bad.

"In our meeting on Wednesday, I'd like to discuss why communications is the beginning of most cause and effect cycles in management."

Brent concluded the session. "In all organizational communications hierarchies, whether information is gathered at the top of the management pyramid or at the bottom, the information must be combined with managerial ability, experience, and intuition to arrive at managerial assumptions upon which decisions are then made.

"There's a very important message here. Communications are only the beginning of a cause and effect cycle. Communications lead to assumptions, which in turn lead to decisions, implementation, and finally results. Therefore, the quality of each step in the cycle is largely a function of the quality of communications, and managements' ability to interpret these communications and arrive at valid assumptions."

· ·

The Essence of Management

● ●

Management by Assumptions

● ● ● ● ● ● ● ● ● ● ● ● ● ● ● ● ● ●

Assumptions and Decision Making

"In all organizational communications hierarchies," Brent began, "whether information is gathered at the top of the pyramid, or at the bottom, the information must be combined with managerial ability, experience, and intuition to arrive at managerial assumptions upon which decisions are then made.

"I've developed a management technique which I refer to as 'Management by Assumptions,' and I've found it to be very effective." Brent then referred to the board on which he had earlier written the following diagram:

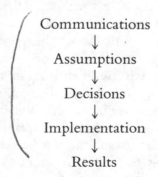

Communications
↓
Assumptions
↓
Decisions
↓
Implementation
↓
Results

"There's a very important message here. Communications are only the beginning of a cause and effect cycle. Communications lead to assumptions, which in turn lead to decisions, implementation, and finally results.

"Therefore, the quality of each step in the cycle is largely a function of the quality of communications, and management's ability to interpret these communications and arrive at valid assumptions, not only before making decisions, but more importantly, after the decisions are made.

"Our original assumptions almost never remain totally valid throughout the implementation period. The longer the period from the point the original assumptions are made until the final results are realized, the more likely the assumptions will lose a significant amount of their validity.

"Under my concept of management by assumptions, after decisions are made to pursue objectives, the major focus then shouldn't be on our objectives, but rather on the assumptions upon which our decisions to pursue the objectives were based. The focus should continue to be on monitoring these assumptions as we move through the implementation period. If we detect significant changes in the validity of our assumptions, we then have an opportunity to make timely decisions about whether we should alter, or perhaps even abort, our original objectives.

"Since managerial results are the culmination of cause and effect cycles beginning with communications that lead to assumptions, I reject the well-known management philosophy that calls for managing by results. If you wait for the results before evaluating decisions, it's obviously too late to alter them.

"A disastrous example of this was the Challenger space shuttle tragedy. Assumptions were made about the safety of the launch which were not disproved until the Challenger had exploded, and the analysis of the results was nothing more than an autopsy.

"Former Secretary of State William Rogers, the chairman of the committee investigating the Challenger disaster, repeatedly stated in his report that there were flaws in the decision-making process.

"In my opinion, the most obvious flaw was that those who made the decisions involving the launch did not practice management by assumptions. They didn't continuously monitor the validity of the assumptions about their decisions throughout the implementation period until the very moment of the liftoff. If, before the launch, they had reassessed their risk assumption about the effect of the unusually cold weather on the so-called O-rings, the results would probably have been dramatically different.

"What then," asked Brent, "would you say is the most critical assumption about almost every managerial decision?"

"The assumption about the risk involved," Mike answered, "because every management decision involves a degree of risk. Stanley was very conscious of this, and he was always asking the question: 'What's the worst thing that could happen if we make this decision, and what impact would it have on Enfield?'"

Brent added, "You may say to yourself, 'This isn't anything new. I always establish assumptions before making a decision,' and you're probably right. This is one reason you're successful managers. You probably do this unconsciously, if not instinctively. It's likely, however, that some of those answering to you do not consciously establish the underlying assumptions of their decisions, and even many of those who do fail to revalidate them throughout the implementation period.

"I'm convinced without a doubt that if you will focus on management by assumptions and motivate those decision makers who answer to you to do the same, you'll achieve a higher quality of decisions made and results obtained by your organizational groups."

16

• •

How to Use Assumptions in Evaluating Your Associates
The Decision Makers and Production Workers

• • • • • • • • • • • • • •
Evaluating Decision Makers

"How can you motivate decision makers to manage by assumptions?" Alan asked.

"By making it clear that they'll be personally evaluated based more on the quality of the *assumptions* they make about their decisions, than on the decisions and subsequent results," Brent replied.

"Then, make sure they understand why it's to their advantage to be evaluated this way by describing how this provides broader, more realistic, and more fair criteria than evaluating based on their results.

"Results are often a function of factors over which they have no control. For example, unusual weather and other acts of God, labor strikes, technological advances, and unexpected shortages. Because

of these factors, decision makers are often encouraged to avoid making prudent decisions that have significant risks, because the potential rewards for showing good results aren't worth the punishment received for showing bad results."

Mike asked, "How does evaluating based on assumptions tie in with periodic performance reviews?"

"It doesn't," Brent responded. "I believe most periodic performance reviews are counterproductive because they usually result in inconsistent performance. Immediately prior to a review, it's only natural for people to maximize their efforts. Afterward, they slack off until the time approaches for their next review.

"This is why these reviews make no more sense than for a football coach to conduct performance reviews of his players every three to six months. A good coach continuously reviews the performance of his players and takes corrective action as needed, between games and, more importantly, even during games when the action is hot. The fast-moving nature of organizations makes it logical for managers to operate in a similar manner, and evaluate their people continuously.

"Periodic performance reviews for decision makers are illogical because of the time lag between their decisions and the subsequent results of those decisions.

"These two events are out of sync, and there's no significant relationship between the quality of their decisions at the time of the review, and the quality of results being obtained at that same time from their previous decisions.

"In addition, management is an *unnatural* game, because you usually play the best when you're showing the worst scores—and vice versa. On one hand, when I've been in trouble and had circled the wagons, I was receiving the most criticism and showing the poorest results. Strangely enough, it was then that I was working hardest and being most effective.

"On the other hand, when I was showing my best results, I wasn't working as hard and was less effective, even though I was receiving congratulations for the good job I was doing."

Alan said, "I'm going to have to rethink how I manage some of my people, because it has always been drilled into my head that managers should be primarily evaluated based on their results."

"Alan, I'm not in any way discounting the importance of results because that's the way managers are ultimately judged. However,

if a manager and his group do a good job of establishing assumptions and then monitor to insure the continued validity of these assumptions during the implementation period, better results will be achieved as a by-product."

● ● ● ● ● ● ● ● ● ● ● ● ● ● ● ● ●
Evaluating Production Workers

Mike said, "Most of my people do production work, which doesn't require a great deal of thinking. How can we evaluate them?"

"We can continuously monitor the production speeds of those who do routine work and establish standards based on our assumptions about the levels of production we expect from them. This is why I *am* in favor of periodic performance reviews for these people.

"However, I'm not in favor of combining performance reviews with compensation reviews. When this is done, if people are performing well, they'll expect an increase in compensation, and managers should maintain the flexibility of being able to give their people good evaluations during a performance review without feeling that they must increase their compensation at the same time."

Mike responded, "When I review the performance of my people, I also discuss their job descriptions. What's your attitude about job descriptions?"

"They usually make a lot of sense for those in routine jobs at the lower levels, because you often have to describe in detail what's expected of them.

"However, I don't believe in job descriptions for those with thinking-type jobs. This places too much of a limitation on how they perform their jobs. I prefer to arrive at an agreement about their responsibilities, and then give them as much latitude as possible in creatively discharging their responsibilities."

17

●●●●●●●●●●●●●●●●●●●●●●●●●●●●●●●●●●●●●●

How to Make Better Decisions

Gordon asked, "Since we've discussed how to use management by assumptions in improving the quality of our decisions, could we discuss some other ways?"

"What would you say some of them are?" Brent asked.

"Well, one way would be to get all of the facts."

"I don't mean to split hairs," Brent responded, "but you said *all* of the facts. We can probably agree that we never really get all of the facts. If we did, the decision could just as easily be made by a 'bean counter' in the lower ranks.

"We talked about achieving the right objectives with a *sufficient* amount of resources. In making effective management decisions, our focus should be on getting a sufficient amount of facts: an amount consistent with the importance of the decision.

"The more fact gathering a manager does, or has someone else do, the greater is the risk that the cost of gathering additional facts is not worth the improvement in the chances of making the right decisions by doing so."

Richard added, "I often use an approach attributed to Benjamin Franklin. I draw a vertical line down the center of a sheet of paper. On the left side, I list the advantages of taking a certain course. On the right side, I list the disadvantages.

"However, unless each of the advantages and disadvantages is weighted as to importance, the number of advantages compared to the disadvantages is irrelevant. We could have many advantages on the left side of the paper, and only one disadvantage on the right.

115

However, if the *one* disadvantage of making the decision is the risk that it could put us out of business, we should obviously reassess the situation."

Alan commented, "I'm hesitant to admit this, but I probably spend much less than half of my time making decisions, and even then they are usually small ones."

Brent smiled and responded, "Then I would give you good marks as a manager. Managers who are constantly making decisions, particularly a lot of big ones, usually aren't on top of their jobs — their jobs are on top of them. Effective big decisions are usually the natural by-products of several small ones, and most of the small ones are often wrong."

Gordon asked, "How could you make more wrong decisions than right ones and still be an effective manager?"

"I read that Thomas Edison made over two thousand wrong decisions trying to invent a practical electric light bulb, before he made the one right decision that made the bulb a success.

"I used to be a member of the Chicago Board of Trade, and I speculated in commodities. It didn't take me long to learn that when it became obvious that I'd made a wrong decision, I should immediately close out my position and take a loss. On the other hand, when I made a right decision, I maintained my position until the profitable trend appeared to have run its course. The profits from that one right decision would often offset the losses incurred by many smaller wrong decisions."

Richard added, "We can also often improve the quality of our decisions by not making them too quickly. I once read that Napoleon didn't open his mail for 30 days. By that time, most of the problems described in his mail had gone away and required no action. I don't recommend following Napoleon's management style, but there's an interesting message here. For example, I've often found that while I'm in the process of deciding what to do about problem employees, they resign."

Brent said, "People I've worked with know that I will not make a decision on the spot if I have the option of sleeping on it overnight. A good night's sleep often seems to provide the opportunity for thoughts to ferment in my mind and improves the quality of my decisions.

"Stanley used to say that his office was in this remote location of the building because he liked to make decisions away from the action in the same way that generals in combat tend to do. He said it helped him maintain his perspective without getting caught up in the emotions of others when he was thinking about decisions that needed to be made. It was Stanley's influence that made me decide to move my office.

"I believe the very best way to make effective decisions is to combine management by assumptions with the objectivity and participation of others."

Gordon asked, "Would this be management by committee?"

"Not really, Gordon. Management by committee does involve participation from others, but decisions are made based on a majority vote of the group. Under participative management, a decision is made by the one person who has the accountability for the final results.

"However, this person can delegate any or all of the responsibility and a related amount of authority to his associates, and hold them accountable for their part of the responsibility.

"For example, on the eve of the Normandy invasion during World War II, General Dwight Eisenhower met with a roomful of his top military advisors and weather experts to obtain their participation. Because of the strong probability of bad weather and disastrous results, some of them urged that the invasion be postponed.

"The assumptions, including a risk assessment, were established and discussed. Then Eisenhower alone made the decision to launch the invasion, because he was accountable for the final results."

● ● ● ● ● ● ● ● ● ● ● ● ● ● ● ●
The Right Way to Delegate

Brent continued, "Once the decision was made, Eisenhower was no different from any other manager—his success or failure depended on how well he delegated the responsibility for achieving the objectives.

"I've found the following steps to be effective in delegating responsibilities to associates:

1. Discuss assumptions, including an assessment of the risk involved. This will usually eliminate misunderstandings, loopholes, and excuses later if the desired results aren't produced.

2. Determine the extent of authority they'll have over the resources of people, time, money, information, and physical resources.

3. Make clear the extent to which they'll be held accountable for achieving their part of the objectives, how they'll be monitored, and how they'll be expected to report back on their progress.

4. Obtain their commitments to achieve their part of the group's objectives. The best forum for this is in tape-recorded meetings among their peers. These tapes eliminate any possibility of future debates about previously made commitments."

Mike commented, "Delegation can be a two-way street. For example, Sam Oliver, my first-shift supervisor, told me he was having scheduling problems and was thinking about putting some of his people on four 10-hour days, instead of five 8-hour days. I told him that some of the members of my production managers' trade association had done this. Sam asked if I would phone them to see how this had worked out and give him my recommendation about whether or not I thought he should do the same thing.

"After phoning some of the members, I told Sam what they had said and I felt it was probably a good idea to make the change. As a result, *Sam* made the decision to change the shifts, because *he* had the accountability."

• •

How to Obtain Meaningful Participation When Making Decisions

Brent said, "At times, I've had strong opinions and made decisions without the participation of my people. As a result, I received less commitment from those I was depending on to implement the decision.

"Other times, I've felt just as strongly about decisions but went through the exercise of getting participation for the sole purpose of obtaining commitment. Then, because of what was expressed during our discussions, I became convinced that my preconceived opinions were wrong and I changed my mind.

"Whenever I've made bad decisions without obtaining participation, there's no assurance my decisions would've been better with participation, but the chances are they would have."

Alan asked, "But when managers are looking for participation, if they have the authority and have a strong preconception about what should be done, why would their people risk expressing a contrary opinion that might backfire? It seems as if they would just give a rubber stamp approval of the managers' position."

"You're right, but managers usually shouldn't telegraph their opinions when looking for participation. Although it is *unnatural* for me, I usually try to conceal my opinions, at least until I've heard from the group, and often even after the decision is made."

"Why would you conceal your opinion after a decision is made?"

"Barbara told us about how she attempts to obtain the participation of her prospects, making them coauthors when she's drafting her proposals to them: The prospects then have more of a vested interest, because they're in essence buying their own proposals.

"Good managers should do the same thing. When managers obtain participation from their associates, and the consensus of their associates is consistent with the managers' preconceived opinions, then the managers should let their associates believe it was their idea. By doing so, their associates become more deeply committed to achieving the objectives."

Brent then pointed to the quotation over the rolltop desk and quoted: " 'When the great leader's work is done, the people say, "We did it ourselves." ' "

Alan pressed the point. "Well, what happens when managers conceal their opinions and their people unanimously disagree? Then the managers are faced with the difficulty of convincing their people that they should reverse their positions."

"That rarely happens," Brent answered. "In my company, while those of us in the management group were in the process of discussing proposed decisions, we often modified our respective positions to some degree and arrived at mutually acceptable solutions.

"Nevertheless, let's take your example. Suppose we as managers are in strong disagreement with our staffs. First, we can try to persuade our people to accept our positions. If that fails, in a much smaller way our situation would not be unlike that of General Eisenhower at Normandy. Like Eisenhower, we have the authority and are ultimately accountable. Therefore, once we make decisions, even if our people disagree with the decisions, they have a responsibility to support them. If they don't, it's insubordination, and we should deal with it accordingly." Brent smiled and added, "If that sounds like a threat, you're right."

Gordon asked, "You said that managers should *usually* try to conceal their opinions about a decision when it involves participation. When would they *not* do that?"

"Alan pointed out the difficulty of convincing people to reverse their positions. When I know a necessary decision will be unpopular, I want to avoid having people take a contrary position, only to have to reverse themselves later.

"In this instance, participation should be deemphasized. At the outset, I take a strong position about what must be done, and my objective then is to obtain agreement and commitment, even when it is somewhat cosmetic and involuntary."

Richard gave an example. "When we installed our first automated production line, Stanley and I knew it was going to be an unpopular decision, particularly with Mike, because it involved laying off a number of his people. So we let the management group know from the very beginning that this was something we must do, and then we proceeded to convince them we were right."

Mike smiled, "I'll admit I did an about-face on that one. At first I was very much against automating, but I finally realized we had to do it to stay competitive."

SEVEN

How to Obtain More Leverage from Your Resources

The Benefits of Hands-off Inspirational Management

The Only Justification for Management

"Everything that we've talked about and done since I've been at Enfield has been directed toward achieving *more* and *better* results. What we are dealing with then is *leverage*.

"Being able to obtain leverage by working together in concert, instead of as individual performers, is our only justification for working in a organizational group.

"One benefit of working together in establishing objectives and planning, is to obtain the *leverage* of the combined thinking of the group. However, a less obvious—but perhaps more important—benefit is that performing these activities is a great potential source of inspiration.

Developing an Attitude and an Atmosphere for Providing Inspiration

"The objectives we establish and *expect to achieve* are more inspiring than those that we've *already achieved*. What we have already achieved may be very satisfying, but is hardly any longer inspiring. The plan-

123

ning process for achieving these objectives is also very inspirational because we *always* plan to succeed — we *never* intentionally plan to fail.

"Top management is often deluded by assuming that those at the lower levels are also inspired by *our objectives*. This isn't necessarily so, and this possibility becomes even less likely the lower people are in the organizational structure. The reason is that they perceive less of a direct relationship between their own personal well being, and that of the organizational group, and unfortunately, they're right!"

Gordon asked, "How then can we inspire them?"

"Their inspiration, or lack of inspiration, is a reflection of the atmosphere and the attitude that's generated within top management and inevitably seeps down throughout the organization.

"Our associates at the various levels will become inspired if this atmosphere and attitude displays that we

- Care about them
- Feel that they're important
- Believe in them
- Offer them an opportunity to realize a sense of accomplishment.

"We can also enhance the chances of our associates becoming inspired if we'll practice effective hands-off management by maintaining a low profile and orchestrating their results by giving them guidance, instead of telling our people what to do."

Richard said, "I believe the great hidden resource in most organizations is the difference between the *average* jobs that some of their people are doing and the *outstanding* jobs they *would do* if they were more inspired.

"I would also add that organizations are always faced with the obvious threats of sales being down, costs being up, and more pressure from competition. However, I'm convinced that the greatest potential threat exists inside of organizations, and is rarely even recognized or addressed. That threat is the loss of our own inspiration, and the inspiration of our associates."

Alan posed the question, "Why then isn't the power of inspiration given more attention by most managers?"

Brent responded, "Because inspiration is an intangible *emotion* that's not directly measurable and is often even thought of in the spiritual realm. The word *inspiration* is derived from the words that mean to 'breathe spirit,' and when people are inspired, their energy and enthusiasm is at a much higher plane than is natural or normal. I have observed this phenomenon within myself and in others many times.

● ●

When to Be Hands-On and When to Be Hands-Off

"This brings us to the subject of *hands-off management,* which is much more conducive to our associates being inspired in their work."

Gordon commented, "Brent, hands-off management seems to imply that these managers don't do any work and are only figureheads."

"I perceive hands-off managers," Brent responded, "as those who develop attitudes and disciplines that will enable them to keep their hands off those nonmanagement activities they shouldn't be involved with, and who'll delegate as much responsibility and related decision-making authority as possible down through the hierarchy to the lowest appropriate levels.

"These managers can be contrasted with hands-on managers who tend to spend too much time on nonmanagerial activities and require or encourage responsibilities and related decision-making authority to rise to the highest possible level in the organization.

"This isn't to say that hands-on managers can't be effective and provide inspiration to their people, so let's take a closer look at these two extremes of management style.

"Hands-on managers provide inspirational *leadership* by giving *direction* to their people.

"*Leadership* under this concept can be described as the ingredient of personality that causes others to *follow.*

"*Direction* under this concept is a direct course of action that is imposed as *authoritative instruction, order, or command.* Translation: These managers *tell* their people what to do!

"At the other extreme we have hands-off inspirational managers who provide *leadership* and *guidance* for people to generate their *own* inspiration."

"Are you suggesting," Alan asked, "that all managers should aspire to being hands-off managers?"

"I am to the extent that it doesn't become counterproductive or result in the abdication of your responsibilities.

"This isn't some abstract, off-the-wall textbook theory, because I was very much of a hands-on manager and I went through the transition of becoming a hands-off manager. My *once successful* hands-on management style had destroyed my effectiveness as my time, energy, and inspiration became increasingly more diluted among too many responsibilities.

"However, I'd be the first to admit that during the early stages of new ventures, and from time to time thereafter, situations will occur that demand our hands-on attention. Then, we *must* be like 'bell-cows,' leading the way with a high profile, showing and telling people what to do, and perhaps putting in longer hours and *directly* producing more results than anyone else in our group.

"Nevertheless, after our hands-on attention is no longer required, if we don't revert to being hands-off managers, and if our responsibilities continue to increase, we can't simultaneously focus more broadly and more deeply on these responsibilities.

"If we don't delegate some of these responsibilities, we'll be limited to the time and effort we can *personally* expend. We'll also eventually become less focused on those few top priorities that represent the greatest potential in results and we'll then be faced with the threat of the loss of our own inspiration—which will inevitably seep down to our people."

Richard contributed, "Stanley used to talk about how when we take on a new management challenge, we begin as hands-off managers, not by design, but rather by necessity, because we must devote most of our time and thoughts to the future in establishing objectives, and planning how to achieve these objectives. We also give a high priority to attracting the right people, and how we should organize their responsibilities to achieve our objectives. These are *all* hands-off management activities."

Brent added, "When I first met Stanley, he pointed out to me how I was in this position when I started my first business, but how I had then begun a gradual, unconscious, and counterproductive, transition to focusing more on my work of *today*. I was giving *hands-on direction* to my people, and Stanley convinced me that because of my inertia, I would continue this trend unless I made a *conscious* effort to reverse it.

● ●

The Transition to Hands-Off Management

"As a result of the effective management practices I learned from Stanley, I very quickly discovered how I could program myself out of my major problems by becoming a hands-off manager.

"I've observed that an occupational hazard among too many managers is their failure to make the transition at the appropriate time from hands-on to hands-off management as their responsibilities increase.

"This process is a transition, as opposed to a sudden shift, because it's a process that normally occurs over a period of time.

"Ironically, when hands-on managers' responsibilities increase, these managers become even more hands-on, which only serves to compound the problem."

Why Managers Fail to Make the Transition

Gordon asked, "Brent, why do so many managers fail to make this transition?"

"There are several reasons:

1. The heritage and inertia of being hands-on managers.
2. They don't *recognize* or *accept* the need to make the transition.
3. They often don't have the *right* organizational structure for making the transition.
4. They have a conscious, or a subconscious, fear of losing control.

The Hands-on Heritage of Most Managers

"First, what's the hands-on heritage of most managers?"

Alan responded, "I came directly out of business school into a management position in our family-owned business. I had hands-on responsibilities as a part of my management training."

Mike answered, "Some of us were promoted into entry-level management positions from hands-on nonmanagement and still retained some of our hands-on responsibilities."

"Then, there are entrepreneurs like Brent," Richard said, "who start their own businesses without any previous management experience."

Brent responded, "Those are good examples of the hands-on heritage of most managers, so now let's address the issue of how managers can *recognize* and *accept* the need to make this transition.

When to Begin or Accelerate the Process

"I believe you should begin or accelerate the transition

If your *organizational group*
- Isn't meeting its objectives

If your *best people*
- Are obviously losing their inspiration, and/or
- Are leaving the organization

And if *your management style* is
- A bias for too much action, and you aren't spending enough time on the thinking component of your management job, and if
- You're overcommitted to the work of today, if not to yesterday's still uncompleted work, and if
- You have a tendency to allow distractions to divert you from your more important priorities, and if
- You've allowed yourself, or any of your key people, to become irreplaceable, or approach this condition."

• •
Management Hierarchy Is Taking a "Bum Rap"

Brent continued, "Some managers don't make the transition to being more hands-off because they don't have the *right* organizational structure.

"It's very popular for management writers and speakers to bash management hierarchy and extol the virtues of having a flat organizational structure. However, in my opinion, management hierarchy is getting a 'bum rap.'

"I believe that the fad of bashing *management* hierarchies was brought on by the tremendous strides that have been made in information-processing technology. This has resulted in the flattening of *communications* hierarchies, which has been very beneficial. This, however, is not the same as management hierarchies.

"Historically, the *art of management* was often intuitive, 'fly by the seat of your pants' management, and subjective decision-making authority was vested in very few people.

"However, the introduction of the computer has enhanced the *science of management* and often makes more levels of management desirable, as managers throughout the organization have instant access to databases of information to aid them in more objective decision making.

"*All* organizations are hierarchies and *must* have one or more levels of hierarchical management. A management hierarchy is nothing more than a pyramid of command and has been the only effective way to organize a group of people going all the way back to the beginning of recorded history.

"This isn't to say that all management hierarchies are effective. Some organizations have too many levels, others not enough. When in doubt about the right number, opting for fewer levels is usually more efficient and cost effective."

Gordon asked, "How then could an organization have too few levels?"

Brent answered, "Highly autocratic organizations usually have too few, and they also have too few managers at the upper levels. This results in very little participative management down through the ranks and provides a breeding ground for irreplaceable managers. These managers also have more people answering to them than they can effectively manage."

Richard added, "The other side of the coin is that too many levels often create bureaucracies which slow up and break down communications. Also, organizations, like people, take on fat in the middle. Organizational fat usually shows up in the form of too many levels of *middle* management, and too much cost for managerial overhead. This makes for inefficient operations."

Brent commented, "Whereas, most of the stodgy, old-line *Fortune* 500 companies probably have too many levels of management, based on my experience, many smaller organizations have too few levels."

"Is the right number a function of size?" Gordon asked.

"Sometimes, but not always," Brent responded, "it depends on the organization. The United States Army has at least 13 levels of management, but the Catholic church only has five: the pope, cardinals, archbishops, bishops, and parish priests.

"Enfield also has five levels, beginning with the office of president, Richard as executive vice-president, then the rest of you in this room as senior managers. Each of you, in turn, has a line of managers answering to you, and some of those have still another line of managers answering to them.

"Managers should keep an open mind and *not* assume that the ideal is to have the fewest possible levels of management, because adding more levels has been a potentially valuable hands-off management tool, which, according to the Biblical records, goes back at least 3,500 years to Moses. In Exodus, Chapter 18, verses 25 and 26, you can read about how Moses established a management hierarchy of five levels and was able to increase his 'span of control.' "

How to Leverage Your Span of Control

Alan commented, "The right number of hierarchical management levels is one thing, but a manager's 'span of control' is something much different. Our textbooks in business school described the span of control as the number of people one person can *directly* manage effectively, and I've read that five is the ideal number. Would you agree with that number?"

Brent answered, "I don't believe there is an *ideal* number, and only hands-on managers need to concern themselves with how many people they can *directly* manage. Hands-off managers focus on how many people they can manage *indirectly*.

"Herein, is the *primary* justification, objective, and benefit of hierarchical management. Specifically to enable managers to increase their span of control over the responsibilities and results of all of the people in their lines of authority by obtaining their

- Participation in establishing objectives
- Agreement about the amount of authority they'll have over the resources of the group in achieving their part of the groups' objectives.
- Commitment to achieving their part of the groups' objectives
- Written—or more preferably, taped—documentation of this commitment
- Understanding and agreement about a feedback mechanism for reporting their progress, or lack thereof, on an interim basis, and subsequent notification to the manager when the objectives have been achieved.

"The extent and effectiveness of the ability of managers to do this is a function of the

- Style of the managers, and their strengths and managerial competence
- Competence level of those in their group
- Degree to which they practice hands-off management
- Structure and effectiveness of their managerial hierarchy
- Control mechanisms within their organizational groups for achieving results.

"Managers' own styles, strengths, and managerial competence can almost always be improved, as can the competence level of their groups. However, this improvement can't provide the dramatic leverage that's potentially available by combining hands-off management with hierarchical effectiveness.

"The curse of hands-on managers is that when they *tell* people *what to do,* they can only leverage their effectiveness to the extent they can control the *activities* of the people who answer to them directly.

"However, hands-off managers are able to increase their span of control over the responsibilities they can handle by allowing each of those who *directly* answer to them to participate in assuming a part of their groups' responsibilities.

"Then, if these hands-off managers combine participative management with hierarchical effectiveness, they create the potential to *exponentially* increase their span of control over responsibilities and results indefinitely.

"For example, I've done some consulting with a friend whose name is Wayne Proxmire. He's an effective hands-off manager and has built a highly successful frozen food manufacturing company.

"When I first met Wayne, the management staff consisted of Wayne and four other managers who answered to him, and he was a strong advocate of participative management among his group.

"Wayne's organization continued to grow very rapidly, and now he still has the same four managers answering to him. However, each of these four managers now has four managers answering to them. By continuing to practice participative management and adding another level of management hierarchy, Wayne was able to increase his overall span of control from four managers to 20 managers—the original four plus 16 additional managers.

"Effective hierarchies provide hands-off managers with even more leverage on their span of control by enabling those down through the hierarchical levels to assume increasingly more responsibilities.

"With sufficient levels of hierarchy, those in the lower levels can assume these responsibilities in more reasonable increments. This is a more logical progression than the quantum steps people must take in assuming responsibilities when there are too few levels of hierarchy."

Gordon asked, "Should managers attempt to maximize the number of people who *directly* answer to them as long as they can manage them effectively?"

"Not necessarily. If managers have the option of having more people answering to them *or* adding another level of hierarchy, it's often better to add another level of hierarchy. This is particularly true in the three top levels of the management hierarchy.

"The fewer people managers have answering to them, the more these managers can *focus* and become *committed* to those objectives that are highest on their list of *priorities*. If managers focus on everything, they haven't focused on anything.

"More hierarchy can also enable managers to focus their *own efforts* on those priorities where they can apply their greatest strengths, and neutralize their weaknesses by delegating other priorities to better qualified people."

How to Structure an Effective Management Hierarchy

Alan asked, "We've discussed how to structure an effective communications hierarchy, but how can we determine the right hierarchical management structure?"

"These are two key questions in determining the right hierarchy:

1. How many levels of management *should* your organization have?
2. How many people *should* answer to the various managers in *your* organization, particularly to those managers at the top two levels?

"If you have more than three or four managers answering to any other manager in your top three levels, I suggest that top management should take a hard look at the possibility of doing some restructuring.

"Based on my experience, the CEOs of smaller, growing companies usually have too many managers answering to them. Therefore, the most effective place to add a level of management is often directly below the CEO.

"For example, when I began working with a CEO in Michigan, whose company manufactures machine stampings, the CEO had six people answering to him. It was immediately obvious to me that he was suffering from the same three common managerial pitfalls we discussed earlier. He was overcommitted, irreplaceable, and with six managers answering to him, he had too many intruders on his turf.

"More hierarchy was the quick and easy solution. Two of the six managers who previously answered to the CEO were selected to continue answering to him directly, and the other four managers would then answer to the two managers who answered to the CEO. He retained the same number of managers and simply added a level of hierarchy.

"The first level of managers, strangely enough, are commonly referred to as supervisors. The next most likely place to add another level of management is directly under this existing level of managers, because except for the CEOs of smaller companies, these first-level managers are usually the only ones who have too many people answering to them. There are two reasons for this. One is that because they only have direct producers answering to them, they are not able to leverage their efforts through other managers. The other reason is that first-level managers are often required to spend an inordinate amount of hands-on management time directing, then monitoring and inspecting the activities of their production people.

"To summarize, the appropriate question for management then is *not* 'How can we reduce the number of levels of management?' but rather 'Does our organization have the most effective number of levels?'

"Although some organizations obviously have too many levels of management, this doesn't usually represent the great potential threat to the survival of organizations by having too few levels."

"Why is that?" Barbara asked.

"On one hand, I mentioned earlier that most of the stodgy, old-line *Fortune* 500 companies probably have too many levels. However, they evolved into this condition over an extended period of time. Even when they arrive at a point of having too many levels and perhaps operating somewhat inefficiently, this is rarely life-threatening to the organization, and there is usually ample time to take corrective action.

"On the other hand, when smaller, growing organizations have too few levels, they're usually quite young in their life cycles, and if corrective action is not taken within a fairly short period of time, it can literally cause the demise of the organizations.

"These smaller organizations are usually growing because their hands-on managers have a strong bias for action and attempt to maximize the amount of responsibilities they can personally handle and minimize the responsibilities they entrust to others.

"I speak from experience when I say that learning to become hands-off managers and establish effective management hierarchies is very often the last, and yet most important managerial skill they develop—if it's not already too late!"

● ●
Monitoring and Controlling: The Managers' Choices

Brent said, "The last reason I mentioned why managers fail to make the transition to hands-off management is that they have a conscious or subconscious fear of losing control.

"There's a story about the CEO of a construction company who was visiting a construction site, and he asked a bricklayer what he was doing. The bricklayer responded that he was laying brick. He asked another the same question, and this bricklayer responded that he was making $15 an hour. He asked a third bricklayer what he was doing, and the bricklayer raised his arms to the sky, and with a far-away look in his eyes, responded: 'I'm building a magnificent cathedral.'

"The sad sequel to this story is that the bricklayer who was building the magnificent cathedral was fired because he was supposed to be building a post office.

"Many of us walk around at times with the fear that some of our people are building cathedrals when they should be building post offices, and this can be a very valid fear.

"Therefore, there's often a *natural* tendency to attempt to maintain tight control over the activity of those who answer to us.

"However, by becoming effective hands-off managers we can have the best of both worlds. Not only will our associates be more inspired to produce more and better results, the managers will be able to

- Delegate more responsibilities and
- Maintain better control."

Gordon commented, "To say that you can delegate more responsibilities and still maintain better control sounds like a contradiction in terms. It seems to me that the more responsibility managers delegate, the more vulnerable they are to the potential damage their people can do by virtue of their decision-making authority, and the authority they have over the resources of their groups."

Barbara added, "I agree, and it also appears to put managers in the position of having to make a difficult choice. If we delegate more responsibility, we risk being damaged by losing some of our control. The other choice is to delegate less responsibility and maintain better control, but lose some of our leverage."

Gordon added, "I would also think that hands-off managers automatically lose a great deal of control over the activities of their people, particularly those in the lower levels."

"You're right, Gordon, and unfortunately, in an attempt to maintain better control, too many managers make the choice of delegating fewer responsibilities.

"Managers have the choice of either controlling more activities and fewer results, or controlling fewer activities and more results.

"Hands-on managers attempt to control activities, which is very difficult and time consuming. This is because they must have more detailed knowledge of the work of those who answer to them, and they must also maintain close surveillance to insure that people are doing what they have been told.

"Hands-off managers spend very little time attempting to control activities. They focus on monitoring and controlling the validity of assumptions about decisions, and the subsequent results."

When to Monitor; When to Control

Gordon asked, "Several times you have used the expression 'monitoring and controlling,' and you included this in describing the seven managerial functions. I'm familiar with the concept of control from business school and management books I've read, but I don't recall that any particular emphasis was ever placed on monitoring. What's your perception of the difference?"

"To me, Gordon, *control* implies something that's punitive or restraining, and most of us don't like to be controlled in this sense. This is why we should focus on monitoring assumptions and, to a lesser degree, activities. We should only attempt to control the activities of people as a last resort by imposing restrictions or restructuring jobs. If this fails, you may have to consider terminating these people."

Richard commented, "Some people can't be managed effectively without being monitored. With others, the better the results and the more confidence I have in a person's ability to produce results, the less inclined I am to monitor their activities closely, if at all."

Gordon responded somewhat critically, "That sounds like you're avoiding an essential management function, and I've always heard that 'people do what we *inspect*, not what we *expect*.'"

Richard smiled and said, "The fallacy of that statement is that the higher someone is in the management hierarchy, the less prudent it is to try to monitor their activities, because we can't *inspect* the thinking activity that takes place in the minds of those very few people within any organization, who, as Brent pointed out, will determine its future success or failure.

"In my own case, I can't monitor the activities of some of those who answer to me, because I don't have the vaguest idea what they're doing. This is certainly true with those in engineering, or research and development, or in your case, Gordon, when you are programming a computer."

Brent added, "Unlike Richard with some of his people, Barbara is able to monitor her salespeople because she has a sales background, and often understands what her people are supposed to be doing better than they do."

"I monitor the results of *all* of my people," Barbara replied, "but I spend very little time monitoring the activities of my veteran salespeople, because they are meeting their quotas. In the case of my rookies, I spend a lot of time monitoring and analyzing their activities as well as coaching them, because they're not yet producing the results I am expecting.

"I also require my people to keep very simple sales call records in three-ring notebooks. On the top of the preprinted call report form, there are four questions:

- Who did you call on?
- What did you talk about?
- What do you plan to do next?
- When are you going to do it?

"I read and initial these reports at irregular intervals. Since my people never know when I'll ask for the records, it disciplines them to keep their reports current while the calls are still fresh in their minds, instead of trying to reconstruct them later.

"This basic information takes very little of their time, and although the information is helpful to me, the real purpose is to help my salespeople discipline themselves to plan and stay well organized."

Brent concluded, "Thanks, Barbara. You have an impressive system. I'll see all of you again on Monday at four."

EIGHT

••••••••••••••••••••••••••••••••••••

How to Deal with the Unnatural Relationship Between Managers and Direct Producers

19

● ●

How to Maximize Your Leverage from Direct Producers

Brent opened the meeting. "Mike asked if we could talk about the relationship between managers, and those who aren't in management. When I first met with you, I pointed out that since we're only managing when we're producing results *indirectly* through our resources, I'd like for us to continue referring to those who aren't in management as *direct producers.*

"Mike, how about starting us off?"

"You said we often fool ourselves by assuming that people at the lower levels are also inspired by *our objectives,* and that the lower they are in the organizational hierarchy, the less they see a direct relationship between their own personal well being and the well being of the organizational group. This really got my attention because most people who fall within my area of responsibility are the 'workers' in the lower levels, and I would like to know how I can maximize my leverage through their efforts."

Brent responded, "I believe the key is in

1. Developing an understanding of effective management among managers at all levels;

2. Accepting that although most direct producers will never develop a good understanding of management, steps can be taken to improve the relationship, if not the understanding;

141

3. Accepting that the first-line managers (commonly referred to as supervisors) are managers in every sense of the word and have perhaps the toughest management jobs;

4. Recognizing and making allowances for the uniqueness of the job of the first-line managers; and

5. Developing an attitude and an atmosphere in top management that will permeate the organization and enable those in the lower levels to become inspired or motivated.

"The focus of most of our discussions has been the ongoing process of developing an understanding of management among managers.

"In spite of a strong interdependence between management and direct producers, direct producers rarely understand what managers do. Furthermore, most of them *never* will have a good understanding because their jobs are so inherently different.

● ●

Management: From the Perspective of Direct Producers

"In order to deal with this specific challenge, I believe we should recognize the negative perspective that many direct producers have of managers, and how we in management tend to foster this unfortunate perception.

"During the Civil War, a Confederate private named Sam Watkins wrote the following in a letter:

I always shot at privates. . . . It was they that did the shooting and killing, and if I could kill or wound a private, why my chances were so much the better. I always looked on officers as harmless personages.

"Interestingly enough, Union General William Tecumseh Sherman, in referring to Confederate General Nathan Bedford Forrest was quoted as having said:

Forrest must be hunted down and killed if it costs 10,000 lives and bankrupts the federal treasury.

"What marvelous examples these were of the contrast in perspective about the value of those in positions of authority, such as managers and army generals, who produce results indirectly through their resources.

"Whereas Private Watkins placed great value on his direct-producing enemy counterparts, General Sherman was willing to trade the lives of 10,000 directly producing troops for the life of one of his indirectly producing counterpart generals in his enemy's army.

"In referring to officers as 'harmless personages,' Private Watkins was being much more charitable than my grandfather was in referring to those in positions of higher authority. He, like many others in the lower ranks, openly distrusted and resented management, and didn't understand what, if any, value a manager had.

"My grandfather was never a manager—he was an active member of a labor union that was always fighting management. I can remember as a young boy hearing him complain about management and how they made most of the money, while he and his coworkers did all the work.

"I doubt if his managers ever spent any time with my grandfather trying to develop his understanding of management, and although it might not have helped, it couldn't have hurt."

Resentment of Management Compensation

Mike said, "Some of my people share your grandfather's resentment about management making too much money. They also resent company profits, because to them, profits represent income to others that my workers in the plant have generated.

"To compound the problem, they see no relationship between profits and their own take home pay or welfare, and for the most part, they're right! Supply and demand determines what they're paid for their services.

"For example, a machine operator is usually paid a fixed hourly rate with only an occasional cost-of-living increase.

"Even if Enfield's profits double or triple, it doesn't make any financial difference to the machine operator. His contribution is the same, because once he learns to run the machine routinely, he becomes a slave to the machine. His productivity can't increase because it's governed by the constant speed of the machine he operates."

How Managers Hurt Their Own Image

Brent said, "I'm still trying to break Mike's habit of referring to some of those within his area of responsibility as 'workers.' We hurt ourselves when we refer to those not in management as workers, laborers, or doers. This implies that managers don't work or labor or do anything, and this only contributes to the image problem of managers.

"We're often even guilty of referring to our people as *subordinates*. By definition, this means they aren't as good as we are. Then, to remove any doubt, we refer to ourselves as their *superiors*.

"Most managers aren't familiar with the term *direct producers* because I coined it. Nevertheless, I encourage managers to accept this term, because I believe it's more descriptive, if not more flattering, than our more common descriptions."

Mike responded, "I really do like your new name for my people, but I'm still trying to get used to it. I'd like to point out another problem with my *direct producers*," he said with a smile. "It's the way they see themselves compared to management. They work in the plant where it's usually too hot in the summer and too cold in the winter. They get dirty on the job, have 15-minute coffee breaks twice a day, and a bell rings to let them know when to start and stop working.

"Now, think of how they see most managers. They see them dressed in suits, sitting in air conditioned offices, drinking coffee, talking, and even laughing. They can't see us actually producing anything, so they naturally assume we aren't working.

"They don't understand that management is a thinking job, and that Richard could be working hard even when he has his feet up on his desk, staring out of the window."

"Gimme a break, Mike," Richard responded with a laugh.

● ● ● ● ● ● ● ● ● ● ● ● ● ● ●

Why First-Line Managers Have the Toughest Management Jobs

Barbara asked, "Would you elaborate on your statement that first-line managers are commonly referred to as *supervisors,* and yet have perhaps the toughest management jobs?"

"I wish the word *supervisor* could be removed from our vocabulary, because it only confuses the understanding of management. The common perception of supervisors are those at the lowest level of management who deal primarily with direct producers. However, they're still managers in every sense of the word, and one of the best managers I've ever known had the title of *production supervisor.*

"One reason their jobs are difficult is because of their heritage. They typically came up through the ranks and have never seen the inside of a business school. Because they did good jobs as direct producers, they were promoted into management, which is entirely different from the labor-intensive work they did before.

"Unfortunately, we usually don't tell them there's a difference. We erroneously assume they either understand management or will figure it out, but they rarely do. This is why, and how, we lose a lot of direct producers and gain a lot of substandard managers.

"People usually go through a form of culture shock when they first become managers. Previously, they might've gone home at night physically tired, with empty lunch boxes, whereas now they go home mentally tired with bulging briefcases full of unfinished projects.

"They haven't discovered that management is a thinking job, and they've become victims of the 'in-basket' mentality. They stay busy during the day responding to whatever is immediate and is demanding their attention at the time, instead of working on the more important part of their jobs: thinking about and performing their managerial functions.

The Twilight Zone of the First-Line Managers

"To make matters worse, these first-line managers are in the twilight zone between management and direct production. They're like sergeants in the Army, who're ludicrously described as non-commissioned officers—whatever that means.

"Enlisted personnel view sergeants as officers, but the officers consider sergeants to be enlisted personnel. In organizations, direct producers usually think of first-line managers as a part of management, whereas management views them as being more a part of direct production.

"They aren't even treated like managers. If they have an office at all, it's usually in the plant, and they also don't dress like most managers. Finally, just to make sure they don't feel like managers, we call them *supervisors.*"

● ●

How to Deal Effectively with First-Line Managers

Alan commented to Mike, "It sounds as if your first-line managers start off in management behind the eight ball."

Mike responded, "You're right, but my biggest problem is knowing how to manage these people.

"They have to wear two hats—manager and direct producer—and they're caught in the middle. While I'm pressuring them to spend more time managing, their production people are pulling on them for more help. Since they came from a vocational background, they tend to spend too much time using these skills in performing activities that others should be doing.

"The direct production they do always involves exceptions. For example, machines need to be repaired or adjusted, or new runs have to be set up on the production lines. I had a meeting with Richard and Brent and they convinced me that although these activities have to be performed, trying to figure out if the first-line managers should do them is a lost cause."

"That sounds like abdication," Alan commented critically.

Mike laughed, "That's what I used to think. When we talked about monitoring activities and controlling results, Barbara explained how she keeps up with her people—for example, by reading their activity reports. I don't have a similar way of monitoring my first line managers."

Alan responded more sympathetically than before. "Sounds like you have a problem without a solution."

"Not really. As a result of some of our discussions about management, instead of attempting to monitor the *activities* of my first-line managers, as I used to do, I have now started monitoring their *results*. I do this based on our quality, time, delivery, and cost standards, and on our other built-in assumptions."

Brent added, "I alluded earlier to the Chinese proverb that suggests we should teach our people 'to fish for themselves.' Mike is teaching his first-line managers to fish for themselves by treating them as the managers they are. He's continuing to develop their understanding of management and the managerial functions, and how they need to be aware of keeping that delicate balance between managing and direct production.

"By meeting regularly with your first-line managers, you're getting recommendations and participation in establishing the right objectives for your production operation. In these same meetings, you're obtaining their acceptance of, and commitment to, their part of achieving your group's objectives. Most importantly, this helps you keep in touch with your first-line managers. These managers are the vital motivational and communications link to the direct producers at the lower levels—who are usually the most difficult people to manage.

● ●
First-Line Managers: Vital Links to Production Workers

"If I were a first-line manager, I'd put a sign on my desk that read: 'Upward communications, motivation, monitoring, and controlling.' This would serve as a constant reminder that these are my most valuable tools for achieving and leveraging results through my people.

"One of the first-line managers' greatest challenges is to obtain upward communications, because in the lower levels, particularly, these communications often have to be induced.

"Here again, this can be done by practicing MPA—Management by Poking Around. Instead of showing and telling their people what to do, first-line managers should focus on poking around in the production area, observing, and asking questions.

"Production workers, and most others, will only *voluntarily* communicate to their managers what they believe is in their own best interests. Therefore, in responding to what their people communicate to them, managers can induce further open communications by displaying why it's to their people's advantage to continue communicating with their managers. Otherwise, they'll be inhibited from speaking up in the future.

"Some first-line managers try to be part of the gang in order to induce upward communications, but this is an ineffective sham that may cause them to lose the respect of their people. As a part of management, the first-line managers should echo higher management's thinking and support their decisions."

Gordon asked, "But if first-line managers always side with management, doesn't this inhibit upward communications?"

Richard answered. "Gordon, their situation is no different from this management group. The first-line managers can side with and fight for their people during the decision-making process, but once the decision is made, they have an obligation to support and echo the decisions made by those in higher authority who have the overall accountability for the final results. If this were not the case, instead of an organization we would only have a mob of people pulling in different directions."

Mike added, "For example, my first-line managers wanted more space for the lunch and break area in the plant. We had to turn them down because the space was needed to enlarge the shipping department. Only one manager didn't accept and support the decision. After it was made, he continued to side with his people and blamed higher management for not getting them more space. This only hurt him, because it made his people—and me—view him as one of their peers rather than as their manager."

Brent closed the meeting by saying, "On Wednesday, I would like to discuss the differences in how first-line managers and managers at higher levels can motivate their people."

How to Effectively Motivate Your People

• •

20

The Unique Motivational Challenge of First-Line Managers

"Of all of those in management," Brent said, "the first-line managers usually have the most difficult challenge when it comes to motivating their people.

"As *unnatural* as it seems, although first-line managers have this difficult motivational task, they're the least equipped with management experience and expertise and have fewer ways to motivate their people.

"Those at the upper levels are exposed to a wide array of motivators such as self-fulfillment, a feeling of importance, money, power, or social standing. They're also more often motivated by the objectives of the organization, because they can more easily relate to the way they can benefit personally if the objectives are achieved.

"These motivators aren't nearly as readily available at the lower levels, where they're needed the most. However, first-line managers do have the strong motivational tool of being able to make their people feel important."

Gordon asked, "But how can you convince the lower-level employees that their jobs really *are* important?"

"By describing to them the reasons why they *are*. Think in terms of economics. Let's say that Enfield earns a six percent profit on sales, and a floor sweeper makes $15,000 a year. If the floor sweeper isn't important, we could eliminate this job, and the $15,000 we would save is the equivalent of the profit on $250,000 in sales. This, my friends, *is* an important person."

"Another way is to follow the advice represented in an acronym I developed that I call 'DCAB.' This stands for Displaying that you Care about, Appreciate, and Believe in your people."

Richard said, "Gordon referred to the management axiom that 'People do what you *inspect*, not what you *expect*,' and I pointed out that this doesn't apply to decision makers. However, a way that first-line managers can display to their people that they care about what they are doing is to inspect the results of those in a production capacity. By comparing these results against production standards and bringing this to the attention of the production workers, the more these people will be motivated or will just react in the way the managers want them to."

Barbara commented, "That reminds me of the Hawthorne experiment."

"What was that?" Mike asked.

"Starting in the late 1920s, the Western Electric Company conducted a series of management experiments at its Hawthorne plant. The objective was to determine the effect of environmental conditions within the plant on the productivity of the workers. As experiments were conducted on the effect of changes in light intensity, break periods, noise levels, and so on, production continued to go up no matter what adjustments were made on factors being tested.

"The final conclusion was that production went up simply because management was paying attention to the production workers. This was evidence that just displaying interest in what people are doing is often a valuable management tool."

Mike asked, "I'm curious about whether production increased because the workers were motivated by a feeling of importance, or because they were being watched."

"I couldn't say," Barbara answered. "I believe what matters is that it worked. The focus should not be so much on the behavioral theory, but rather on *what* produces results. At one end of the motivational spectrum, the workers were probably motivated by a feeling of importance. At the other end, they were probably motivated by fear, or by feeling insecure because they were being observed."

Brent added, "There are behavioral scientists who contend that fear and a feeling of insecurity aren't strong motivators. However, fear was the strongest motivator I ever experienced when I was on the verge of bankruptcy and faced with the very real possibility that my business, along with everything else I had worked for, was about to be lost.

"My grandfather was also very strongly motivated by wanting to be free from the fear of the *absence* of money. He was motivated on his job to earn enough money to satisfy his strong need to feel secure."

Gordon said, "It's interesting to me that you referred to the 'absence of money' as a strong motivator because I've never thought about money in those terms. I have a good income, live comfortably, and don't feel motivated by the *absence* of money, but rather by its *presence,* and I'm strongly motivated to earn enough extra money to buy some things I want but really don't need."

Brent responded, "The *presence* of money is a very strong motivator for many people, but like my grandfather, I was strongly motivated by the absence of money when I didn't have enough to satisfy my wants and needs. However, once I had enough, money was no longer a strong motivator as a means of obtaining goods and services."

• •

Intimidation and Manipulation as Motivators

Gordon asked, "If fear and a lack of security are motivators, would you say that intimidation and manipulation can be used as motivators?"

"I say they can, although many would disagree with me. When people are motivated, the action comes from *within.* When people are intimidated or manipulated, they are motivated by something that's done *to* them, but this in turn causes them to be motivated from within to take action. Intimidation moves people to action through pressure or fear of punishment. Sometimes this is the easiest, if not the only, way to motivate them."

Gordon asked, "Then are you saying that as long as you're around to continue intimidating people, the results are as good or better than when they motivate themselves?"

"No way," Brent said. "Self motivated people will push themselves harder than they'll allow someone else to push them to become motivated through intimidation.

"With manipulation, managers use their skills to induce action. The con artist negatively manipulates people by appealing to their greed while he's fleecing them."

Gordon then asked, "Are you implying that there's no place in good management for manipulation and intimidation?"

"I don't mean to imply that at all."

"That surprises me," Alan said, "and I'd like to hear more about that. One of the reasons I left my previous job was that I felt I was being manipulated."

"Alan, I don't believe in manipulating managers. I assure you that I'd terminate a manager before I'd ever resort to the negative motivation of manipulation. I have too much of my own work to do without having to deal with managers who can't become positively motivated.

"However, we manipulate some of Mike's people, and we even create situations where they are intimidated. Why don't you tell them how you did this, Mike?"

"Shortly after Brent came to Enfield, I talked to him about some of my direct producers who weren't self motivated. When I asked him what I could do about it, he said I probably couldn't do anything. I told him I thought he was supposed to be an expert on motivation, he laughed and said I'd just heard an expert's opinion.

"Brent had to do a lot of talking before he convinced me that manipulation and intimidation can be valuable management tools for motivating those who aren't self-motivated.

"He also gave me a book to read entitled *The Human Side of Enterprise,* by Douglas McGregor. The book describes how to deal with people in an organization using what the author referred to as Theory X and Theory Y.

"Theory X assumes that people don't want to work, and controls have to be imposed on them to make sure they do their work. Theory Y is at the other extreme and assumes that people want to work and will push themselves harder than they'll let someone else push them, and they'll also exercise self-control.

"Theory Y is better for dealing with managers, other decision makers, and many production workers. The reason is that the majority of these people can be self-motivated to manage themselves to various degrees.

"Many people aren't self motivated. At Enfield, this was the case with some of our assembly line workers and some who are paid based on the number of pieces they produce. So we figured out a way to positively manipulate and intimidate them to become motivated, but we did it for their own good, as well as for the company."

Alan was still very skeptical as he said, "I'm still waiting to hear how you do this."

Mike continued, "I met with Brent and Harry one day and we discussed those who are doing piecework, and how we were paying them a fixed amount for each piece they produced. We decided to make a study and determine the average level of production on each of our piecework jobs. These averages became our standards, and we agreed to pay our people a bonus whenever any of them exceeded these standards by 10 percent. We also agreed to pay an extra bonus if the whole department went over the group standard by more than 10 percent.

"Immediately, everyone not only met the standards, they exceeded them. As production went up, we raised their standards. We finally leveled off at close to a 40 percent increase in productivity, and the bonuses we paid out only increased our costs of labor by 25 percent. The result was that these production people made more money, our productivity increased, and we lowered our cost per piece.

"We also began posting individual and group results on the bulletin board. This causes pressure on everyone in the group to meet the standards. Those who don't, feel intimidated by those who do. The bottom line is that we're positively manipulating and intimidating them to meet higher standards.

"We manipulate our assembly line workers the same way by figuring their average production speeds and making these the standards for the line. Again, as the production increases, we increase the standards and pay a bonus for going over these standards. This goes into a pool and is shared by everyone on the production line."

Alan asked, "How can assembly line workers be motivated to work faster when their production is governed by the speed of the products coming down the line to their stations?"

"No sweat," Mike answered with a smile. "We tested the speed of each worker and made the fastest ones lead operators. We put them on the first station of each line. Then, if those farther down the line don't keep up with the ones on the front, they're soon covered up to their eyeballs with products. The slower ones are intimidated by their fellow workers to speed up and meet the group standards, so their assembly line will earn the bonus. We do give them a break by grouping those people on each line who tend to have similar aptitudes."

"I'm glad I don't work for you," Alan said with a smile, "but I have to admit that your approach makes sense.

"The word *manipulate* has always had a negative connotation for me, and I never considered manipulating people positively, but now that I think about it, I manipulate my kids all the time."

Brent said, "Except for the first-line managers, most managers have similar challenges and motivational tools to work with, so why don't we discuss motivation in general?"

●●●●●●●●●●●●●●●●●●●●●●●●●●●●●
Motivational Tools Available to All Managers

Gordon asked, "Could you rank the factors that motivate people?"

"I couldn't begin to," said Brent. "We, as managers, and everyone else, are often unaware of what motivates us, much less what motivates others. We are also motivated by different things at different times, depending on our moods and circumstances. Employees who believe they may lose their jobs are undoubtedly more motivated by fear than by a need to feel important. An ambitious man lost in the desert loses his ambitions and is motivated by his basic need for water.

"However, once the man in the desert satisfies his thirst, he becomes ambitious again because a satisfied want or need is no longer a motivator. It's a mystery to me why so many managers never learn this simple truth.

"Too many managers try to solve a problem with unhappy employees by increasing their compensation, even when the employees are satisfied with their present income. But they have a much greater need to feel more important and derive more satisfaction from their jobs."

Alan asked, "If you feel so strongly about the motivational value of a feeling of importance, do you disagree with behavioral scientists like Abraham Maslow that a sense of self-fulfillment is the strongest motivator?"

"I don't disagree with that at all, because my strongest motivation is a sense of self-fulfillment. The problem I have with self-fulfillment is that it is in such short supply in the great majority of jobs. Therefore, managers usually have to look for something else as a motivator—and simple ways to give people a feeling of importance are readily available in great abundance.

"In the final analysis, wants and needs motivate all of us. Often we do things without being fully conscious of the reasons why we are motivated. For example, I was motivated to come to Enfield because of my friendship with Stanley. After I arrived, I was motivated by a variety of additional wants and needs."

Brent concluded, "So how do we motivate others? I mentioned DCAB. We can motivate people by *displaying* that we *care* about, *appreciate,* and *believe* in our people. We can motivate people by picking up signals about what motivates them as individuals. We can motivate by our own examples—by striving to be good role models, and by the energy and enthusiasm we display toward our own jobs, and in pursuing worthwhile objectives. Finally, we can motivate them by managing *unnaturally* by keeping a low profile and giving them as much credit as possible, so that when *our* work is done, our people say: 'We did it ourselves.' "

21

•••••••••••••••••••••••••••••••••••

The Motivation of Inspiration

••••••••••••••••••••••

How to Develop an Attitude and an
Atmosphere for Creating Inspiration

Brent said, "Since intimidation and manipulation are the extremes at the negative end of the motivational spectrum, let's look at inspiration at the other extreme on the positive end of the spectrum.

"I used Stew Leonard's as a classic example of an effective communications hierarchy. This organization is also an excellent example of how the attitude of top management is communicated to the people at the lower levels and creates an atmosphere for them to become inspired.

"I find it ironic that the top management of organizations presumably cares the most about their customers, and yet it's the direct producers who have by far the most contact with them. At Stew Leonard's, its the cashiers. In other organizations, the direct producers might be retail clerks and other types of salespeople, customer service personnel, maintenance people, or reservations and food service personnel.

"So let's pose the question. If those who care the most about customers have the least contact, how do they convey this attitude of caring to these direct producers who spend the most time with customers?

"Stew Leonard likes to quote Bill Marriott, Jr., of the Marriott Corporation who said, 'If you take good care of your people, your people will take good care of your customers.' I believe there's a profound message here about customer relations. It suggests that perhaps we in organizations are guilty of putting too much focus on the customers."

The management group looked surprised if not shocked. "Now I've heard everything," Alan remarked. "For you, of all people, to suggest that we are putting too much focus on the customer, is unbelievable."

"Then I'd like for you to think about this. Most people who become financially successful do so because they focus not on making money but rather on doing other things well and they made money as a by-product. If more organizations put more emphasis on their own people, they would have happier customers as a by-product— and make more profits. *(yes)*   *yes*

"Stew Leonard's has over 800 employees, referred to as *team members,* who display an attitude of really caring about their customers. In my opinion, it's impossible to hire this many people who have a *natural tendency* to care about customers.

"Stew's father used to tell him that 'the best fertilizer is the farmer's shadow,' and Stew has been able to cast the shadow of his attitude about caring for customers. I believe Leonard's team members care about the customers because Leonard cares about them. More importantly, he displays in every way possible that he also cares about his team members and gives them the credit for the success of his organization.

"It's just that simple. We could talk about this for a month and cover hundreds of examples of attitude and atmosphere seeping down from the top, but Stew Leonard's is a classic example that says it all.

● ● ● ● ● ● ● ● ● ● ● ● ● ● ● ● ● ● ● ●

Inspiring Others by Believing in Them

"Whether we like it or not, we as managers are not only authority figures, we often serve as role models. If we are positive role models, we can inspire people by communicating to them with our words and by our actions that we care about, appreciate, and believe in them.

"When we display that we care about people, this tends to develop loyalty. This may generate inspiration to some degree, but people will be more inspired when we display to them that we appreciate and believe in them.

"As managers, we often find that we believe in our associates *more* than they believe in themselves, because we aren't privy to to their self-doubts. If we display belief in them, they'll believe in themselves even more, and will tend to subordinate their self-doubts to their inspiration of wanting to live up to *our* expectations of them.

"I developed this belief long before I discovered that psychologists refer to this as the 'Pygmalion effect.' In George Bernard Shaw's play, *Pygmalion,* a cultured English gentleman created an elegant lady from a poor, ignorant young girl. He did this by believing in her more than she believed in herself, and she became motivated to be that which he wanted her to become."

● ● ● ● ● ● ● ● ● ● ● ● ● ● ● ● ● ● ●
Why You Must Trust Your People

Alan said, "I see trust as closely associated with loyalty, but quite different as a concept. To me, trust means depending on or having confidence in your people. I'm loyal to some people that I wouldn't trust with certain responsibilities. There are others I would trust with these same responsibilities, but I don't have strong feelings of loyalty toward them."

"That's true, Alan, but in order for us not to assume too many responsibilities ourselves, we must trust our people. However, even though we must trust them, we can't relinquish control because we are still accountable for the results.

"Built-in monitoring and controlling mechanisms such as budgets, financial reports, and regular meetings don't create trust, but rather help promote and maintain trust."

Richard commented, "Trust is extremely fragile and takes much longer to build than to tear down. Whenever I begin losing trust in people who can still make a contribution, I warn them of my concern, and I attempt to cooperate in rehabilitating that trust."

Gordon asked, "If they don't regain your trust, do you terminate them?"

"Very rarely, particularly if they've been with us for any length of time. Assuming we can justify their cost and they can still be productive, I try to restructure their job responsibilities accordingly. I also put them—at least in my mind—into 'organizational limbo.'

If they regain my trust, I give them additional responsibilities. Otherwise, I leave them where they are. I never want to be too quick to terminate people who find themselves in this position, because I often share the blame."

"How is that?" Barbara asked.

"Frequently, people *think* they want more responsibility or just give lip service to wanting more responsibility. As their manager, I should be better qualified to determine if they can actually handle the additional responsibility. If I decide that they can, and then they fail, the blame is partially mine for making a wrong decision about their ability. Therefore, I feel that I owe them another chance to become productive again handling different responsibilities."

● ●

How to Gain the Trust of Your People

Mike said, "Alan spoke of trust in the context of depending on someone, but how can managers gain the trust of people?"

Brent said, "Stanley used to say that the best way to build trust is by applying the Golden Rule to a *human relations continuum*. He defined a continuum as individual parts united by a fundamental common character. He said that the human relations continuum in organizations is comprised of six major groups: your fellow workers, prospects, customers, vendors, creditors, and the public at large. He believed that the application of the Golden Rule is the fundamental common character that organizations should consistently display in treating all of these groups as we would have them treat us.

"He felt that it makes good business sense to adopt this philosophy, forgetting any moral considerations. I agree with his attitude that the application of the Golden Rule is often the only real uniqueness that makes an organization successful, and in my opinion, is the foundation of Stew Leonard's success."

Richard said, "Stanley also used to say that you can't be 'two-faced.' If you aren't consistently fair and honest with those groups outside of the organization, those inside of the organization won't trust you, because fairness and honesty aren't sometimes virtues.

"Stanley said that you gain the trust of your associates by displaying a consistently positive demeanor. Managers jeopardize the trust others have in them if they display negative emotions such as anger, worry, and frustration. This is inhibiting and intimidating and causes people to attempt to anticipate the managers' moods before approaching them."

Brent commented, "A consistent demeanor also enables your people to learn to read you like a book. They'll know what you like and what you don't like, and this will enhance the nonverbal communications between you. This will also make them feel more comfortable coming to you whenever they feel it's necessary without having to first analyze your mood."

Barbara added, "Richard, when we lost the Baker account, I knew it would dramatically affect our profits. I dreaded telling you because I'd recently been promoted to sales manager and this was the first time I had to give you any bad news. But you didn't seem to be particularly concerned and that was very reassuring. I decided if *you* could take the bad news that calmly, I was probably overreacting."

Richard smiled. "I reluctantly admit that when I heard this news, my stomach was in knots. Nevertheless, when managers display negative emotions it creates uncertainty. Since we *are* role models, people will react to our emotions and attitudes. I knew you would read my reaction as a barometer. I try not to cheer too loudly at good news or show too much displeasure at bad news. People look for a steady hand on the helm, particularly when in troubled waters."

Barbara responded, "That's admirable, Richard, but when I suppress negative emotions I feel stressful."

"Wait a minute, Barbara," Richard said with a smile, "I didn't say I suppress negative emotions—I only conceal them in front of others. After you told me about the Baker account, I went to my club and vented my frustrations by hitting tennis balls."

Brent said, "As managers, we can build trust by maintaining a positive attitude and communicating this to our people by our words and performing *unnatural* acts such as giving credit to others—even if *we* deserved it, and by taking blame when it wasn't our fault but was our responsibility. We can also build trust by making our associates feel important and improving their working conditions, compensation, and growth opportunities when it's deserved.

"I could summarize all of this saying that the best way to build the trust our associates have in us is by keeping our focus on them and what they're doing and not on ourselves. President Ronald Reagan had a plaque on his desk that read, 'There is no limit to what one can do or how far he can go if he doesn't care who gets the credit.'"

22

•••••••••••••••••••••••••••••••••••••••

Showdown with Alan Braswell

The regular Friday afternoon meeting was canceled because Richard and Barbara were out of town. Brent took the opportunity to inform Alan about his decision concerning the #4000 series. Late in the afternoon, Brent phoned Alan and asked him to come to his office. He anticipated a touchy session, so Brent closed the door to his office after Alan arrived and took a seat.

"Alan," he began, "we've discussed the #4000 series in several meetings, and I've discussed this individually with each of you in the management group. Richard and Mike feel we should close the new production line and discontinue the #4000 series. Gordon doesn't have a strong opinion either way, and you and Barbara think we should keep it.

"After weighing all the pros and cons, I've decided to close the line, sell off the equipment, and discontinue the series.

"Since you were primarily responsible for the logistics of installing the equipment, Richard and I would like for you to be responsible for developing a plan to phase it out."

Alan was silent for a few seconds. Then he replied angrily, "The first day we met, you said you had temporarily assumed Scott Wilson's authority and were accountable to Helen Wilson. You also said that the implementation of any of your decisions was subject to her approval, and I can assure you that Scott would never allow his mother to approve this decision."

Brent responded quietly, "I talked with Helen about this, and she authorized me to do what I think is best. In my opinion, we should discontinue the line."

"You don't know this business well enough to make that decision, and it would be a terrible mistake. Furthermore, if you do, you'll have to find someone else to come up with a plan to phase it out, because I'll resign."

Brent stared at Alan for a few seconds, then said calmly, "As I said, I've already made the decision. Does this mean you'll be resigning?"

"I . . . I guess so," Alan stammered.

Brent leaned forward in his chair as he asked abruptly, "What do you mean 'you guess so?' Either you're resigning or you're staying. In spite of the fact that you answer to Richard, if you meant what you said as an ultimatum, as far as I'm concerned you can go back to your office and clean out your desk right now—because I don't take well to ultimatums.

"I'm committed to help save this company, and I intend to do it with or without you. I would prefer to have your help, but if you want to resign, that's your decision to make."

Brent's reaction came as a shock to Alan. After a long pause, he responded almost apologetically, "I really don't want to resign, but I believe discontinuing the #4000 series would ruin Enfield."

"I don't see it that way, and in our Monday morning meeting I'm going to address Enfield's future position in the marketplace. If that discussion would have any bearing on your decision to leave, you're welcome to attend—but that's entirely up to you.

"Now if you'll excuse me, I have an appointment." As Brent picked up his briefcase and started toward the door, Alan said, "I guess I'll wait and decide after the Monday meeting."

"Suit yourself. I'll see you on Monday."

With that, Brent walked out of the office and down the hall, and Alan slowly returned to his own office.

• •

TEN

Why People Really Buy Your Products and Services

● ●

How to Analyze Your Organization's Value Added in the Marketplace

"In order to survive and prosper, every profit-making organization must have one or more characteristics that give its products or services value in the marketplace," Brent stated as he opened the meeting. "What characteristics do our products and services have that provide market value?"

Several seconds of silence suggested to Brent that this subject had not been previously discussed in a management meeting.

Finally, Barbara replied hesitantly, "We offer better prices than the foreign competition when you factor in their shipping costs to the United States market."

Brent walked over to the board on which he had earlier drawn three columns headed "market advantage," "equal in the market," and "market disadvantage." In the first column he now wrote "price."

"What else?" he asked.

Richard said, "We sell to both large and small companies."

Brent wrote "large market segment" on the advantage side.

Mike smiled and said, "We produce and ship orders faster than the competition, thanks to the pressure from the sales department to ship everything out of here yesterday!"

Brent added "fast delivery" on the advantage side.

Alan added, "Our customer service is far superior to the competition's." Brent included that on the list.

"Is there anything else?" he asked.

"Product quality," Barbara contributed.

Brent added that to the advantage side.

"How about reputation?" Richard added.

Mike asked, "Isn't reputation the same as the quality of our products and services?"

"Not necessarily," Richard answered. "The Edsel automobile was *not* a quality product, but many people bought it because of Ford's reputation."

Brent wrote "reputation" on the advantage side. Then he said, "You've covered most of the characteristics that can make up market value for *any* organization, but let me ask you about some others.

"How about location?"

Barbara said, "Well, being located in the United States gives us an advantage over our foreign competition because of our faster response time, and we also have branch sales and service offices, which brings us even closer to the market."

"You're right, and location is often the only market value an organization has." He wrote "location" on the advantage side, then he asked, "How about uniqueness of products?"

The group agreed that Enfield's products were not unique compared to those of the competition, so Brent wrote "unique products" under the "equal" heading.

"How about technological capability?" Brent asked.

Barbara said, "We're probably equal now that we have our new production line for the #4000 series."

Brent wrote "technological capability" under the "equal" heading.

Then he asked, "What about management and marketing expertise?"

Richard said, "I would certainly give us the nod on marketing expertise, but in light of our recent financial performance, we don't stack up too well on management expertise."

Brent responded, "Management and marketing expertise are inseparable. If you're weak in one, the other is inevitably affected. Based on your comment, I'll put management and marketing expertise under the disadvantage heading." Brent stepped away from the board and turned to the group. "Let's take a good look at the board and see what it tells us."

This is what the group saw.

Market advantage	Equal in the market	Market disadvantage
Price	Unique products	Management and
Large market	Technological	marketing expertise
segment	capability	
Fast delivery		
Customer service		
Product quality		
Reputation		
Location		

"Richard described the Ben Franklin approach as a way of making decisions. I've taken the same approach here by writing the advantages on the left, the disadvantages on the right, and the equals in the middle. What did Richard caution us about in using this approach?"

Gordon responded, "He said that unless each of the advantages and disadvantages are weighted as to importance, a comparison based on the number in each column isn't meaningful. A single disadvantage on the right might represent a threat that could put us out of business."

"Then what does this suggest to you?"

Gordon answered "That all of those characteristics listed under advantages don't mean too much if the quality of our management and marketing expertise could ruin the company."

"Exactly, Gordon. In my opinion, a profit-making organization will ultimately succeed or fail based on this one characteristic. All of the other characteristics are really only components of management and marketing expertise.

"However, I must tell you that this was the greatest area of disagreement between Stanley and me. Stanley was genuinely fascinated by machinery and production technology, and his primary focus was on producing exceptionally good products with unique characteristics.

"I'm interested in producing products and services of high quality, but I don't particularly care what they are as long as they have value in the marketplace. The value added that I'm most interested in, in any organization, is management and marketing, and a marketable product is only a prerequisite.

"I also don't like to get involved with products or services that require an inordinate amount of time and effort dealing with how to produce them. I accused Stanley of falling in love with his products, whereas he accused me of falling in love with management and the marketplace.

"In any organization, you have to look at what you're providing to the marketplace and ask the question: Are we a market-driven organization, a production-driven organization, a customer service-driven organization, or some combination of the above?

"In my opinion, Enfield is primarily market driven. Customer service is not a major factor here, because unlike an automobile dealer for example, our products require very little maintenance from us. Also, our products don't have any significant advantage over our competition.

"Now, let's talk about how we can move our management and marketing expertise from the right-hand column into the left-hand column.

"What market advantage does the competition have over us?"

After several seconds of silence, Brent was about to answer his own question when Barbara answered, "I would say producing larger orders for the *Fortune* 500-type companies."

Brent smiled. "That's exactly the way I see it. Now, why do you suppose I said management and marketing expertise are inseparable?"

Barbara, having gained confidence from her last reply, responded, "Management has to decide what makes up our market value, and then apply this to a niche in the marketplace where we're stronger than the competition."

"Okay Barbara, let me ask you this. If the competition has market value over us in producing larger volume orders for larger customers, what does this suggest to you about where our market niche might be?"

For the first time since Brent came to Enfield, Barbara smiled at him and answered in a friendly tone, "Why do I feel you're leading me into another trap? The obvious answer is that the advantage is in marketing smaller volume orders to *all* of our customers."

"Precisely—and I have another observation. We've identified only one characteristic where we're weaker than the competition, two where we're equal, and seven where we're stronger. Is there a message here?"

"Maybe we are providing too much market value," Richard suggested.

"You've got it, Richard."

"How can you ever have too much market value?" Alan asked.

Brent replied, "Market value always carries a cost. If you give too much in the way of market value, you can't remain competitive. For example, Neiman Marcus doesn't try to compete with K-Mart on price, large market segment, or location.

"Deciding on the right balance of these characteristics is where the market value of management itself comes into play. I believe we're paying more than we can afford in the way of market value. This is why our costs are increasing more than our sales, and we're losing money.

"When Stanley was here, Enfield's prices were higher than the competition, and the company was very profitable. Now our prices are virtually the same, if not lower, than the competition, when you factor in their shipping costs."

Barbara said, "We had to cut our prices to meet the foreign competition."

"And where do we compete with the foreign suppliers?"

"On larger orders to the larger companies."

"So, what should we do about our prices?"

"I suppose we could increase them without losing any business on the smaller orders. However, if we did increase prices, we would probably have a decrease in our overall sales volume because we would lose some of the less profitable larger orders."

"You're right, but '*more* is often the devil.' I'd rather have lower sales volume and be highly profitable, than have more sales and be less profitable."

Barbara responded, "I really can't disagree with that. We're saying that instead of competing with the big guys in their ballpark, make them compete with us in ours."

"Good for you, Barbara," Brent commented with a smile.

After some further discussion, although Alan remained silent, the rest of the group expressed enthusiasm for developing a marketing plan to determine the impact of raising prices and shifting the marketing emphasis toward selling more smaller orders to customers of all sizes.

After the meeting, Alan stayed behind to speak with Brent. He appeared nervous as he said, "Brent, I've done a lot of thinking over the weekend, and I want to apologize for overreacting on Friday and behaving like such an idiot.

"Unless I've damaged myself beyond repair in your eyes, I'd like very much to stay with Enfield. I'll do whatever is necessary to help phase out the new production line, and anything else that will be of value to the company—even if I don't always agree with you," he added with a smile.

"I'm delighted, Alan, and I assure you no damage has been done. On the contrary, I admire you for speaking up and not being hesitant to disagree with me. You have all the makings of an outstanding manager, but you need to learn to control your razor-sharp tongue and your tendency to overreact."

"I'm working on it, Brent, and this isn't the first time I've heard that criticism."

As Alan stood to leave he said, "When I came into the meeting this morning, I was still in strong disagreement with your decision to discontinue the #4000 series. However, I recognize that it was *your* decision to make.

"Then, during our meeting, after we went through the analysis of our market value, I suddenly realized how wrong I've been. This may sound like an excuse, but I'm inexperienced in marketing, and Scott and Barbara convinced me that in order to remain competitive, we had to be state of the art. However, the market value characteristics you listed on the board, and where we should position ourselves in the market, make perfect sense to me.

"I was also very impressed with Barbara's perception of the market and how quickly she saw where you were going with your analysis of our market niche. She also agreed with you about our market position, and that's why I can't understand why she's been so adamant about keeping the #4000 series."

Then they shook hands, and Alan returned to his office with a sense of relief. A few minutes later, Brent phoned Barbara and asked if he could come to her office.

When he arrived she said, "I can guess why you wanted to see me. You must have talked with Scott."

"I don't understand."

"Scott phoned during our meeting this morning and left a message for me to call him. When I did, he asked about my reaction to your plans to discontinue the #4000 series. Then he said he was also going to call you."

"He hasn't yet, but I wonder how he knew about the #4000 series?"

"Alan phoned him Friday night after his meeting with you."

"Barbara, the reason I wanted to see you was to tell you about my decision on the #4000 series. I'm sorry you had to hear it from Scott first, but there was a problem involving Alan that I wanted to resolve before I spoke with you."

"I didn't hear about the #4000 series from Scott. I heard about it from Alan. He called me Friday night at home and we discussed the #4000 series, as well as the problem between the two of you."

"What *was* your reaction when Alan told you about my decision to discontinue the series?"

"That you had made a very bad decision!"

"Scott must have been delighted to hear that."

"On the contrary, I told him this morning that I thought eliminating the #4000 series was a great idea."

"I'm confused."

"You really finessed me in the meeting by using the 'Ben Franklin' approach to persuade me where we should be positioned in the market, and I walked into the trap with my eyes wide open. You asked leading questions until I convinced myself that we should concentrate on selling smaller orders and discontinue the #4000 series."

"Barbara, I'm glad you came to that conclusion on your own. I'm highly impressed with your perception of marketing, and I believe you can make a very significant contribution to Enfield's overall marketing strategy."

"That is an area of particular interest to me, and I'd enjoy being able to spend more time on it," Barbara replied. Then she said, "If you have another minute, I just want to apologize for my attitude toward you since you've been here. I now believe you've been on the right track all along, and I'm anxious to do anything I can to help make Enfield successful again."

"Your apology is greatly appreciated, but certainly not necessary, Barbara. You're doing an excellent job, and I welcome and need your support."

After Brent returned to his office, he began reviewing financial statements. February would show a loss, and although March would also show a loss, it would be a small one. After shutting down the #4000 series production line at the end of March, Enfield should show a nice profit for April and, based on his conservative projections, should continue to be profitable thereafter. For the first time, Brent was confident the company would be in a sound condition before he left.

As he returned the financial statements to his briefcase, the phone rang.

"Brent Powell," he answered.

"This is Scott Wilson."

"Hello, Scott. How are you feeling?"

"I was feeling fine until I found out you're trying to destroy my company."

"What are you talking about?" Brent responded, knowing full well what Scott had on his mind.

"I'm talking about your plans to discontinue the #4000 line and sell the production equipment at a loss. Do you have any idea what that will cost?"

"Well, we still owe about $2 million on the equipment, and we can probably sell it for at least $1.2 million."

"If we did that, we would still incur an $800,000 loss."

"That's right, but it's less than we'll lose over the next 12 months by continuing to operate the line."

"You're wrong, and I'm sure as hell going to be back soon enough to prove it. In the meantime, I'm ordering you *not* to shut down the #4000 line."

"Sorry, Scott, but that's precisely what I'm going to do at the end of the month."

Wilson was now furious. "You're trying to put Enfield back in the dark ages like you tried to do when my father was running the company, and you were always hanging around his office exerting your influence on him."

Brent felt this was a cheap shot but responded matter-of-factly, "You could do worse, Scott. Enfield was highly profitable when your father was running the company."

With that, Scott slammed down the phone.

Less than 30 minutes later, Brent's phone rang again. This time it was Helen.

"Brent, I know that I told you to do whatever you felt was best about closing down the new production line, but Scott just called me, and he's very angry. Alan Braswell let him know that you planned to shut down one of the production lines, and Scott believes this will ruin the company. He said you wouldn't listen to him, so he wanted me to tell you to continue running that line. Connie and Sandra agree that we can't jeopardize Scott's health and our family's relationship over this."

"So what do you want me to do, Helen?"

"I don't want you to close down the line."

"I'm sorry, Helen, but I can't go along with that."

"What do you mean, you 'can't go along?'" she snapped. "Have you forgotten who controls the stock in Enfield?"

"Not for one minute, and that's the only reason I'm here. No offense intended, but you can run this company yourself, you can let Richard Thompkins run it, or you can let Scott run it by telephone. But until you tell me to get out, I'm going to run Enfield exactly the way I think is best. If you want a puppet on a string just to follow orders, you don't need me here."

There was a long pause, then Helen said unemotionally, "I'll call you back."

Brent hung up and thought, "Sounds like I'm about to be fired."

He turned in the old leather-covered chair and gazed at the hills. "Well, Stanley," he said aloud, "I wonder if I'm doing what you would've wanted? You were right when you told me that good management is an *unnatural* act. My natural inclination would be to give in to Helen and Scott, but you always said that whenever I had a strong conviction, I should stick with it—as unnatural as it might seem at the time."

Brent now realized how much he wanted to stay until this job was finished, and he wondered, "Was I too harsh with Helen? Maybe I should phone her and compromise." Then he thought, "No, I can't. Scott is a misguided missile on an ego trip with this #4000 series. If Enfield doesn't drop the line, I'm convinced the company is headed for bankruptcy, and I'm not going to be a party to that."

Brent turned his chair back to the worktable and began doing paperwork, but his heart wasn't in it. A few minutes later, the phone rang. It was Helen again.

"Brent," she said solemnly, "I'm in a difficult position. I'm forced to choose between what my son wants me to do and what my husband told me to do. Stanley assured me that I could depend on you if Enfield was ever in trouble. I realize now that you can't be expected to save Enfield if we're trying to tell you how to do your job.

"I've talked with Connie and Sandra, and we're in agreement that for Scott's own good, he shouldn't be involved in making any further decisions about the management of Enfield.

"What I'm trying to say is that you have our support in your decisions about the company. Somehow I'll try to calm Scott down. All I ask is that if he calls you again, please don't be too tough on him."

"I won't, Helen. I have no desire to hurt Scott. I appreciate your trust in me, and I'll try not to let you and your family down."

"Just do the best you can, Brent. That's all Stanley would ever have asked, and all that we ask."

•

SECTION

ELEVEN

••••••••••••••••••••••••••••••••••

Effective Staffing: Skill or Russian Roulette?

●●●●●●●●●●●●●●●●●●●●●●●●●●●●●●●●●●●

How to Hire the *Right* People

Brent came to the Wednesday management meeting well prepared. He had reviewed the personnel records and was concerned about the high employee turnover. He decided to cover the subject and distribute some material that might help the group during the hiring process.

"Employee turnover," he began, "is usually a result of managers not dealing effectively with their people or a result of hiring the wrong people in the first place. Today, let's talk about how to hire the *right* people."

Gordon commented, "I sometimes wonder if hiring the right people is a matter of skill, intuition, or a form of Russian roulette. I seem to keep hiring and losing people, always attempting to maintain the right staff."

"Hiring the right people is, at best, an inexact science," Brent responded, "and it's easier to identify those applicants who probably would *not* make it, as opposed to those who probably *would*. Nevertheless, you can learn techniques that will enable you to improve your odds."

Barbara said, "When I make sales calls, the prospects are usually very much at ease, and I'm focusing on *their* best interests while I'm trying to persuade them to buy our products.

"When I interview a prospective salesperson, it's like a whirlwind courtship. We're both somewhat uneasy, acting unnaturally, and concentrating on our own interests, trying to get well enough acquainted in a short period to determine if we have a good match."

Mike added, "One way I try to put applicants, and myself, at ease is to let them know at the beginning of the interview that I'm sorry we have to try to get to know each other so quickly. Just bringing this out seems to help both of us.

"I also ask about things I picked up from their resumes, such as where they have lived most of their lives, where they went to school, or how they spend their spare time."

"How do you deal with this unnatural situation?" Barbara asked Brent.

"I developed a list that I review before interviewing an applicant. This helps me keep the hiring process in perspective," Brent said as he passed out copies.

The Right Attitude About Hiring

1. Beware of the self-fulfilling prophecy. There is a natural tendency to be overly influenced by applicants' good traits and to disregard their bad ones. The danger of this is that after they are hired, they may never look as good to you again as they did the day they were interviewed.

2. Focus on hiring those who can best fill the position rather than attempting to match people to the jobs. Though this sounds obvious, there is a natural tendency to fall victim to hiring people we like, or those who seem to most closely resemble our self-images.

3. Do not hire someone because you are tired of the interviewing process. It is better not to hire anyone than to hire the wrong person.

4. Keep in mind the high costs of hiring the wrong people, over and above their salary and fringe benefits. These costs can take the form of

- Foul-ups
- Lost opportunities and loss of momentum by having the wrong people
- Morale problems they cause among coworkers
- Loss of other employees because of their negative influence.

5. Do not oversell the job opportunity. Hiring a person involves risks to the organization and to the prospective employee, so be as realistic as possible.

Alan asked Brent to elaborate on not overselling the job opportunity.

"As the hiring manager, you have a better understanding of the requirements of the job being discussed than do the applicants, and you can better evaluate the applicants' qualifications. If they're qualified, assume an attitude that you're interested in buying their services, and the applicants are interested in buying job opportunities.

"Most applicants don't know how to go through this buying process very well, so you have a responsibility to them, and to the organization, to help lead them through a rational decision about whether to accept positions with us. It's better for the applicants, and for us, to know before the applicants are hired what can be expected, rather than have unpleasant surprises later.

"Before I start interviews, I often ask the applicants if they have any objections if I turn on my tape recorder. If they do, this could be a signal that they aren't open communicators or aren't very straight-forward and are therefore uneasy about being recorded."

"Why would you ever tape interviews?" Gordon asked.

"For the same reason I tape many discussions about any important decisions I'm about to make. Before offering applicants jobs, I often review the tapes to pick up anything I might have missed during the interviews and to give me another chance to review the representations they've made about their qualifications."

Brent continued, "I ask about their acceptable salary range early in the interview. It's useless spending a great deal of time with these people before discovering that we're miles apart on compensation. If their salary ranges *are* acceptable to me, I briefly cover the major provisions of our fringe benefits."

Alan asked, "Isn't this very early to be discussing fringe benefits?"

"Not, for example, if our hospitalization plan doesn't provide maternity benefits, and that happens to be one of their prerequisites.

"Next, I describe what the job involves, what is expected of them, and how they'll be evaluated. When I'm interviewing decision makers, I also get in agreement with them about the assumptions relative to their responsibilities, the authority they will have, and how I'll hold them accountable. I make sure that the applicants and I have a mutual understanding of what is expected of them. Then I offer to answer any questions."

Seeing the relevance of the discussion to his own situation, Alan said, "Thinking back to my interviews with Stanley and Richard before I came to Enfield, Richard reviewed the assumptions involved as he described my job. Now I realize he was fashioning a weapon to beat me with later if I didn't live up to his expectations."

"You're more intelligent than you look," Richard responded with a laugh. "And even though Brent wasn't here, he shares the blame. He's the one who introduced the concept of management by assumptions to Stanley and me.

"When you were hired, we outlined the responsibilities and the assumptions about how much authority you would have over our managerial resources. We also established assumptions about how you would be measured and evaluated on your performance."

Alan added, "I always like to know where I stand, even if it's knee deep in hot water. On my previous job I never knew, and I felt as though I was misled. One of the major reasons I came with Enfield was that you let me know where I stood on the front end, by nailing down the assumptions."

Richard said, "You were right when you said that employees often never look as good to you again as they did the day they were interviewed. It's incredible how some people can be on stage during an interview and their real characters aren't revealed until they're on your payroll."

Brent said, "I've developed a list of questions that might help you to avoid being misled by those who are 'on stage,' as you put it. I can remain more objective and less emotionally involved with applicants by focusing on the quality of their answers."

Brent then passed out copies of this list.

Questions to Ask Job Applicants

1. How did you learn about us?
2. Why do you have an interest in possibly coming with us?
3. What did you consider to be your most significant contributions in your last job?

4. What did you like most about your previous jobs?

5. What did you like least about your previous jobs?

6. Why did you leave your previous job?

7. What did you think of your previous managers?

8. What is the highest level of education you completed, and how were your grades in school?

9. What are your strengths?

10. What are your weaknesses?

11. What are your personal goals?

12. Would this job represent a compromise compared with any other job you might be able to have?

13. Would you view this job as a possible career path for you, or are you viewing this job only as a means of financial support?

14. Do you have any reservations or concerns about our organization or anyone you have met here?

15. How does your spouse feel about this job, and what is your spouse's occupation?

16. Is there anything in your personal life that could cause us a problem? For example, problems with health, finances, marriage, children or other dependents, alcohol, drugs, and so on.

17. If you are a smoker, would you agree not to smoke on the job?

18. Are you a high achiever, or do you have an eight-to-five mentality?

19. Do you feel that you are persistent and have a high energy level?

20. Do you feel you are streetwise? Do you tend to catch on to new things quickly? Do you have good common sense?

21. Do you have good work habits; Are you punctual? Are you often out of work due to sickness or personal reasons? Are you well organized?

22. Are you dependable? Do you fulfill your commitments without someone following up on you?

23. Are you willing to do whatever is necessary, within reason, to handle your responsibilities?

24. How do you spend your time when you are not working?

25. Are you overly emotional and tend to overreact? Or do you keep a cool head?

26. How well do you accept constructive criticism?

27. Do you have trouble admitting when you are wrong?

28. Do you have a good sense of humor?

29. How well do you handle money, both yours and that of others?

30. Is our location convenient to your home?

31. Are your personal objectives compatible with the responsibilities you would have here and with our corporate objectives?

32. Are you straightforward, or do you have a tendency to cover up things?

33. Do you feel comfortable with me?

34. Do you feel we could communicate effectively?

After the group reviewed the list, Brent asked for comments.

Alan spoke up. "The answers to some of your questions are so obvious, I question their value. For example, people would have to be idiots to admit they had eight-to-five mentalities, couldn't be depended upon, or didn't take criticism well."

"You're right, Alan. Many of the answers are predictable, and some of the questions on my list are for the sole purpose of letting applicants know immediately what's important to me and how they'll be evaluated."

Mike added, "I use some of the same questions in a job interview just to put applicants on notice about things I won't put up with. I always ask if they are punctual. Then if they're hired and come in late to work without a good excuse, I give them one warning, then get rid of them if it happens again."

Gordon asked, "Why do you ask their opinion about previous managers?"

"For several reasons. Criticism of previous managers could suggest mavericks or hotheads who can't work well in a structured environment. It also might indicate a tendency to blame others for their own deficiencies or reveal that they don't understand or might even resent management. Furthermore, they aren't being very street-wise by being critical of former managers to someone who might be their next one."

"Now that I think of it, when Richard interviewed me," Alan recalled, "he asked about my personal weaknesses. This took me by surprise, because no one had ever asked me that question in a job interview."

"What was your answer?"

"I told him I needed to improve my human relations skills. I don't have to tell you that I can be rather abrasive at times, and I also need to learn to be a better listener. Another weakness is that even though I'm good at math and finance, I don't have a technical aptitude—For example, for computer programming."

"That sounds like an excellent answer," Brent responded.

"Do people ever tell you they can't think of any personal weaknesses?" Alan asked.

"Only rarely, and then I assume they're trying to bluff me, are unrealistic, or aren't introspective, and I probably wouldn't hire them."

Gordon questioned, "Why do you ask how their spouses feel about the job?"

"I want to determine how strongly the applicants are influenced by their spouses. If our people are constantly being goaded by their spouses about how unfairly the organization is treating them, they tend to lose their objectivity about their contribution to the business. The only perception spouses can really have is through the eyes of our associates, and I can promise you that this is usually a very biased perception in favor of our associates.

"I once had a conversation at a company Christmas party with the wife of one of my lower-level managers. Her erroneous perception was that her husband practically ran the organization. In the spirit of Christmas I didn't tell her any different."

"Why do you ask how the applicants spend their time when they aren't working?" Mike asked.

"I want to know if they take any initiative on their own time to improve themselves, particularly in the way of any 'self-help' reading."

Mike commented, "I can't imagine people admitting they don't have a sense of humor."

"Here again, I always receive the obvious answer, but I want to indicate to the applicants that this is important to me. Without a sense of humor, they may not get along well with others, or they may tend to take themselves and/or their jobs too seriously."

"The applicants' responses to these questions and their non-verbal communications often send up what I refer to as *red flags*, that I want to clear up before I would decide to make job offers."

"For example?" Alan questioned.

"I just happen to have a list," Brent said, as he smiled and passed out copies to the group.

"Red Flags" During the Interview Process

1. *Late for the appointment.*

   If the applicants are late, that is bad. It is near fatal if they do not call ahead and indicate they will be late or do not apologize when they do arrive.

2. *No resume.*

   This is nearly fatal, unless there are extenuating circumstances. For example, the applicants may still be employed elsewhere, have been there for a long time, are not actively seeking other employment, and we sought them out. Also, many hourly workers are not expected to have resumes.

3. *Disturbing appearance.*

   This takes many forms:

   - Inappropriately dressed
   - Unsightly hair on their heads or faces
   - Evidence of nail biting
   - Poor eye contact
   - Obvious anxiety and other distracting mannerisms.

4. *Poor communicators*

   This too takes many forms:

   - Poor or inappropriate grammar
   - Do not express themselves well
   - Indecisive or off-the-wall responses to questions
   - Do not ask intelligent questions
   - Either talk too much or not enough.

5. *Cannot name any personal weaknesses, or name them hesitantly, defensively, or unintelligently.*

   Applicants who cannot identify any weaknesses obviously are not making any attempts to improve them.

6. *No evidence that they take any initiative to improve themselves on their own time.*

7. *Unexplained gaps in their employment or educational history without a satisfactory explanation.*

8. *Low level of formal education without a legitimate reason.*

9. *Frequently changed jobs with little if any progress in their careers for the time spent.*

10. *Overqualified for jobs at this level of responsibility or compensation.*

11. *Unsolicited criticism of former employers and managers.*

12. *Unable to verbalize realistic personal goals.*

    This may indicate that they are task oriented instead of being goal oriented.

13. *Very little interest in the scope of the job, the present well-being of our organization, or in its future outlook.*

14. *Have personal problems that could affect their performance, such as with health, children, personal habits, and finances, or have spouses who are subject to being transferred.*

15. *Greater concern about compensation and benefits than about the job opportunities.*

16. *Openly expresses radical opinions.*

    Job interviews are inappropriate forums for applicants to express radical views on race, politics, religion, rights of women and minority groups, and so on.

17. *Do not need to work.*

    When people have this flexibility, they are much more subject to change jobs frequently or abruptly resign without a known source of other employment.

"If the applicants display any characteristics that send up any of these red flags, I give them an opportunity to alleviate my concerns with an explanation.

"However, no matter how well applicants answer your questions and deal with your concerns, if you still have bad intuitive feelings, don't hire them. When you go against these feelings, you'll probably regret it later."

Alan looked concerned, "Aren't you skating on thin ice from the standpoint of legal exposure when you start expressing concerns about age, personal problems, or your question about a spouse's opinion of the job?"

"I'm not suggesting that you *ever* ask any questions, or express any opinions that could possibly cause you legal problems. However, in the final analysis, we decide to hire or not to hire applicants based on our intuitive feelings about them—and you can't be hanged for what you are thinking.

"After the interviews I spend some time evaluating whether the applicants fit the jobs and how well I believe they'll relate to our other associates. I also think about my perception of their value systems, their goals, their motivations, and their attitudes.

"One more question I ask myself, particularly in the case of hiring managers, is 'Do they have class?'—that undefinable intuitive feeling we develop about others. If my overall evaluation is positive, I check their references."

Gordon commented, "At times I question the value of checking references. Why would applicants use those as references who would give negative responses?"

"They wouldn't on their personal references, and I rarely check them. Current and even previous employers are also usually reluctant to risk being critical. However, you can usually obtain useful information by asking these questions," Brent said as he passed out the last of his lists.

Questions to Ask Present or Former Employers

1. What were the applicant's strengths?
2. What were the weaknesses?
3. Was the applicant dependable? Was he or she absent much? If so, why?
4. Would you rehire this person if you had the right position open? If not, why not?
5. Why did this person leave your organization?
6. Could the applicant have progressed if he or she had stayed with you? If not, why not?

7. Did this person leave under favorable circumstances?

8. Did the applicant get along well with his or her manager?

9. Did this person get along well with his or her fellow workers?

10. Was the applicant a team player, or did this person just look out for himself or herself?

11. Was the applicant stronger in managerial skills and relations with people or in vocational skills?

12. How did this person respond to constructive criticism? Could he or she admit to being wrong?

13. Was the applicant well organized and punctual, and have good working habits?

14. Was this person loyal? Did you trust him or her?

15. Did the applicant have any personal problems or habits that caused any trouble in the workplace? (Here, again, think what you wish but be careful of what you say because of potential legal exposure.)

16. Was this person: ambitious, a high achiever? goal oriented? Did the applicant ever take work home? or show evidence of wanting to improve himself or herself?

17. Was the applicant a good communicator?

18. Did this person ever tend to get emotional or overreact to situations?

"If the applicants' references are acceptable," Brent concluded, I ask one or more other people in the organization to interview them in order to obtain more objectivity.

"If that exercise is positive, I'll make job offers to the applicants. If they accept, two or three days later I phone them to ask if there are any other questions or concerns that they would like to discuss."

"Why do you do that?" Gordon asked.

"Barbara, will you answer Gordon's question, since we had a similar discussion involving prospects?"

Barbara replied, "When applicants 'buy' your offer of jobs, it's not very different from a sales situation. Sales aren't really made until the products are delivered. Applicants haven't really bought their jobs until they deliver themselves to work their first day.

"The period between accepting the jobs and coming to work is precarious. Even though they accepted, they may have second thoughts, or their present employers may offer salary increases or other incentives to keep them. I've lost a couple of good sales applicants this way.

"It's also reassuring to applicants for me to display a personal interest by calling them after they have accepted the job offers, and it gives me an opportunity to alleviate any concerns they may have developed."

● ● ● ● ● ● ● ● ● ● ● ● ● ● ● ● ● ● ● ●

The Real Key to Effective Staffing

"As important as the hiring process is," Brent continued, "the real key to effective staffing is retaining the right people after you hire them. Few things are more costly to an organization than employee turnover. Never take your people for granted or assume they're in the safe column. There are always other organizations looking for good people, and you don't want them to hire yours.

"We have an opportunity through effective staffing to create an environment for our people to be inspired in their work, and stay with the organization.

"As managers, we can do this when we focus on

- Hiring the right people
- Retaining the right people
- Training them to assume more responsibilities
- Attempting to rehabilitate those who have become counterproductive
- Eliminating those uninspiring misfits who we have determined cannot be made productive, and any others who are counterproductive, and do not belong in the organization.

••••••••••••••••••••••••••••••••••••

TWELVE

The Five Greatest Human Relations Problems for Managers and How to Solve Them

• •

How to Identify and Deal with Problem Employees

As a change of pace, the management group was unanimously in favor of canceling the Friday meeting and instead having an all day-discussion on Saturday about problem employees. Brent took this initiative on their part as an endorsement of his management philosophy.

They chose the Colonial Inn, in the hills overlooking Enfield, as an informal setting for the meeting, and they gathered there early on Saturday morning for breakfast. After breakfast, the group convened in the Inn's comfortable and attractive meeting room, which provided a panoramic view of the surrounding hills.

Richard opened the meeting by thanking Brent on behalf of the management group for his efforts during his six weeks at Enfield Manufacturing. Then he turned the session over to Brent and suggested that he first cover the group that *can be* problem employees, and who Brent refers to as *failure avoiders*.

• • • • • • • • •

Failure Avoiders

Brent began, "There is an identifiable group of people in almost all organizations that we could characterize as *failure avoiders.*

"Thomas Edison said, 'Those who are afraid to fail are afraid to succeed.' I was a manager for several years before I realized the importance of recognizing that difficult-to-detect group of people who are afraid to fail and who will go to great lengths to avoid ever doing so."

"Why are they difficult to detect?" Mike asked.

"They tend to be loyal and hard-working and are usually among the better-liked people in the organization because they don't represent a threat to others. They avoid confrontation or making enemies and even avoid offering constructive criticism to those who answer to them.

"In meetings, they'll answer direct questions but won't take the initiative to contribute anything innovative—and, they won't speak up when they're in disagreement or when the subject is controversial."

"Are these people aware that they're failure avoiders?" Mike asked.

"Not usually. They aren't imaginative enough to realize that they're failure avoiders. They equate being busy or efficient with being effective. They don't think in terms of failure or success but rather in terms of failure and the avoidance of failure.

"They strive for objectives that represent no real risk to them if they aren't achieved, and they resist being put in positions where they'll be challenged or be in the spotlight.

"Failure avoiders are rarely found in top management, but they can represent menaces as middle managers because they'll only make safe decisions. They simply cannot, or will not, make those more important decisions involving inherent risks that should be made.

"These decisions then become decisions by default to continue following what could be counterproductive paths of inertia, which at times could put the organization at risk."

"Could you give us an example?" Gordon asked.

"Not making personnel changes is one of the most prevalent examples. Failure avoiders don't like change, because it represents uncertainty and the possibility of failure. Decisions to terminate, move, or add people all spell 'bad news' to failure avoiders, so they'll make personnel changes only as a last resort.

"Show me managers who are failure avoiders, and it's a good bet that among their staffs you have some square pegs in round holes, as well as some people who probably shouldn't be in the organization at all."

Barbara asked, "How can failure avoiders progress high enough in an organization to become menaces and do a lot of damage?"

Brent responded, "Instead of being *pulled* up through the ranks by their achievements, they're *pushed* up by maintaining their record of avoiding failure. They tend to display steady, reliable performance instead of showing initiative and taking prudent risks. As a result, they're pushed up too high in the management hierarchy."

Alan asked, "Would you say that this is a common problem?"

"No," Brent responded, "and the failure avoiders are usually responsible for preventing the problem. According to the so-called Peter Principle, some people are promoted to their level of incompetence and are left there.

"Since failure avoiders are motivated by the fear of failure, they insulate themselves from becoming victims of the Peter Principle. They do this by consciously or subconsciously resisting promotion to higher positions where they might find themselves either incompetent or overly challenged.

"As a result, you have the ironic situation where failure avoiders are usually overqualified and are quite happy remaining in jobs that would become boring to you."

"How would you describe those jobs?" Alan asked.

"We've discussed how the management job is bifocal in that it deals simultaneously with the work of today and the work of tomorrow. Failure avoiders are better suited to those jobs only having to do with the work of today, particularly in those positions where the objectives have been well defined, and they can take mechanical approaches to implementing solutions.

"Most failure avoiders have trouble seeing the overall picture. Not only are they prone to wander into the wrong part of the forest, they often aren't even sure where the forest is. Therefore, they're more effective away from the cutting edge of tomorrow, where subjective and creative decisions need to be made about the future progress of the organization."

Richard spoke up. "Some managers condition their people to become failure avoiders because they prefer staffs who do only what they're told. This is tragic when the result is the stunting of the promising careers of those who have natural inclinations to be innovators and to take reasonable risks."

Gordon commented, "I experienced that kind of conditioning after I was drafted into the army. I soon learned never to volunteer for anything and to do only what I was told—nothing more, nothing less. Fortunately, I wasn't in the army long enough for my failure-avoiding syndrome to become chronic."

Richard asked, "Brent, how can managers improve the effectiveness of natural-born failure avoiders?"

"By delegating properly. A manager who delegates by telling people what to do only compounds the problem, because failure avoiders want to be totally dependent on others for direction.

"Their managers can force-feed changes in some people for their own good, by making them accept and commit to responsibilities, preferably in front of their peers. Although their managers still need to exercise sufficient control to ensure that these commitments are fulfilled, although not meeting their commitments is seldom a problem.

"The reason is that once failure avoiders commit to responsibilities, they're usually strongly motivated to carry them out because they know their managers are depending on them. If they don't fulfill the responsibilities, this represents failure, which is exactly what they are attempting to avoid."

Mike said, "I certainly wouldn't say my production workers are failure avoiders—but they aren't innovators, so how would you classify them?"

"Mike, the activities of all people in an organizational group can roughly be divided into conformers and decision makers. Failure avoiders, as well as production people, are usually *conformers* to the directions of *decision makers.*

Alan frowned and said, "The word 'conform' carries negative connotations for me. I see myself as a free thinker, and I joined this organization because of its reputation for encouraging people to be innovators and mavericks."

● ● ● ● ● ●
Mavericks

Brent responded, "It's interesting that you grouped innovators and mavericks together, because I see them as quite different. Organizations need innovators, but the need for mavericks is questionable.

"According to my dictionary, the word *maverick* was derived from a Texas rancher by the name of Samuel Maverick who lived in the 1800s. Unlike other ranchers, Maverick didn't brand his cattle or fence them in; instead, he let them wander all over the range.

"All organizations need a team of people willing to pull together by working in concert, rather than as individual star performers. As I pointed out before, the only justification for an organization is for people to be more productive working together than they would be as individual performers.

"Although mavericks can make significant contributions in the right jobs, they have to be controlled. These nonconforming loners can be menaces if allowed to wander around in the organization unbranded, without any fences, doing what they please.

"At one time in my computer services company, my best computer programmer was a maverick. He wouldn't keep records of how he spent his time, and he worked on whatever was of most interest to him. Because of this, we finally had to let him go. The last I heard, he was working alone, doing freelance contract programming. That's where he belonged—not within an organization.

"There are many examples of individual star performers in the sports field, who aren't real assets because they aren't team players."

● ● ● ● ● ● ● ● ● ● ● ● ● ● ● ● ● ● ●
Those on the Road to Obsolescence

Alan spoke up, "You described failure avoiders as often being overqualified for their jobs. My biggest problems are with those who are underqualified. These are marginal employees who aren't performing well enough to keep but aren't doing badly enough for me to feel justified in terminating them.

"Sometimes in meetings with them, they'll claim they're victims of circumstance and convince me they'll do better. I fall victim to my own optimism, and if there's even a glimmer of hope, I talk myself into giving them another chance.

"However, there's rarely any improvement, and by then I've invested even more of my time in them and if I do terminate them, I'll have to begin the training process all over again with others who might not be any better. Therefore, I tend to hang on far too long. Do you ever have this problem?"

Brent said, "Most of us in management have been guilty of avoiding a resolution to this problem and of spending a disproportionate amount of time and thought trying to decide what to do about those who are marginal."

Richard added, "Marginal employees are like a dull but persistent ache. On occasion, I've had something bothering me but wasn't aware of what it was until I realized I was subconsciously stewing over a marginal employee. Worst of all, I'm even uncomfortable being around these marginals because they represent a problem without a clear-cut solution.

"It's much easier to decide to terminate misfits who obviously don't belong in the organization. Although quite unpleasant, it's swift, and the ache leaves as they walk out of the door."

Brent commented, "We always hope somehow the problem will correct itself, but the negative trend continues, and it evolves so gradually that there's no sense of urgency to take corrective action until the problem becomes quite serious. By then, we've usually reached a point of no return. The employee is beyond any hope of rehabilitation, and termination or early retirement are the only remaining logical options.

"Let's take a look at the real cost of having marginal employees on the payroll. Their salaries may be the smallest part of the cost. The real cost is the counterproductive time we spend agonizing over what to do about them, and the untold damage they can cause: the sales that should have been made but weren't, the customers the organization loses because of them, and the morale problems they cause among productive people who can't understand why we tolerate employees who aren't productive and who represent such a distraction.

"I'm convinced that marginal employees are the greatest waste of time, money, and opportunities within any organization. They're menaces that should be dealt with without delay. So let's talk about what can be done about them.

"Years ago, I'd been agonizing over a marginal employee. Then one morning, he came to my office, said he was quitting, and told me in no uncertain terms what I could do with his job. He made my day. I was delighted, and the experience taught me a valuable lesson. Ever since then, whenever I have marginal employees I ask myself if I'd be just as happy if they quit. If the answer is yes, I take one of the following steps:

- Put them in different positions,
- Downgrade their present jobs,
- Attempt to make them productive, or
- Terminate them.

"In the same category with those who are marginal are those who are burned-out and bored. The heart of the problem is that they're on the road to obsolescence, and all three types can be effectively dealt with in a similar manner."

"What are the symptoms we can look for in these people?" Gordon asked.

"Many of them live in the past by dwelling on, defending, and clinging to the way things used to be. At times, they even continue to perform tasks that are no longer necessary.

"Like failure avoiders, they cling to the status quo and show signs of not being interested in anything innovative or in the future of the organization. However, unlike failure avoiders, they often display a low level of job satisfaction and initiative. Failure avoiders usually display a high level of satisfaction in jobs for which they are well qualified, and they'll display a great deal of initiative by working hard to avoid failure."

Barbara asked, "After you've identified those becoming obsolete, what do you do about them?"

"Employees who have been with the organization only a short time probably shouldn't have been hired to begin with, and termination is a logical option. In the case of long-term employees, termination is usually a much less desirable solution, and the organization has more of a moral obligation to try to make them productive, perhaps by moving them to more suitable positions. If they're terminated without making this effort, the company could appear to be unappreciative, inhumane, or uncaring, which would have an adverse effect on the morale of others.

"As with alcoholics, they're usually the last to recognize or admit they have a problem and agree to take the cure before it's too late. Therefore, the first step is to sit down with them and discuss the problem. This is often enough to motivate them to face up to the situation and accept that something must be done. Make it clear that their jobs are in jeopardy, and that they should have a positive attitude about the organization's attempt to make them productive again.

"At the same time, keep their egos intact by emphasizing their importance to the organization and your desire to continue working with them. Reassess their strengths and weaknesses and discuss the possibility of restructuring their jobs or training them for other positions where they can be more effective. If they aren't innovative, look for areas that require little, if any, imagination. If they're victims of burn-out, consider giving them different challenges and areas of responsibility requiring new types of thinking."

Richard added, "Sometimes you can cosmetically structure different job assignments as lateral promotions or reduce the employees' compensation consistent with their contributions.

"I don't subscribe to the theory that you either have to move employees up or out but *never* down. Employees usually find reassignment to lower positions more desirable than termination. If properly presented, they should feel more secure knowing they can pay their own way at a lower compensation."

Mike interrupted, "Richard, I believe you just solved a problem for me. Fred Fisher, the quality control inspector on the #3000 line has been making a lot of mistakes, and his supervisor wants to fire him. Fred's been with Enfield for a long time, and he really tries hard but he isn't getting the job done.

"Before being promoted to quality control inspector, Fred was very happy in his maintenance job. The shift supervisor has been against putting him back in his old position, because he feels it would create a morale problem if Fred made more money than the others in maintenance. I'm going to talk to the supervisor about putting him back with a pay cut. I believe the supervisor will like this approach, and Fred will probably welcome the change."

Brent added, "People who become obsolete at Fred's level are bad enough, but with managers it can be particularly dangerous. If they're in the executive suite, they can be menaces because of the widespread negative effect they can have on others. If you can put these managers in staff positions with fewer people answering to them, it helps minimize, or eliminate, the potential damage.

"The greatest menace of all can be the chief executive officers who are the founders, or majority stockholders, and are becoming obsolete—but can't be removed unless they agree to it."

Barbara said, "I can understand how CEOs could be menaces if they were promoted to that position through nepotism but it seems that founders who have the ability to build organizations would always be assets."

"You might be surprised how often these CEOs are a problem, and I speak from first-hand experience," Brent answered. "My first company reached a point in its maturity where I felt my entrepreneurial flair had outlived its usefulness."

Brent looked a little sad as he added, "I learned to deal with this problem from both sides of the desk. I had dealt with some of my associates who were marginal, becoming burned out or bored. Then one day, I came to the sobering realization that I was losing interest in my job, and boredom was leading to my obsolescence.

"Although I wasn't marginal or burned out and was still making a significant contribution to my company, I found myself beginning to cling too much to the past and avoiding some of the innovative risks that presented themselves. Fortunately, I was able to sell my stock to the employees and pursue other interests before I became a menace."

Alan commented, "It seems as though a person in your position would have difficulty recognizing that you had outlived your usefulness."

"This became painfully obvious to me because of my background with Delta Air Lines and IBM. These organizations owed their success during their formative years to the entrepreneurial spirit fostered by C. E. Woolman at Delta and Thomas J. Watson at IBM.

"Nevertheless, during the twilight years of Woolman and Watson each of their companies had reached a point in growth and maturity where they needed the infusion of new management.

"Watson, at IBM, didn't believe computers had significant potential in the commercial market and felt they had only limited appeal in the scientific market. As a result, he had serious reservations about IBM making a strong commitment to entering the computer business. Imagine the great lost opportunity and serious repercussions that could have had on IBM's future.

"It was Watson's son, Thomas, Jr., who became the driving force behind IBM's entry into the commercial computer market. Watson, Sr. was a great businessman, and you can't say enough about his contributions to the company, but he was potentially a misguided missile in IBM's executive suite.

"I saw a remarkable, yet uncomfortable, parallel on a smaller scale with my situation, and I decided to leave my company before I became counterproductive.

"Stanley and I talked about this a lot. At times he'd be critical of other managers who knew they were approaching obsolescence but didn't do anything about it. His aversion to computers and other newer technology was a sign to me that perhaps he was becoming obsolete, but like most of us, he wasn't able to be objective about himself."

Richard asked, "Was there one major reason that you decided to leave your organization?"

"Yes. It was the realization that my focus was no longer on my company but rather on writing and speaking about management, and about human relations within organizations and in the market place. So I decided to leave before I found myself on the down side of the bell-shaped curve."

Mike asked, "What's the bell-shaped curve?"

"Since you're from Pennsylvania, visualize the Liberty Bell in Philadelphia. Where it slopes sharply up on the left, this represents the period when you're growing in your job and increasing your contribution to the organization. Then the bell levels out at the top. This is where I saw myself in my company.

"The bell then begins a sharp, sloping descent on the right side. This is the down slope of effectiveness, where you find most of your problem employees, and they'll continue to slide farther down the slope as they become less effective and more of a problem."

Gordon commented, "That sounds pretty grim to me. Is there any way to avoid eventually being on the down slope?"

Brent smiled. "Not unless you find a way to live forever and still remain effective. Athletes are acutely aware of this cycle, although they may not relate to it as a bell-shaped curve.

"Managers, like athletes, can often extend their careers by changing their style and work habits to avoid the road to obsolescence, but I want to emphasize that your location on the bell-shaped curve is not necessarily a function of your chronological age. Finding yourself on the down slope can occur at any time and at any age.

"If any of you are ever in positions where you detect signs of obsolescence within yourselves, and you answer to other managers, your jobs may already be in jeopardy. The chances are that your managers have probably already recognized the problem but haven't yet decided how to deal with it.

"Therefore, I recommend that you go to your managers and ask about possible restructuring or retraining to reverse the trend. This will probably come as a relief to your managers because *you* showed the initiative and brought up the problem. By doing so, there's a good chance it will save your job. You should also encourage your associates to come to *you* if *they* ever begin feeling obsolete.

"The earlier you can detect oncoming obsolescence, the better the chances of correcting the problem. I suggest you ask yourself these questions on a continuing basis:

How to Detect Oncoming Obsolescence

- What changes are taking place or will take place, either outside or within the organization, that can cause human obsolescence?
- Who among those in my organizational group, including myself, are susceptible to becoming obsolete because of these changes?
- What steps can I take to deal with this problem?
- Do I have a program that gives me and my associates a fair chance at remaining productive?"

Barbara asked, "What if they don't remain productive?"

"My attitude is that if you and your organization have met your obligation to keep people productive, the burden then shifts to these people to do their part in remaining productive. If they don't, and you aren't able to move them to more suitable positions, they'll continue to be misfits or distractions, and they should be terminated."

"Dealing with obsolescence can be a heavy burden, but helping my associates to remain productive has been one of my most satisfying management experiences."

• •

Egomaniacs in the Executive Suite: Assets or Misguided Missiles?

"At my former company," Gordon commented, "the CEO wasn't on the road to obsolescence but rather on the road to counterproductive egomania. He wouldn't listen to anyone, and he eventually drove the company into bankruptcy."

Brent responded, "Egomaniacs in the executive suite are an interesting paradox. They can be assets or liabilities."

"I don't think of egomaniacs as ever being assets," Barbara said with a surprised look.

"Barbara, it sometimes takes egomaniacs to implement new ventures or to solve organizational problems against overwhelming odds. Their determination, persistence, and the drive of their own egomania can also provide the much-needed strength and leadership an organization requires in times of stress or turmoil.

"However, since we're concentrating on personnel problems, let's discuss how these egomaniacs can be menaces to organizations."

Barbara asked, "Except through nepotism, majority stock ownership, or being the founders, how can egomaniacs work themselves into the executive suite?"

"Many of them go undetected as they move up through the ranks because they're 'closet' egomaniacs. They don't show their true colors until they get into a position of power. Their egos and their strong, if not stubborn, determination propel them into the executive suite. Once there, these same qualities begin to cloud their good judgment."

Gordon asked, "How can you identify these egomaniacs?"

Brent responded, "There are several ways:

How to Identify Counterproductive Egomania

1. *They pursue objectives far beyond the point at which they should be altered or abandoned.*

   The more their efforts fail, the more obsessively they pursue objectives without regard to the cost in managerial resources, or the cost of not pursuing more worthwhile objectives.

2. *They tend to be too autocratic.*

   They rule with iron fists, insisting that everything be done as they direct, discounting any ideas that are not their own. They don't listen to upward communications because they don't care what other people think.

3. *They display poor human relations skills.*

   They tend to be insensitive to the feelings of others and rarely admit to being wrong. This, in turn, makes their people so paranoid about being wrong, that they avoid making decisions involving prudent risks.

4. *They pay only lip service to participative management.*

   They hold meetings to *tell* people what to do instead of arriving at a consensus about what should be done and then giving people their own responsibilities.

5. *They strive to be irreplaceable.*

They feel threatened by any potential encroachment on their power base and don't help their people develop for fear they will become a threat."

Brent continued, "Misguided egomaniacs are such poor role models because of these tendencies that they cause organizations to lose many of their best people."

Alan asked, "If we identify these tendencies within ourselves, or within others, what can we do about it?"

Brent responded, "I suggest the following steps.

How to Neutralize Counterproductive Egomania

1. Recognize the characteristics and accept that there is a problem.
2. Continuously challenge the validity of your objectives and those of your people. More importantly, challenge the assumptions underlying the decisions to pursue these objectives.
3. Encourage a policy of participative management through regular meetings.
4. Induce upward communications by
   - Keeping your associates informed. The more you tell them, the more you'll receive in return.
   - Asking your associates for their opinions without telegraphing your own.
   - *Not* intimidating people. Too many managers suffer from a 'king's messenger' attitude of 'off with their heads' when people bring them any bad news. Once this happens, people will only tell their managers what they think their managers *want* to hear, thereby depriving the managers of valuable upward communications, particularly about any bad news.
5. Delegate properly. Instead of telling people what to do, obtain their commitment to achieve their part of the objectives, preferably in taped meetings, in front of their peers."

● ●

Those Who Have Conflicts with Others

Mike said, "I have problems with some of my people who always seem to be fighting with others."

"*Fighting* isn't the problem," Brent responded. "Here again, it's only a symptom. You can be the referee and stop the fighting temporarily, but unless you deal with the causes, they'll soon be at it again, so ask yourself, why are they fighting?"

Mike thought for a moment and responded, "It's usually about who has a certain responsibility."

"That is a management problem, and we can program out a lot of conflicts by clearing up company policies, having better descriptions of job responsibilities, and clarifying the authority people have in the handling of their responsibilities.

"Conflicts between people that can't be *programmed* out are more difficult to resolve. These conflicts arise among

- Those who answer to the same managers,
- Those who answer to different managers, and
- Managers and their staffs.

"You should approach these conflicts with the attitude that they *will not be tolerated*, and they *will be resolved*. As a manager, you can't afford to allow this type of disruption to continue.

"With a conflict among employees answering to the same managers, the managers should make it clear that to stay in the department, and perhaps even in the company, the employees must learn to work harmoniously among themselves. If this fails, the managers should separate them by either transferring one or more of them to other departments, or by termination.

"There are often personality conflicts among people who answer to different managers but who must work together—for example, sales and production people. In this type of conflict, their respective managers should agree on a position, then meet with the people having the conflict and show a united front by issuing an ultimatum that if those involved can't learn to work in harmony, their jobs will be in jeopardy.

"In conflicts between managers and their staffs, the managers should do all they can to resolve these conflicts, but if that fails, termination is the only logical answer."

At this point, Richard interrupted. "Unless anyone has any other types of problem employees they would like to bring up, this might be a good time to adjourn the meeting, and we can get together again in the lounge before we have dinner."

Later everyone relaxed in front of the fire in the lounge, and the group had an opportunity to become acquainted with Brent on a more personal basis.

● ●

Criticizing Others as You Would Have Them Criticize You

● ● ● ● ● ● ● ● ● ● ● ● ● ● ● ●

*How to Use Criticism
as a Positive Management Tool*

"During our session at the Colonial Inn," Brent began, "we discussed various types of problem employees. In addition to the solutions we discussed, offering constructive criticism can often be the best method of dealing with problem employees.

"Nevertheless, other than terminating people, many managers find that criticizing those who answer to them is their most unpleasant task. Therefore, they avoid it except when they become angry, in which case, criticism is an emotional and counterproductive negative reaction.

"This type of criticism can be a strong negative push for people to decide to leave an organization and is probably the cause of losing more good people than any other single factor.

"Being able to criticize unemotionally and positively without offending is a greatly underrated motivational tool and is part of the rapport managers need to build with their people. This takes time, and it's based on the mutual respect, trust, and understanding that the criticism is offered in good faith.

"I believe that offering criticism is an obligation, not simply an option. Therefore, we're being unfair and doing our people a great disservice if we don't offer criticism when we feel it's justified. However, if it's carried to excess, people will resent and even become immune to criticism."

Richard added, "We're all prone to make mistakes, and these are often only isolated instances, so I attempt to avoid being excessively critical by looking for patterns and waiting until there have been two or three similar instances of a certain problem before taking any action.

"For example, if there's a complaint about a customer service representative, I may just write a memo to the department manager. If there are repeated complaints that form a pattern, I talk to the manager."

Brent added, "After making a fool out of myself a couple of times, I learned that I could also reduce the amount of criticisms I was inclined to offer by always confirming my assumptions.

"I remember one instance when I criticized someone in my shipping department because a customer hadn't received a shipment on time, only to find that we'd made the shipment *before* the scheduled date. In fact, the shipment had been sitting on the customer's receiving dock for several days before the customer called and complained to me."

Richard said, "Your example emphasizes the importance of verifying facts, instead of acting on hearsay and impressions. This helps eliminate the emotion and makes matters less subjective."

"Could you give us any guidelines," Barbara asked Brent, "for when the offering of criticism is justified?"

Brent answered, "Whenever your people have done something that

- Makes themselves or others less effective,
- Creates a problem or a potential problem, and
- Reflects unfavorably on the organization."

Alan said, "One of my former colleagues used to say that constructive criticism is fine as long as you're giving it, but isn't worth a damn when you're receiving it."

Brent responded, "I don't subscribe to that philosophy. I've found that your best and most enlightened people *always* want to know how they stand, even, as you previously said, when it's 'knee deep in hot water.' They don't enjoy the process, but they prefer being criticized rather than experiencing the uncertainty and the counterproductive stress when they detect that we *feel* dissatisfied with them but don't *express* it. In addition, few things cause me more stress than not expressing criticism when I feel it's warranted.

"Our associates never do anything intentionally to warrant our criticism, so letting them know how you feel gives them an opportunity to correct the problem. Therefore, I believe you'll find that they'll tend to welcome your criticism if you'll follow these 'Golden Rules.'

● ● ● ● ● ● ● ● ● ● ● ● ● ● ● ● ● ●

Five "Golden Rules" of Criticism

"Before being critical of our associates, we need to try to mentally put ourselves in their shoes and ask how we would prefer being criticized. I believe our answers would be that

1. We prefer that the criticism be unemotional and constructive.
2. We would prefer to be able to maintain our self-respect and not be put in a position where we'll become defensive.
3. We prefer not to be criticized personally but rather to be criticized about a problem situation where we've had a responsibility or some involvement.
4. We prefer to be able to apologize if we deserve the criticism, and have our managers understand that we'll be more critical of ourselves than they would be of us.
5. We prefer the criticism to be one on one, not in front of others."

Richard smiled and remarked, "When Stanley felt inclined to be critical toward any of us for causing him a problem, he had an effective way of never really criticizing us, but instead was able to make *his* problem *our* problem.

"Let's say that by a Monday I had committed to give Stanley the specifications and costs on some new equipment to include in next year's budget. Then on Monday I hadn't met my commitment. Stanley would come to me and say, 'Richard, I promised the bank and our board of directors that I'd give our proposed budget to them this week. I did this based on your commitment to give me a report by today of our estimated equipment costs for the coming year. Since I don't have the report, what do you suggest that I tell the bank and our board?'

"This approach invariably made me feel guilty and more motivated to solve the problem than if Stanley had stormed into my office and criticized me for not having the figures, in which case I would have tended to become defensive and make up excuses.

"An exception to your rule about criticizing one on one," Richard continued, "might be times when I'll criticize a manager and one or more of his or her people in the same session."

"When would you do that?" Gordon asked.

"For example, if I received more than one complaint from a major customer about our customer service representative. To emphasize the seriousness of the problem, I might meet with the manager and the customer service representative and criticize *both* of them for mishandling this very important account. However, I'd never single out and reprimand only *one* person in front of another.

"I also might be critical about someone who answers to another manager. For example, I may express dissatisfaction to Barbara about how one of her salespeople handled a particular customer."

"However, I would caution managers that when they do complain about others to third parties, they should be particularly sensitive not to appear 'catty.' I assure you that although people may tolerate catty remarks from colleagues, managers who are catty will soon lose the respect of their associates. Before expressing yourself, the acid test is always to ask yourself, if your remarks were repeated later, would you be embarrassed?

"When being critical of someone to a third party, I usually indicate that I don't mind being quoted verbatim, as long as it's kept in the right context. This way, if I'm later confronted by the person I criticized, I won't be on the defensive or uncomfortable admitting that I'd been critical—and furthermore, had said I didn't mind being quoted."

Brent said, "Before we conclude our discussion, I'd like to share an idea with you about how to criticize people for the first time, and how to put the criticism, as well as any future ones, in the right perspective.

"New employees usually go through a honeymoon period when they're insulated from criticism. Even after this, the first time you criticize them can be touchy, because you don't know how they'll respond.

"It's important that the criticism be accepted positively, so I say something like this: 'We haven't worked together very long, but I'd give you good marks for your performance to date. So far, you haven't received any constructive criticism from me, but I'd like to offer you some now. How you react is more important than the criticism itself. If you become defensive and react negatively, I'll be hesitant to offer you any criticism in the future. That would be to our mutual disadvantage and would create a barrier in our ability to communicate.'"

As the management meeting adjourned, Brent asked Barbara if he could speak with her. After the others had left, Brent said, "Barbara, since we talked today about the obligation of managers to their people to offer criticism when they feel it's justified, I believe this is an appropriate time for me to offer you some.

"After reviewing the sales reports, I'm concerned about Chuck Abernathy. He's behind on his quota, and based on his previous performance I'm disappointed that you haven't either gotten rid of him or talked to me about his poor performance."

Barbara had anticipated this discussion, and she was embarrassed to answer Brent's question with a painfully honest answer.

"I haven't fired Chuck . . . because I can't."

"Why not?"

"Shortly after my promotion to sales manager, I fired one of my sales representatives—or, more accurately, I destroyed him. This was my first experience with terminating anyone. It was so traumatic for me that I asked Scott to let me return to my position as sales representative. He persuaded me to remain as sales manager, but only with his assurance that he'd handle the terminations of any salespeople in the future."

"Then why didn't he fire Chuck?"

"Scott doesn't like to fire people either. We discussed Chuck's performance the week before Scott's heart attack, and he felt we should give Chuck another chance. As you've discovered, it hasn't worked!"

"You said that you and Scott didn't like to fire people. Barbara, in my opinion, any manager who enjoys terminating people is perverse. If it's of any comfort, the first time I terminated someone was my all-time worst management experience. I still hate the chore, but I'll do it when necessary, and without delay.

"I'm not going to force you to terminate Chuck or anyone else, and as long as I'm here, I'll handle any of your terminations that are necessary, but only because Scott promised that you wouldn't have to. In your defense, some other managers at Enfield must have your same reluctance to terminate people, as evidenced by some of the 'dead wood' around here.

"Nevertheless, having someone else handle this important part of your job will eventually cause you to lose the respect of others. To be highly successful as a manager, sooner or later *you* will have to learn to deal with this unpleasant task."

Barbara replied, "I don't like to admit that I'm unable to cope with any facet of my job, but I can't stand the thought of having to go through the experience of firing someone again."

Brent said, "I believe that a discussion of how to go through the termination process effectively would be a good topic for our management meeting on Wednesday."

As Barbara got up to leave, Brent said, "Let me know if I can help you in dealing with the Chuck Abernathy problem."

"Thanks, let me think about it, and I will get back to you."

• •

How to Terminate People with Less Trauma

Brent opened the session. "We've had discussions about problem employees, and how to deal with them. If all else fails, there's only one obvious answer—they should be terminated.

"I don't know of a more unpleasant task for a manager than having to terminate someone, but this is an integral part of the management job. I've had to terminate many people over the years, and I've developed some techniques that I believe can make the process less traumatic for some of you, *and* for those being terminated.

"The first time I dismissed one of my associates, I did everything wrong from beginning to end. It might be helpful if you heard the story of that disaster.

"I had a production manager whose name was Simpson. He wasn't meeting his schedules, and some of our key people left because they couldn't get along with him. My other managers agreed that Simpson should be terminated, but I dreaded going through the ordeal.

"Late one Friday afternoon, I asked Simpson to come to my office. That was my first mistake—I should have gone to his. After an hour, Simpson was still sitting in my office.

"My second mistake was opening the session by gradually working up to my reason for wanting to see him. I began by telling him he was being too rough on his people, and that customers were complaining about late shipments.

"Then he stood up as he assured me that he'd do better in the future and started to leave. Then the terrible realization hit—I'd been so vague, Simpson thought he was just being reprimanded, and now he was about to walk out of my office. I quickly asked him to please sit down again. Now I was on the defensive, and I thought, 'Maybe I'm being too hasty and should give him another chance.' But I knew I was just kidding myself. Simpson didn't belong in my company, and I'd look like a coward and lose the respect of my associates if I didn't go through with this, so I told Simpson he was being terminated. Then I made my third big mistake by adding that the other managers all agreed that he should leave the company.

"Simpson became incensed and said he thought he'd been answering to me, but if his colleagues had anything to do with this, they should be in my office participating in his execution. Then, in an attempt to fortify my position, I mentioned some more specific examples of why I wasn't happy with his performance, and we got into a debate about points that were no longer relevant.

"Finally I tried to change the subject by suggesting to him that on his next job, he should stay better organized, begin planning more realistically, and quit overcommitting himself. He let me know in no uncertain terms what I could do with my advice. He pointed out that I should have been criticizing and giving him advice *before* deciding to terminate him, not afterward. Furthermore, he said I'd never given him any indication or warning that his performance was unsatisfactory, and I hate to admit it, but he was right, because criticizing my associates was almost as distasteful for me as having to terminate them.

"At this point, I apologized to Simpson for not managing him more effectively, but I stood firm and ended the session by telling him that he would have to leave the company. As I drove home that night, I vowed I'd never go through such an experience again.

"Over the next few days, I kept thinking about how I could develop a discipline that would enable me to effectively terminate people in the future, and I came up with this list that I've used for years and have referred to many times.

S tud y

Fourteen Keys to Terminating Effectively

1. First, develop the right attitude about the task. Immediately before the session, remind yourself that this is best for the person being terminated as well as for your organization. If you do not end this counterproductive relationship, you will be doing this person a disservice by robbing him or her of valuable career time that could be better spent elsewhere.

2. Never terminate anyone when you are emotional, and make certain you have reached a rational decision. To obtain more objectivity, solicit the opinions of others who may have meaningful input. You have a responsibility to do all of your homework carefully, because you are dealing with a human life, and being fired can be a traumatic blow to a person's self-esteem.

3. State the purpose of the session immediately to avoid the building of tension.

4. Never be tentative or defensive. Once the decision is made, do not second guess yourself. Begin the session with the mindset that the decision is irrevocable—and make this clear to the person being terminated.

5. Be firm and act unemotionally. Give straight, honest reasons for the dismissal. Emphasize that this is *your* decision, because blaming others will only cause resentment.

6. Acknowledge that this is a mutual disappointment and, to the extent it is justified, assume the blame for the relationship not working out.

7. Emphasize that this termination is not a reflection on the strong skills and aptitudes of this person that can be put to more effective use elsewhere. If you can do so in good conscience, offer to provide references that will emphasize his or her good qualities.

8. Ease the blow to the person's ego by focusing *not* on personal deficiencies, but rather on situations that exist, such as a need to cut back on personnel.

9. Be careful about offering unsolicited advice. It may only cause resentment by being offered so late.

10. Avoid being drawn into an argument or a counterproductive discussion. If this happens, give additional reasons for the ter-

mination that can't be challenged. For example, that you are no longer comfortable with your working relationship. Someone obviously cannot argue that you *are* comfortable.

11. If the session becomes a court of final appeal and the person grasps at straws and becomes defensive about minor points, ignore this distraction and continue to focus on the real reasons for the termination.

12. Conduct the session at the end of a day, as soon as possible after you have made the decision, and not necessarily on Fridays as is traditional. Delaying the session will only make you feel stressful and will dominate your thinking as the anticipation builds up.

13. Meet one on one. It is unfair and embarrassing to have third parties present. Whenever possible, have the session in his or her office. This will enable you to control the length of the session by leaving after you have stated your position.

14. End the session as quickly as possible. Wrap everything up in one session, including the obtaining of office keys, files, and other important documents. After this, encourage the person to leave as soon as possible.

"When people are put into a managerial position for the first time, I suggest that you ask them that if it becomes necessary to terminate someone, would they be reluctant to do so. Although the inevitable response is that they wouldn't, I find this hard to believe because of the anguish of my first experience. Nevertheless, this will give you an opportunity to point out to new managers that if they retain those who should be terminated, this will reflect unfavorably on them."

Brent added rather sadly, "Many terminations are necessary because when we hired these people we misjudged their abilities, so we're at fault. However, this is no excuse for keeping someone in the company who doesn't belong. It's also only a cop-out for managers to justify their procrastination, or failure to terminate employees, by claiming they're too warm-hearted and compassionate.

"When decisions aren't made to terminate when necessary, they become decisions by default to keep the wrong people. This isn't fair to them, to the others in the organization, or to the organization itself."

• •

Dealing with Those Who Become Hostile When Terminated

Brent answered his phone, and it was Barbara Lansing asking if she might see him for a few minutes.

"Sure," he said. "I'll drop by your office on my way to the plant."

Ten minutes later, Brent walked into her office. "Hi, Barbara, what's going on?"

"A sales candidate who appears to be very well qualified is coming in for an interview first thing in the morning. If you're available, I'd like for you to meet her."

"Why are you talking to a sales candidate? We have a full complement of salespeople."

"Not any more—Chuck Abernathy is gone!"

"Did he quit?"

"No—I fired him," she said with a faint smile.

"You almost look as though you enjoyed it."

"I didn't enjoy firing him, but I used your technique, and I *am* pleased that it worked."

"So, it went smoothly?"

"Well, not entirely. After I told him I was letting him go, he became very hostile and said he didn't understand why he was being fired."

"That's a natural reaction," Brent said casually.

"But what can I do in the future to reduce the hostility and make people understand why they're being fired?"

"I can answer both of your questions with one sentence. You probably can't reduce the hostility, because those being terminated usually don't understand, or even try to understand, the reason."

"You're going to have to explain that."

"As a psychology major, you should know that fair is in the mind of the beholder. I had a computer programmer who became obsolete at the age of 32. Even after we tried without success to train him on newer equipment, he wouldn't adapt to the changes in computer technology. When his manager told him that he was being terminated, the programmer immediately invoked the open-door policy and came to me. As a result, I met with him and his manager.

"We told the programmer that we could no longer justify keeping him because he wasn't qualified to handle the newer equipment. We went to great lengths to explain why, but we just couldn't get through to him. He felt he'd been loyal, and now we were firing him. He didn't understand us, because he didn't want to understand.

"Some people become hostile as a defense mechanism. The only way they can maintain their self-respect *and* accept termination is to believe that the *organization* has been unfair.

"You should just assume that some of those you terminate are going to become hostile and claim they don't understand the reason, no matter what you tell them. Therefore, as *unnatural* as this may seem, don't worry about it."

"But I'm not sure I can learn to do that."

"Then let me tell you how I learned.

"Late one afternoon, I was sitting in my office reflecting on a termination I'd just concluded. This person had been very hostile and claimed he didn't understand why he was being terminated, so I was experiencing the same type of concern you expressed and having a difficult time coping with it.

"Then I recalled a situation involving someone whose name was Cliff Alexander and who had been with my company for a long time. When we installed a new type of computer, we spent a lot of time and money training Cliff to program this equipment. Shortly afterward, he resigned unexpectedly and went with our largest competitor to program the same type of equipment.

"We paid for his education, and the competition received the benefit. Cliff was almost irreplaceable at the time, and although I concealed my feelings, I was very upset with him for leaving without giving us more notice. What did the people in our office do? They gave him a going-away party.

"Thinking about Alexander's situation made me realize that *he* had 'terminated' us—yet *we* had given *him* a party. Following this same logic, I reasoned that when the company terminates someone, perhaps that person should give us a party.

"Of course, that was an absurd thought, but it put things in perspective for me. When people terminate us, they should rightfully expect no hostility in return. By the same token, when we terminate them, we have a right to expect no hostile feelings from them. Since then, whenever I terminate people and they become hostile, my attitude is that the reflection is on them, not on me—and it makes me damned glad to be rid of them."

As Brent stood to leave, Barbara said, "Thanks, Brent, you've made me feel much better about Chuck."

●●●●●●●●●●●●●●●●●●●●●●●●●●●●●●●●●●●

Dealing with the Question of Loyalty to Problem Employees

Brent opened the meeting. "As you all know, Chuck Abernathy is no longer with Enfield. Barbara terminated him on Thursday afternoon. I know this was a very unpleasant experience, Barbara, but I congratulate you on how well you handled this situation.

"Chuck had been with the company for quite awhile, and Barbara told me later that her biggest concern was about how much loyalty she and Enfield owe to someone like Chuck, who was loyal, but who should be terminated.

"This is one of the toughest questions managers have to face, because the answer is subjective and involves human emotions, and the careers and lives of people.

"In the case of problem employees, loyal or not, if they cannot be rehabilitated, their managers have a *duty* to terminate them or force them into early retirement."

Alan asked, "In my family's insurance business, after my uncle's loyal secretary was no longer productive, he kept her on the payroll for several years until she reached retirement age. Do you believe my uncle should have given her 'the sack'?"

Brent smiled and responded, "Alan, just for a change of pace, I wish you would occasionally ask me a question that is easy to answer.

"Nevertheless, in response to your question, was your uncle's secretary a problem?"

"Not really. She was actually very well liked by everyone."

"Then I'll answer your question two ways.

"If the secretary had created a problem for the organization, and your uncle had kept her on anyway, this would have been unfair to the others in the company. In this case, he should have terminated her or forced her into early retirement.

"Since his secretary wasn't a problem, and because he was an owner of the business, he had every right to make a decision to underwrite the costs of his unproductive secretary. However, let's assume your uncle did *not* have a substantial equity in the business. If he'd decided to keep his secretary on the payroll out of his loyalty to her, without the authorization from those with the fiduciary responsibility, this would be tantamount to stealing money from the company."

Richard commented, "There are managers who have stronger loyalties to those who answer to them than they do to the organization, only to discover later that this loyalty is misplaced. The reciprocal personal loyalty these managers had perceived existed with their people goes away when these people leave the company. In fact, these managers later often find themselves competing fiercely with these same people in the marketplace."

Gordon asked, "Nevertheless, as long as these people were on the payroll, didn't their managers and the company deserve a high degree of loyalty in return?"

"Gordon," Richard answered, "I'm leery of any suggestion that an organization can expect, deserves, or can buy loyalty with paychecks. Most people look on paychecks as compensation for the work they perform, not as the price for their loyalty. Managers and companies have to earn loyalty from their people through fairness, decent treatment, and many other ways—but not with paychecks."

Brent added, "The first loyalty of all of those in an organization is almost always to themselves. Then, however, the strongest loyalty of managers is usually to their organizations, and finally to their people.

"For most direct producers, their strongest loyalty, other than to themselves, is to their peers, then to their own managers, or their customers. Finally, it's to higher management and to their organizations, both of which they view as rather vague abstracts."

Alan asked, "Since the priorities between managers and direct producers are so different, how do you explain the strong loyalties that often flow between managers and their people?"

Brent answered, "I believe it's because of the interdependence between them, similar to that of a football coach and his players. Another reason is that although their priorities are much different, they are compatible."

"Why," Gordon asked, "do those closer to the top have stronger loyalties to the organization than those in the lower ranks?"

Brent responded, "Because the personal objectives of those at the higher levels are more compatible with those of the organization.

"I would add that as a manager, I have no right to impose my priorities on others. However, if the priorities of any of those who answer to me are incompatible with my managerial priorities, the differences have to be resolved, or I'll terminate my relationship with them."

"I can give you an example," Richard said. "Several years ago, one of our largest customers wanted our sales representative to call regularly on their branches, which were all over the country.

"Our salespeople were answering directly to Stanley at the time, and our representative handling this customer told Stanley that traveling would mean being away from home too much, but he didn't want to give up the account either.

"I was at this meeting, and Stanley told the rep that he would either have to travel or give up the account to someone who would. Then the rep asked Stanley if he had any other choices. Stanley looked at him very calmly and said, 'Well, you could always leave the company.'

"The sales rep looked shocked and told Stanley that he'd been loyal to him and to Enfield, and that he'd expected more loyalty in return. Stanley then explained that as his manager, his obligation to the company transcended any personal loyalties that he had to the people at Enfield. He went on to say that the employees could only depend on his loyalty as long as they conformed to the needs of Enfield.

"The conclusion of the story is that the sales rep decided to travel, learned to like it, and continued to be very successful with us for several years before leaving to start his own business."

· ·

Managing Yourself and Your Life

30

● ●

Managing the Stress Out of Your Job and Your Life

Brent opened the meeting. "Up until now, all of our discussions have dealt primarily with *how* to perform the job of manager. This afternoon I would like to discuss a real personal threat in the job of a manager. That threat is when the inherent pressures of the job result in the negative emotional reaction we refer to as *stress*.

"Pressure is a paradox. On one hand, it can be a positive force that causes people to be more committed to achieve objectives and enables them to accomplish more than they thought possible. The absence of this type of positive pressure in many people can even result in them feeling stressful, if not severely depressed. Professional athletes often experience this emotion when they retire from active participation in sports.

"On the other hand, pressure is most often thought of as a negative force that causes mental or physical stress. If you don't keep your perspective and learn to deal with it effectively, stress can ruin your health or perhaps even kill you.

"Another interesting aspect of pressure and stress that a manager should be aware of is that the *pressure* in the management job, and in many other occupations, is a fact, whereas the *stress* you might feel from the job is an emotion. This suggests that it is how we

227

view the pressures of our job that will determine if the job will be stressful. People can have identical management jobs and some will be enjoying themselves immensely, while others will be feeling highly stressful.

"I'm not exaggerating or speaking hypothetically. I worked very closely with one manager who had a stroke and died in his forties. I'm convinced that the stress of his management job contributed to his death, and this has had a profound effect on me.

"Managers have to learn to live with the potentially lethal pressure that surrounds their jobs in the same way that electricians have to learn to live with the high voltages of deadly electricity that surround their jobs.

"Good management is largely a matter of practicing good human relations, and those who don't learn to practice this create stress within themselves and in their associates, because stress is as contagious as a virus.

"In organizations, stress normally flows downward from the top. This is why many surveys have indicated that there's more stress at the middle and lower levels of organizations than at the top.

• •

How Managers Can Make "Stress Transfers" to Relieve Stress

"At times, stress flows upward when those at the lower levels cause stress for those at the higher levels. As a young manager and CEO, I tolerated my share of this. However, I later discovered that when people who answer to me cause me stress, I can eliminate the problem through a process I call a 'stress transfer,' and I've never found a better way to instantly relieve the stress that others cause within me. The object is to take the stress others have imposed on me and transfer it back to them in kind, and I highly recommend it to you."

"I tell my associates that two things I will absolutely not tolerate are a bad attitude and for anyone on my payroll to cause me stress over any significant period of time. I always let someone know immediately when he or she is causing me to feel stressful, and I tell this person why. Then I tell the person that one of two things is going to happen: either he or she is going to eliminate the cause of my stress, or one of us is going to leave the organization—and it won't be me.

"I find that the more calmly I tell a person this, the more dramatic the impact, and at this point, the stress transfer is largely achieved. I end the conversation by explaining that this should be taken not as a threat, but as a simple statement of fact."

Barbara laughed and said, "You used those exact words on me the first day you came to Enfield when you calmly told me that if anyone displayed any resentment toward you to the extent that it was counterproductive, you would make it your business to get that person out of Enfield Manufacturing. I remember the conversation like it was yesterday, but I didn't realize until now that you were making a very successful stress transfer to me."

Mike added, "I made a stress transfer to Bud Randall after he was causing me stress by trying to become irreplaceable. It worked like a charm. As you suggested, I met with him and told him very calmly that the next time he was away from the plant, if the large punch press went down and I had to fix it, he was through at Enfield.

"I could tell that Bud was feeling a lot of stress for the next couple of weeks while he was training someone else to maintain and repair the press, and I really hate to admit it, but knowing that he was feeling stressful gave me a perverse sort of pleasure."

"Mike, if that's perverse," responded Brent, "then I share your perversion, because knowing that you've transferred the stress is part of the therapy. I find it very cathartic to see evidence that the transfer was successfully accomplished, and that the person who caused me stress is now feeling the same, if not a higher degree of stress, than he or she caused in me."

Brent continued, "Except for stress transfers, where people have brought the stress on themselves, I'd never consciously do anything to create stress in those who answer to me. On the contrary, I want to do everything within reason to help my people avoid or relieve stress, because the less stress they feel, the more effective they're likely to be.

"I also don't want to carry the moral burden of thinking I might have created stress in someone to the extent that it could cause a heart attack, a stroke, ulcers, or even death.

"It's only natural for people to feel some stress in their relationships with their managers, who by virtue of their managers' authority can have such a significant influence on their careers. Managers should be very sensitive to this and to how easily they can create stress within their associates by how they deal with them.

"Everyone is strongly influenced by managers because we live in a society of organizations, the largest of which is the United States government. All organizations, regardless of size, are run by managers. Almost everyone in our society is a manager, answers to a manager, or is married to or lives with someone who either is a manager or answers to a manager.

"As a manager with years of experience, I'm convinced that much of the stress within our organizational society is a direct result of a lack of understanding about management, among direct producers as well as managers. This lack of understanding creates stress in the relationship between these two groups."

Richard commented, "I believe that most stress among those in organizations is self-imposed and is a result of people being unable to handle their responsibilities. These people naturally don't want to blame the stress on themselves, so the most logical candidates for taking the blame are their managers for imposing too many responsibilities on them."

● ●
Stress and the Myth of the Overworked Manager

"Another major cause of stress within organizations," Richard continued, "is that many people work too hard. By definition, if they're working 'too hard,' they're working harder than they should. Stanley used to say that managers can't work effectively when they're 'so busy they can't think.'

"Too many managers assume that hard work, if not overwork, is an integral part of becoming highly successful in management. I don't agree with this assumption. On the contrary, overwork and perhaps even hard work interferes with a manager's effectiveness.

"I believe the myth of the overworked manager is fostered by managers and those not in management who aren't successful. They use the excuse of being unwilling to sacrifice their personal lives by putting in the long, hard hours they claim are necessary to be successful in management."

Barbara was visibly irritated by Richard's remark. "That's easy for you to say, Richard, but I don't happen to agree. After calling on untold numbers of managers in my career, I've observed, and have heard many of them complain about, how overworked they are. Furthermore, although you never seem to show any signs of stress from being overworked, some of your people do."

Richard smiled and calmly asked, "Would you care to mention any names?"

"I'm afraid I'm the culprit," Gordon volunteered. "Barbara and I had a discussion a few weeks ago, and I was complaining about the stress I was feeling—not because of you, but because of the responsibilities of my job. Since then, our management discussions have helped me to greatly alleviate this stress and have made me realize that the stress I still feel is self-imposed, as you suggested."

Brent looked very serious as he said, "Gordon, it's obvious to me that you and some others at Enfield are feeling much more stress than you should. In your case I believe it's your attitude about your work. I don't mean this critically, but I see you as a perfectionist. Before you became a manager, this characteristic no doubt helped you in your accounting career. The debits always had to equal the credits, and you were trained to make sure the books always balanced perfectly.

"However, when you're managing, something is always out of balance, and you'll *never* be able to balance the books. Managers spend most of their time dealing with exceptions. These are often in the form of problems and complications that arise while trying to achieve their objectives.

"As a manager, you're kidding yourself if one of your objectives is to strive to make everything always run smoothly and to eliminate the deviations from normal that keep coming across your desk. By doing so, you're trying to eliminate an integral part of *every* manager's job.

"Organizations are as imperfect as the rest of the world we live in, and now that you're a manager, you should learn to do what comes *unnaturally* for you. This includes accepting as normal the *imbalances* inherent in your job. Until you learn this, you'll probably continue to feel stress and cause stress within your people.

"The key is to develop the right attitude about your job. This is a prerequisite to enjoying your work as a manager. Norman Vincent Peale said, 'Change your thoughts and everything else changes. Your life is determined by the kind of thoughts you habitually think.'

"You can do very well as a manager by not taking your job, *or yourself, too seriously.* There are many things I'm more concerned about than my career—the health and well-being of my family, for instance."

● ● ● ● ● ● ● ● ● ● ● ● ● ● ● ●

Humor and Relieving Stress

Richard said, "Brent, when you said that no one should take his job or himself too seriously, this reminded me of a conversation you and I had about the use of humor as a management tool. I believe the group would benefit from your thoughts on this subject."

Brent responded, "Humor is often overlooked as a valuable management tool for relieving stress within yourself and others. Some managers make the mistake of trying to force-feed humor even when they don't use it well. Those few unfortunate managers should avoid it, but I would encourage other managers to 'think funny' and look for humor in organizational situations."

Gordon interrupted. "But I take my management job very seriously, and don't believe I could ever make light of it."

"Gordon," Brent answered, "managing the government of the United States is very serious business, but all of our recent presidents have recognized the value of humor in effective leadership. Classic examples are Presidents Kennedy and Reagan. I read a book on presidential humor that pointed out how former presidents have devoted a lot of time and effort to being coached on the effective use of humor.

"When I was in sales, I often used humor to break the ice and to loosen up prospects. I don't necessarily mean telling jokes, but rather the same kind of light humor you might use in talking to a good friend or a relative.

"Managers can use humor in meetings the same way a minister in a church uses it as a change of pace to gain attention and put his audience at ease.

"When talking to larger groups, I always try to use humorous stories to keep the audience on my side and to hold their attention. People are starved for humor. You may work for months to create an eloquent speech, but if the audience remembers anything, it'll probably be your humorous remarks. Every speech and every meeting should have substance, but if you package and deliver your substance wrapped in humor, the audience will be more receptive."

● ●
Managers and Their Personal Lives

"Most of our discussions," Richard said to Brent, "have had to do with management within organizations. Stanley used to tell me how interested he was in your strong beliefs about the benefits of management in the personal lives of people. Could you share some of your thoughts about this with our group?"

Brent responded, "Most of the good managers I've known have been good managers of their personal lives and vice versa. In fact, I once decided against hiring a candidate for an important management position because I could tell from answers he gave during our interview that he was mismanaging his personal life. His wife had a good job, they lived in a very expensive house and drove new cars. In spite of this, he volunteered that he couldn't afford to send his only child to an out-of-state college. I had the uncomfortable feeling that since he managed his personal life poorly, he wouldn't be able to manage his organizational life any better."

Alan asked, "Do you believe most people have to learn to be good managers of their personal lives before they learn to be good managers within an organization, or is it the other way around?"

"That's an interesting question, and it probably can work both ways. I told you about the time that I was so overcommitted that I had almost decided to liquidate my business. I was feeling very stressful at the time, and that was when I began learning about management from Stanley Wilson. From that point on, I applied these principles in my career as a manager as well as my personal life.

"In my personal life, I began to consciously establish assumptions and then to establish and prioritize my personal objectives and make plans based on these assumptions. I developed the habit of continuing to monitor my assumptions until I achieved the results or modified or aborted my plans. I also used sound management principles in leveraging my personal resources of time, money, information, physical resources, and the human resource of my own efforts.

"Then I came to the startling realization one day that by applying sound management principles in my career and in my personal life, I had literally managed most of the stress out of my life in a very short period of time.

"The focus on dealing with stress in our society is on *coping* with stress, not on *eliminating* the cause. I believe the major cause of stress is that we do not effectively manage our lives by the application of sound management principles.

"It is ironic to me that when people become so stressful that they have to seek professional help, they turn to those therapists who only attempt to help them *cope* with stress. I believe many of them would be better served to turn to effective managers for help in dealing with the *cause* of stress.

"If I could leave only one lesson as a legacy from my entire management career, it would be to help more people learn how to manage the stress out of their lives, instead of just coping with the stress that is a symptom of not managing their careers and personal lives effectively."

FOURTEEN

The Conclusion of a Turnaround

31

●●●●●●●●●●●●●●●●●●●●●●●●●●●●●●●●●●●

Brent had been in the plant. On his way back to his office he saw Helen Wilson sitting in the reception area. He tried not to look surprised as he said, "Hello, Helen. How are you?"

"I'm fine, Brent. I apologize for popping in, but do you have a few minutes to talk with me?"

"Sure, Helen. We can talk in Scott's office."

"Could we talk somewhere else? I haven't been in that office since Stanley died, and I'm not up to seeing it right now."

"I understand. We can use the conference room."

Brent knew that Helen had not come by just to check on the status of the business, and it was obvious to him that she was very nervous.

After they were seated in the conference room, he asked, "Is there something wrong, Helen?"

"Oh no. I just got a call from our attorney, Charles Dickey. The attorney for Kilgore Enterprises called him. Kilgore's president heard of Scott's heart attack and expressed an interest in the possibility of Kilgore acquiring Enfield."

"What did you tell Mr. Dickey?"

"I told him I wanted to talk to you before expressing any possible interest."

"Did he mention any numbers?"

"No. Charles said Kilgore wants to see copies of our financial statements before making any offer."

"Does Scott know about this?"

"Heavens no! He'd be opposed to even talking with Kilgore. He dislikes the Kilgore people intensely, as did Stanley. They both felt Kilgore was an unethical competitor. Besides . . . Scott still plans to return to Enfield.

"Brent, you're going to have to tell me what to do. I look to you as Stanley's alter ego, and whatever you recommend is what I know Stanley would have wanted."

"Helen, you've really put me on the spot. Up until now, my interest in Enfield was focused on earning the trust you've placed in me to help put the company back in sound shape."

She sighed. "I don't mean to impose more pressure on you, but you're the only one I can turn to for advice. I really don't know if we should sell or not. Do you believe the company is doing well enough for us to receive a decent price?"

"It depends on what you mean by a decent price. You should be able to get a reasonably good price because Enfield is doing much better financially, and based on my projections it should be consistently profitable starting in April. Our cash flow is improving, and the Enfield Bank isn't giving us any more trouble. My biggest concern is about the future management of the company. What is your current thinking about Scott in this regard?"

"I feel more strongly than ever that he shouldn't come back. Since he's been away, Scott has changed for the better and is more like he used to be.

"I don't think he's aware of how different he is when he's not here. Running Enfield these last three years was the worst thing he ever attempted. He's been obsessed with trying to prove he could make Enfield more successful than it was when Stanley ran the company. Unfortunately, the harder he tried, the more he failed. Even though Scott would be opposed to selling the company, it might end his bizarre competition with the ghost of his father.

"I'll emphasize to you again that what I *really* want is for *you* to stay as president of Enfield and make the company as successful as it was when Stanley was running it."

"You flatter me, Helen, but I don't believe it would be the best answer for you, me, or the company. Getting back into active management is an interesting possibility, but first, why don't we take a look at Kilgore's offer? I believe you should listen to what they have to say, and I'll be glad to sit in on any discussions."

"I would appreciate that very much. In the meantime I want you to please consider becoming president."

"I will, Helen. Thanks!"

As Brent walked Helen to her car, he said, "Don't worry about Enfield, Helen. We'll figure out what's best."

Brent didn't return to his office. Instead, he walked across the parking lot to the path that led along the river. He and Stanley had often strolled along this path, particularly when one of them had something of importance he wanted to discuss. Now Brent was alone, and it seemed strange not having Stanley by his side.

As he stopped and stared at the river, his thoughts returned to Enfield, and how much more deeply involved he was than he had intended. It had all seemed so simple when he started. He would come in for three months, do the best he could by applying some sound management principles, and then leave.

Now Kilgore was interested in buying Enfield and Helen wanted him to advise her about what to do. If the Wilsons did not sell Enfield, Helen would still pressure him to become president.

He began to wonder if he was losing his objectivity, because he was beginning to think about how satisfying it would be if he could make Enfield more successful than it had been when Stanley was running the company. Then Brent remembered what Helen had said about Scott competing with his late father. He wondered if he might be falling into the same trap of competing with the ghost of Stanley Wilson.

As Brent turned back toward the plant, he thought, "What if I tell Helen not to accept Kilgore's offer, recommend someone else as president, and after I leave, Enfield gets back into trouble?"

Brent began feeling very stressful as he thought, "Just the other day, I was talking with the management group about learning to deal with stress, and now I'm feeling it myself. I have to keep my perspective. It's only business, but it's a lot different now that I'm playing with the Wilson's chips. I could always deal with losing what was mine, but I don't know how well I would deal with losing what belongs to them."

As he crossed the parking lot and entered the building, he continued to think about his options.

● ●

"Westport Station . . . Westport Station." As the words came over the train's loudspeaker, Brent reflected on the day exactly nine weeks earlier when Helen had first called him and had met him at this same station. It seemed much longer ago.

Helen was again waiting on the station platform.

"Hello, Helen, how are you?" he asked as she approached him.

"I'm fine. Thank you for coming out."

They decided to return to the Post Road Restaurant. During the 15-minute ride, they reflected on the events that had transpired during the past nine weeks, but there was no reference to the Kilgore offer.

After they arrived at the restaurant and were seated, Brent asked, "Have you had a chance to study the proposal from Kilgore?"

"Yes I have, and I'm amazed that Enfield could be worth so much money. It's more than I could ever have imagined."

"Does that mean you're interested in selling?"

"I'm not sure. I want to know if you think we should, and whether or not you have decided to accept my offer to become president of Enfield."

"In all honesty, I'm seriously considering it, but you should keep that matter separate from your decision about the sale to Kilgore."

"But that's impossible."

"Why?"

"Because if you agree to stay as president, I wouldn't sell."

"I was afraid you might feel that way, so for the sake of this discussion, let's assume I'm *not* going to stay."

"I hope that is only a hypothetical assumption, but that being the case, I'm leaning toward selling."

"I believe that would be a big mistake."

Helen appeared surprised and hesitated before she responded critically, "Just recently you told me your main concern is what will happen to Enfield after you leave. Furthermore, I can't forget our first conversation when you were talking about the phenomenon of organizations getting into or out of trouble within a 90-day period. For all I know, three months after you leave, Enfield could be right back where it was when you took over—then we might not be able to even *give* the company away."

"Helen, whether or not I stay at Enfield is beside the point in regard to the Kilgore offer. Let me explain why it isn't a good offer, and why I believe you shouldn't accept it.

"As you requested, after Mr. Dickey negotiated the best offer that he could with Kilgore, Richard and I tried to negotiate with them for a higher price, but Kilgore wouldn't budge. They're trying to steal the company for less than the value of the land. They can tear down the buildings and sell the land to a developer for condos or apartments for much more than they are offering you."

"But we certainly don't want them to destroy the plant!"

"What did you *think* Kilgore would do?"

"I assumed they would continue operating the company."

"Helen, they'll probably have the bulldozers heading for Enfield before the ink is dry on the contract. I hired a friend to do some checking on Kilgore. They're only running two shifts, and there are only about half as many people on the second shift as on the first."

"How could you know that?"

"My friend counted the cars in the parking lot during both shifts. If I were in Kilgore's place, I would close Enfield and combine the operations at their present location, and I believe this is what they'll do.

"Richard and I tried to get Kilgore to state in their proposal what they intended to do with Enfield's plant and employees. They said it was none of our business what they did after the sale, and I reluctantly have to agree with their position.

"Not only is the land worth more than what Kilgore is offering, but the cash you would receive as a down payment on your stock wouldn't cost them anything, because they could borrow that against Enfield's accounts receivable. After that, Enfield's operating profits would more than cover Kilgore's monthly payments to you on the remaining debt."

"I don't understand."

"I ordered a Dun and Bradstreet report on Kilgore and the company appears to be in a tight cash position. If you accept Kilgore's offer, they could go to their bank, pledge Enfield's accounts receivable as collateral, and probably borrow at least 75 percent of the total amount. That's more than enough to make a down payment to you and still leave them some extra cash for working capital."

"What if Kilgore got into trouble later and couldn't make the remaining payments?"

"You'd be out of luck. Their proposal states that after they make the down payment, their remaining indebtedness to you would be collateralized by common stock in Kilgore. Their stock wouldn't be worth much, if anything, if they went into bankruptcy and the company was liquidated.

"That's why the consideration of whether I become president of Enfield should be kept separate from the decision about Kilgore. You shouldn't accept their proposal, no matter what I decide to do."

Helen said, "I'm sorry if I sounded critical earlier; I'm really extremely grateful for all that you've done.

"It never occurred to me there was even a possibility that Kilgore would close the plant. If that happened, some or all of our employees might lose their jobs, and I would feel I had betrayed them."

"That's for you to say, Helen, but I'm glad you came to that conclusion. After the company starts doing better financially, if you're interested in selling some or all of your stock, I'd much rather see you sell the stock back to the employees, or you could even consider a public offering of Enfield's stock. Either way, you'd come out a lot better than you would accepting the Kilgore offer, and the employees would certainly be better off."

For the next few minutes, Brent and Helen discussed further aspects of the Kilgore offer and the current status of Enfield. Later, at the train station, she thanked him again, then added, "I'm still hoping you'll agree to become president."

"I'm thinking about it, Helen," Brent said with a smile.

Friday afternoon, April 5

Brent was in the plant later in the afternoon when he was paged to answer a phone call. Mike Cline was not in his office, so Brent took the call there. It was Helen, and she sounded as though she had been crying.

"Calm down, Helen," he said. "Tell me what's wrong."

"I have a terrible problem. Stanley would've never believed that Enfield Manufacturing could destroy our family.

"Connie and Sandra just left, and they're furious. They were expecting you to recommend the sale to Kilgore. They don't have any attachment to Enfield—on the contrary, they resent the company for all the nights and weekends Stanley spent at the plant instead of at home. They feel they never really knew their father because of it."

"Then why don't you sell to Kilgore?"

"Because I agree with you that we shouldn't, but the girls have talked with our attorney, and although he knows that the appraised value of the land is more than Kilgore's offer, he pointed out that the land is really worth only as much as someone is willing to pay for it. He also contends that the costs of demolishing the buildings and clearing the land could represent a potential liability to a developer."

"I don't agree with Mr. Dickey about the real estate. In addition, Enfield's book value and ongoing profit potential are also good reasons why you shouldn't sell the company to Kilgore."

"What do you mean by *book value?*"

"In order to determine Enfield's book value, you estimate the liquidated value of all the physical assets, such as the buildings, land, equipment, and inventory. Then, add to that your cash and accounts receivable. From the total of these assets, subtract all the liabilities such as accounts payable, notes payable, and other liabilities. What you have left is the book value, and Enfield's book value is considerably more than Kilgore is offering."

Helen said, "You mentioned profit potential. That subject also came up in the discussion with Charles Dickey. He explained that profit potential is just that—only potential. He said Enfield may or may not make the profits you're projecting.

"He also pointed out that if you leave Enfield in the next few weeks, it could jeopardize not only the future profits, but the company as well. Then Charles proceeded to paint a dismal picture of what would happen if Enfield were forced into bankruptcy."

Brent saw no advantage at this point in debating Enfield's future, so he changed the subject by asking, "Does Scott know about the Kilgore offer?"

"Not yet, thank goodness! But when he does hear about it, there's going to be even more trouble. As I said last week, he wouldn't want to sell, because he's still planning on coming back to Enfield. Although I'm not anxious to sell, I certainly don't want Scott to return to the business. To further complicate matters, my daughters agree that Scott doesn't belong at Enfield, but they *do* want to sell. I can't believe what a complicated mess this is. I really don't know what to do."

"Helen, since there are some differences of opinion among you, would it be of any help if I met with you and your daughters and Charles Dickey to discuss what is best for your family?"

"That sounds wonderful, but should we include Scott?"

"You'll have to deal with him eventually, but perhaps you might first see if you and Sandra and Connie can reach an agreement. Then you can deal with Scott later."

"I believe you're right. When would it be convenient?"

"I'm at your disposal."

"I'll call you back as soon as possible."

Helen phoned within an hour. "Brent, this is short notice and although tomorrow is Saturday, could we meet at Charles Dickey's office in the morning at eleven?"

"That would be fine."

Helen gave Brent directions to Dickey's office. As he hung up, he thought, "This meeting tomorrow could be very critical for the Wilsons, and Helen will be looking to me for advice."

Brent picked up his coat, left his office, and returned to the familiar path by the river. He wanted to think about the position he should take when he met with the Wilsons the next day.

33

● ●

Brent followed Helen's directions to the offices of Clayton, Buchanan and Howard. He knew Winston Buchanan, who had been Stanley Wilson's attorney, but he had never met Charles Dickey, the Wilsons' attorney since Buchanan's retirement.

Brent parked in front of the law offices and entered the one-story brick building. There was no one at the receptionist's desk.

"Anybody home?" Brent called out.

Charles Dickey emerged from the conference room and greeted him. Dickey, in his early forties, was short and slight. His round horn-rimmed glasses gave him an owlish look. Brent had dressed casually in grey slacks, blue blazer, and open shirt. Dickey wore a dark blue suit, white shirt, and conservative tie. He introduced himself and showed Brent to the conference room.

Helen, Connie, and Sandra Wilson were seated around a large table. The empty coffee cups in front of them suggested that they had been there for some time.

Dickey said, "I asked the Wilsons to come in earlier so that we could have a preliminary discussion about the Kilgore offer."

Brent then greeted the Wilsons. He had not seen Sandra and Connie since their father's funeral and had never known them very well. Connie appeared cordial, but cool. Sandra was reserved, but more friendly.

As they began discussing the Kilgore offer, Dickey reiterated his concerns about the value of the land and buildings and the profit potential of Enfield. Brent remained quiet, but he felt Dickey was overplaying his role and appeared to be less knowledgeable about business than he would like for the Wilsons to believe.

When Dickey commented on the possible negative impact if Brent left Enfield, Connie turned to Brent and added rather coolly, "I have the strong feeling you're very interested in staying on as president, or at least that you would like to keep your options open."

"Is that a question or a statement?"

"It was a statement, but I'll pose it as a question. Are you interested in becoming president of Enfield?"

"Connie, I have the feeling that you're challenging me, so I'll respond this way. Helen asked my opinion about the Kilgore offer. She also asked if I'd be willing to stay as president. My answer was, and still is, that these are two separate issues. Whether you accept Kilgore's offer shouldn't have anything to do with whether or not I stay."

Dickey interrupted. "With all due respect, Mr. Powell, I disagree. The Wilsons believe that if they turn down the Kilgore offer, they'll become even more dependent on you. Then, if you decide to leave Enfield in the near future, it could seriously jeopardize the stability of the company. If your plans *are* to leave, my advice to the Wilsons is to accept the Kilgore offer."

Brent looked disappointed and said, "I was afraid that might be your attitude. I had hoped that you would not perceive that I would have that much of an impact on the future of the company. I can understand your concern, but perhaps you can see the position this puts me in. Although I agreed to come to Enfield for only three months, none of us could have anticipated the Kilgore offer, which has certainly complicated the situation. Nevertheless, I'm not willing at this point to commit to staying at Enfield."

Dickey interrupted. "Then it looks as though we're at an impasse, and the only prudent course would be for the Wilsons to sell to Kilgore."

"Not necessarily, Charles. I felt it might come to this, so I'd like to propose an alternative for the Wilsons' consideration."

"What is that?" Helen asked anxiously.

"Even though I'm convinced you would be making a big mistake in accepting the Kilgore offer, I can appreciate your family's concern about missing an opportunity to sell the company. Kilgore proposed that you sell them a 60-day option to purchase Enfield. I'll make you an offer of $150,000 more than they offered for an option to buy Enfield under the same terms they proposed. However, I must tell you that my offer would still be a bad deal for you, even though it's better than Kilgore's. If I were in your position, I wouldn't accept either one."

Helen looked shocked. "Why would you be willing to pay us $150,000 more than Kilgore is offering?"

"Because even then it would still be a good investment for me. I'm convinced that the company will start showing a substantial profit within 60 days and the stock will then be worth much more than Kilgore is now offering. Furthermore, I don't want to invite any lawsuits, or have Scott, or anyone else, accusing me of trying to take advantage of you."

Sandra commented, "Even if it's a good investment, if you haven't made a decision to stay at Enfield, I don't see why you would be interested in buying the company."

"Because Kilgore would probably close the plant, and I would like to see Enfield continue to operate. I also believe that's what Stanley would have wanted."

Connie said, "Why would Kilgore close the plant?"

"Kilgore has excess production capacity, and it makes good sense for them to absorb Enfield's production at their present location, and for them to sell Enfield's land to a real estate developer."

Helen said, "Although I'd be delighted to have $150,000 more for our stock, it doesn't seem fair for you to pay a premium over Kilgore's offer. As far as I'm concerned, you're the one who has saved the company without any compensation."

Dickey interrupted at this point because he was afraid Helen might reject Brent's offer to pay a premium for an option and would propose instead that they sell to him on the same terms Kilgore had offered.

"Mr. Powell, may I ask you to wait in the reception area for a few minutes? I'd like to discuss your offer with the Wilsons."

Brent excused himself. Ten minutes later, Dickey came to the reception area and asked him to return to the conference room.

The Wilsons looked anxiously at Brent as Dickey said, "Mr. Powell, the Wilsons feel your proposal is quite fair, and unless you want to discuss it any further, they're ready to accept your offer."

"As far as I'm concerned, any further discussion is unnecessary," Brent answered.

"In that case, I'll submit a draft of an agreement for your review by the middle of next week."

Dickey then told Brent he had some other matters to discuss with the Wilsons, and as Brent stood to leave, Connie asked if she could walk out with him.

On the way to his car, she apologized for her coolness toward him, explaining that it was because of the stress they had all been under. She then thanked Brent for all he had meant to her father and for what he had done for her family at Enfield since Scott's heart attack.

Brent smiled as he thanked her. He continued toward his car with the satisfaction that at least the positions of Helen Wilson and her daughters were now compatible.

As he turned on the ignition, Brent thought, "What am I getting myself into? This is a situation I wasn't looking for. Now I'm committed to purchase an option to buy a company I'm not sure I even want. And who will run it?—I don't want to. If I did run the company, I wouldn't be able to devote the majority of my time to writing and speaking about management."

He smiled to himself and thought, "Well, here's another example of how the management process applies to individual lives as well as to organizations. I'm always challenging managers to continuously reevaluate their objectives and assumptions, and now *I* am challenged to do this once again.

"What do I really want? I don't need the money, but maybe I do need the challenge of management again. If I stay at Enfield, would I ever devote myself to writing and speaking?"

Brent sighed. "I feel the way generals in the army must feel between wars. They're trained to fight as soldiers, and when there's no war they aren't doing what they were trained to do. I'm a manager, and when I'm not managing, I'm not doing what I was trained to do. It's not an easy adjustment."

Brent was still deep in thought as he drove through the gate at Enfield Manufacturing and parked in the deserted lot. Instead of entering the plant, he walked unconsciously to the river path.

He strolled along the bank of the river, then stopped to watch a stick as it slowly floated down the river. A few minutes later on his way back toward the plant, he stopped again and stared at the stately brick buildings that had stood there for more than one hundred years. The ivy clinging to the sides gave them a look of dignity and permanence, and they reminded him of his first view of Harvard University.

He thought aloud as he considered the possibilities. "How can I resolve this so that everyone will benefit? It would be a shame to destroy these beautiful old buildings and replace them with condos or apartments. Nevertheless, if I buy Enfield, the land is too valuable and the buildings too inefficient for me to want to continue operating here."

"These old structures are too inefficient for a manufacturing plant. Turning them into a school doesn't make any sense. They would be suitable for a museum, but there isn't any money in the museum business. What *would* they be good for?

"Bingo!" he exclaimed. "A shopping center— we could call it the Carriage Works Mall. It's a great location, close to a lot of residential areas. There's ample parking and easy access to the freeway, plus the charm of the old buildings. It's a natural.

"But what about Enfield Manufacturing? Maybe I can make a deal on the land and buildings that would provide enough money to build or buy a more efficient facility. The Sokol Building in the Cannon Industrial Park might be a possibility."

Brent hurried across the parking lot. He could feel his adrenaline pumping as he thought, "If I ever saw a sure thing, I believe this would be it."

He entered the building and rushed through the deserted hallway to his office, picked up the phone, and called George Cannon, president of Cannon Properties, but there was no answer. After finding Cannon's beeper number in his address book, he called and said excitedly, "George, this is Brent Powell. Please call me at 432-9841— It's urgent!"

After ten minutes, Cannon still had not called, and Brent switched off the lights and was about to leave when the phone rang.

"Brent, this is George. What's the matter?"

"Nothing's the matter. I want to talk to you about a real estate idea."

"You damned fool. You said it was urgent. I was on the golf course when my beeper went off—you caused me to three-putt the seventh hole and it cost me five bucks!"

"George, I may have a way for you to recoup your five bucks. Have you sold or leased the Sokol Industries Building yet?"

"Hell no, and the debt service is killing me. When Sokol moved to Minneapolis, it was a real shocker. They were my first major tenant in the park. Sokol put a gun to my head when we wrote the lease by insisting on a 60-day cancellation clause, and I had no choice. Now the building is vacant. Why do you ask?"

"I may have a prospect for the building, but first let me ask you another question. How would you like to have the hottest shopping center location in this part of the country?"

"I'd love it, but I know this area like the palm of my hand, and there aren't any good locations left."

"What about the Carriage Works Mall?"

There was a pause before Cannon answered. "I've never heard of it. Where is it?"

"The Enfield Manufacturing location."

"You're kidding! I heard rumors after Scott Wilson had a heart attack that Enfield was in trouble. Is the company going down the tubes?"

"No, we're not going down the tubes. I thought we might do a tax-free exchange by swapping the Enfield location for the Sokol building, some cash, and an equity position in the shopping center."

Cannon said, "I like what I'm hearing, but what do you mean by 'we'? I didn't think you had anything to do with Enfield except for your friendship with Stanley Wilson."

"While Scott is out, I'm at Enfield doing what I can to help the Wilsons."

There was a short pause, then Cannon asked anxiously, "How soon can we get together?"

"You name it."

"I'm teaching Sunday School in the morning, so how about two o'clock at the Enfield plant? I'd like to look at the property."

"That's fine, George. I'll see you then."

"One other thing, Brent. Could we keep this confidential? This deal has marvelous potential."

"Sure, George. I'll see you tomorrow."

34

• •

As Brent parked his car at the offices of Clayton, Buchanan and Howard, he reflected on the events of the past week. He had met with George Cannon on Sunday and again on Tuesday to discuss the tax-free exchange and the proposed shopping center. Now he felt much more comfortable about the offer he had made to the Wilsons.

As Brent entered the office, Dickey greeted him warmly in the reception room. Dickey was dressed casually rather than in his conservative attire of the previous Saturday.

"How are you, Brent?" asked Dickey.

"I'm fine, Charles," answered Brent, smiling inwardly, because for the first time Dickey had addressed him as "Brent."

When they entered the conference room, Helen, Connie, and Sandra were already seated. Documents were stacked in neat piles on the table. Copies of these documents had been sent by courier to Brent and to his attorney on Wednesday afternoon for their review.

After Brent greeted the Wilsons, Dickey said, "When I talked to your attorney yesterday, he suggested some minor changes in the agreement, and they've been incorporated into these documents. Will he be meeting with us this morning?"

"No, we didn't think that would be necessary. I have a copy of the changes he proposed, and I can check them out as we go through the papers."

Brent then reviewed the documents and verified the changes his attorney had recommended.

"These look fine to me," said Brent.

"The Wilsons are satisfied, so I guess we're ready to start signing."

"Before we do, there's something we should discuss."

"What's that?" Dickey asked with a concerned look.

Brent smiled. "Relax, Charles. You won't have to redraft the documents. It's just that I'm not sure the Wilsons should sign them."

"Why not?" he asked, looking even more perturbed. "They reflect the terms of our agreement."

"I understand that, Charles, but let me explain. After leaving here last Saturday, I drove back to the plant. I took a walk along the river, and as I was standing there, staring back at those beautiful old buildings, I thought about how inefficient they are as a manufacturing plant, but how ideal they would be—for a shopping center."

"A shopping center!" exclaimed Sandra. "What a wonderful idea! Would the buildings be left intact?"

"Absolutely. Their appearance is the real charm. The only visible change would be to enlarge the parking area."

Connie said, "I agree that a shopping center is a wonderful idea, but how does this affect your offer to purchase an option to acquire our stock?"

"This looks like an outstanding business opportunity, and I thought you might want to reconsider selling an option to me, or perhaps we could do a joint venture."

Brent reviewed the plans that he and George Cannon had discussed. Then Brent asked, "Helen, we haven't heard from you. How do you feel about the plant buildings being converted into a shopping center?"

"I'm thrilled with the idea, but I wanted Connie and Sandra to have an opportunity to express themselves first. I'm delighted to hear there's a good possibility that those old buildings won't be torn down. Until now, I assumed it was inevitable. What would the shopping center be called?"

"Oh, I don't know. Maybe the Carriage Works Mall."

"Why not use the original name?"

"What was that?"

"The Wilson Buggy Works."

"That's great! Stanley never mentioned the original name to me."

"Oh yes. Stanley's grandfather founded the original carriage company. After the business was closed, the buildings stood vacant for years until Stanley started Enfield Manufacturing there."

Connie and Sandra both expressed their enthusiasm for calling it the Wilson Buggy Works.

Dickey asked, "If the Wilsons decided to do a joint venture with you, how much cash would they receive?"

"Probably not any, at first, but in a couple of years they should get an excellent cash return from the shopping center, and also from Enfield Manufacturing."

"A couple of years?" Connie repeated. "And what happens if the shopping center isn't successful, and Enfield Manufacturing doesn't do well either?"

Dickey quickly interrupted. "You wouldn't get any cash. Furthermore, if the cash flow from the shopping center is not adequate to service the debt of several million dollars, you could lose your equity through foreclosure."

Brent protested. "Look, anything's possible, but this is as close to a sure thing as anything I've ever been involved with."

Connie said, "The risk is not my concern, because we have a lot of confidence in you. My concern is that I have expensive tastes and can't afford a lot of things I would like to have. The idea of waiting two more years to receive any money is very unappealing."

Sandra spoke up. "It appears that you plan to exercise your option, and if that's the case, I'll have more than enough money to satisfy *my* needs."

Dickey felt he was losing control of the discussion, so he said, "Brent, if you don't mind excusing us, I'd like to discuss your offer with the Wilsons."

"Certainly, I'll get a cup of coffee," Brent responded. As he stood to leave, he said, "Take your time. As far as I'm concerned, we really don't have to resolve this today if you need more time."

Twenty minutes later, Dickey came to the reception area and asked Brent to return to the conference room. As they reconvened the meeting, Dickey said, "Brent, the Wilsons and I sincerely appreciate your candor about your proposed plans for Enfield. Nevertheless, they're uneasy about becoming involved in such a complicated transaction, and they don't want to take the risk of not receiving any cash until sometime in the future, if even then. So they've decided to go ahead with the sale of an option to you to purchase their share of the company."

Brent responded, "Although this appears to be an excellent investment opportunity, I thought perhaps that might be your position. Therefore, in light of my financial projections for Enfield and the shopping center, I do have a suggested amendment to the agreement."

"What's that?" Dickey asked nervously.

"Under the purchase price, I would like to write in: 'plus a 10-percent equity in the proposed shopping center.' "

"Why would you offer to do that?" Helen asked.

"Because even though I'm paying $150,000 more than Kilgore offered, as I said before this is still not a very good deal for you. If we split the 20-percent equity I'll have in the shopping center, it will be more equitable to you over the short-term. However, if Enfield and the shopping center do what I honestly believe they'll do over the longer term, you may look back on this transaction and wish you had kept the company. Although, there's always the element of risk, and I could be wrong."

Helen said, "Having an equity position in the shopping center would be exciting, but I want to be fair to Scott."

Then she turned to Connie and Sandra and asked how they would feel about including Scott in their 10-percent ownership of the shopping center. They were in favor of the idea, so Helen asked Brent, "Do you have any objections if we include Scott?."

"Not at all. That's your decision."

Sandra asked, "Assuming you exercise the option, will you stay at Enfield as president?"

"Not necessarily. I need to see a few more pieces of the puzzle in place before I decide. Right now I'm so enmeshed in trying to run Enfield and deal with this real estate transaction, there hasn't been time to rethink my position.

"If I exercise my option and don't stay, I'll probably sell the stock back to the employees later under their stock ownership trust. I should also tell you that if Enfield lives up to my expectations, I plan to sell the stock to the trust for considerably more than I'll be paying you."

Connie said, "In all honesty, I hope you'll be successful. You deserve it as compensation for what you've done for us.

With a hint of emotion in his voice, Brent responded, "Thank you, Connie, but my real compensation has been the satisfaction of knowing I could help your family as partial repayment for all that your father did for me."

The Wilsons were touched by the obvious sincerity of this expression from Brent. There was an awkward pause, and then Dickey said, "Well, if there's no further discussion, these documents are ready for your signatures."

After the papers were signed, Brent handed Helen Wilson a cashier's check for $500,000.

35

● ●

Brent was in his office when Mary Hastings called from the reception desk. She sounded nervous. "Brent, the sheriff is out here and he asked for you."

"Thanks, Mary. Tell him I'll be there in a couple of minutes," Brent responded casually.

As he approached the reception area, he saw the uniformed sheriff with his holstered pistol on his hip. Brent tried to conceal his irritation at this intimidating symbolism by making light of the situation. As he approached the sheriff, he said, "Hello, officer. Did you come out here to shoot me?"

"No, sir. I came to deliver this," the sheriff answered seriously, and handed Brent a folded document. As the sheriff left, Brent glanced at the document on his way back to his office. Scott Wilson had filed a lawsuit against Brent and Cannon Properties for four million dollars, charging fraud, conspiracy, and a variety of related offenses having to do with the option agreement between Brent and Scott's mother and sisters.

The complaint also requested that the court issue a temporary restraining order to prevent Brent from exercising his option to buy the stock owned by his mother and his sisters. A hearing was set for Thursday, April 25th.

"Damn," Brent muttered. "I'm running out of time, and now Scott has thrown up this roadblock."

Brent turned his chair toward the window and stared out at the hills. He thought of Stanley and wondered what his mentor would have done. Then he said aloud, "I know what you would have done, Stanley, and I'm going to do the same thing. You always told me to go for the throat when someone attacks me or gets on my turf. Scott's on my turf, and I'm going for *his* throat, even if he *is* your son."

As Brent reached for his phone, he thought, "Scott, my boy, you're in way over your head." He called John McCormick, his litigation attorney.

"John, this is Brent Powell. I'm sending you a copy of a four million dollar lawsuit that Scott Wilson has filed against Cannon Properties and me for fraud, conspiracy, and a bunch of other crap. He's also asking the court for a temporary restraining order to block me from buying the Wilsons' stock.

"After you've read the complaint, how about calling me? Unless you can convince me otherwise, I want to file a countersuit against Wilson for five million dollars for tortious interference in my contractual relations with Helen Wilson, her daughters, and Cannon Properties."

For the next several minutes, they discussed the events that had precipitated the lawsuit, then Brent left his office for an appointment in town.

When Brent returned to Enfield, there was an urgent message to call George Cannon. Brent knew full well that he was calling about the lawsuit, and that Cannon had a tendency to overreact when trouble was brewing. Cannon answered on the first ring after Brent dialed his private line.

"Hello, Georgie. This is Brent. What can I do for you?"

"What can you do for me?" Cannon almost shouted. "Have you seen the complaint from Scott Wilson?"

"Yes, I have a copy," Brent answered unemotionally.

"Then what you can do for me is get me out of this mess. Wilson is charging us with fraud, conspiracy, and God knows what else, and I want out!"

"Okay, Georgie, no problem—I'll just do this real estate deal with one of your competitors."

"One of my competitors, like who?" Cannon asked, taking the bait.

"Like Norman Kennedy. He has a building that I believe would be very suitable for Enfield Manufacturing."

"Norman Kennedy! Kennedy would do business with the devil himself!"

"Then I shouldn't have any trouble cutting a deal with him," Brent said with a laugh.

"You may see something funny in all of this, but I don't. There's no such thing as a frivolous lawsuit. What do you plan to do about it?"

"Well, for openers, I plan to file a countersuit against Scott Wilson for five million dollars for tortious interference in my contractual relations with his family and with you, plus anything else I can think of."

Cannon calmed down a little. "That sounds like a good idea, but I'm going to have to think about this for awhile before I decide if I want to stay in this deal with you."

"That's fine, Georgie—I'll give you fifteen minutes."

"Fifteen minutes!" Cannon shouted.

"Georgie, talking to you is like talking into an echo chamber. Every time I say something, you repeat it back to me—It really does waste a lot of time."

"Okay, wise guy! I'll quit repeating what you say if you'll stop calling me Georgie."

"It's a deal. Now look, George, Scott Wilson is bluffing. I know it, you know it, and he knows it. I don't need you as a partner if you can't keep calm. If you back out now, Scott will read it as a sign of weakness and may pursue the lawsuit. In any event, I'm going to beat him, with you or without you. It might take me a little longer without you, but I'll still beat him."

There was a long silence before Cannon responded. "You're right, Brent. He's bluffing, and I agree we can beat him. I'm still in—but I'm depending on you to work this out."

"Don't worry about it."

"Don't worry about it?" Cannon exclaimed.

"There you go again, Georgie! You're really going to have to learn not to repeat everything I say."

"Go to hell!"

"What a thing for a Sunday School teacher to say."

Cannon hung up without further comment.

• •

The phone rang as Brent entered his office.

"Brent Powell," he answered.

"Brent, this is John McCormick. I just talked to Scott Wilson's attorney. Wilson is willing to drop his lawsuit if you'll drop your countersuit—what do you think?"

"That's fine, but I want it buttoned down, with no loose ends. I also want him to pay your legal fees."

"But I haven't spent that much time on this case."

"It's a matter of principle. You tell his attorney that if Scott doesn't pay your legal fees, I'm not dropping the suit. Just tell him I'm acting crazy and irrational, and you're having a difficult time reasoning with me, and I'm anxious to take Scott to court."

McCormick laughed. "Okay, I'll call you back as soon as I talk with Wilson's attorney."

An hour later, Brent received another phone call from Mc-Cormick.

"Brent, Wilson agreed to pay my legal fees, so I'll meet with his attorney and settle this."

"Thanks, John. I'll wait to hear from you." Brent then phoned George Cannon and gave him the news.

37

● ●

Brent stood at the window of his office. He looked again at the hills and reflected on the events of the past week. Scott Wilson had dropped his lawsuit on Wednesday, and on Thursday Brent had exercised his option and purchased the Enfield stock owned by Helen and her daughters.

He had definitely decided to leave Enfield the following Friday, and there were several matters that had to be settled before then. One was the selection of a new president, which had been delayed because of Scott Wilson's lawsuit. He was so deep in thought that he was startled when the phone rang, particularly this early in the morning.

It was Barbara. "Brent, may I come by to see you for a few minutes?"

"Any time."

Five minutes later, she appeared at his door.

"Have a seat," Brent said. "What can I do for you?"

She remained standing and asked, "Are you still planning to leave Enfield next Friday?"

"Of course. I told you that in our management meeting on Monday."

"In that case, I wanted to let you know that I'm resigning from Enfield," she said as she handed Brent a copy of a letter addressed to Richard Thompkins.

Brent glanced at the letter, which simply stated that she was leaving and was giving two weeks notice.

"What was Richard's reaction to this?"

"He doesn't know yet. Even though I answer to Richard, I first wanted to confirm that you still planned to leave before I gave him the letter."

"Why don't you sit down and let's talk about it?"

"Okay," she said solemnly and took a seat.

"This is quite a surprise. What brought it on?"

"I'm sorry if I'm adding to your problems during your last days at Enfield. I want you to know that my decision is because of Scott, not because of you."

"I'm curious. What does Scott have to do with this?"

"The rumors are that Scott took legal action to get you out of the company, and everyone knows that the sheriff was here last week to serve papers on you. Now you've confirmed that you're leaving.

"I don't want to work with Scott again. When you first came here I resented you, because of what Scott had said. I realize now that I was wrong, and that Scott isn't capable of running Enfield."

"What makes you think you would have to work with Scott?"

"Even though I'd answer to Richard, I know that Scott would still be calling the shots."

Brent smiled and leaned back in his chair. "Barbara, we're having a communications problem. Are you assuming that Scott is coming back to Enfield as president?"

"Of course."

"When I first came here," Brent responded, "I said that if you don't tell people what's going on, they'll guess, and they'll usually guess wrong. *You* are guessing wrong. I apologize for keeping you in the dark, but things have been happening very fast around here during the last few days.

"In the first place, Scott is *not* coming back to Enfield. The final decision hasn't yet been made about who will be the next president, but it will be made before next Friday.

"Since you say you are resigning, this is probably the best time to tell you some things in confidence that I was going to tell you later."

Brent then told Barbara that Scott's lawsuit was precipitated by Brent's option agreement to purchase the stock held by Helen and her daughters. He explained that the lawsuit had been dropped and that he had exercised his option and purchased the stock.

Barbara looked surprised and embarrassed as she said, "In retrospect, I should've managed by assumptions, as you always suggest, and confirmed my assumptions before making a decision to resign. In light of what you told me, I'd like to have my letter of resignation back."

Brent frowned faintly. "Barbara, before I give it back, there's another change maybe you should know about."

"What is that?" she asked with a puzzled look.

"I want to replace you as sales manager."

Barbara stared at Brent in disbelief. "Replace me as sales manager! Why?"

"Because I want you to be Enfield's marketing vice-president."

"What are you talking about?"

"Not long after I met Stanley and started visiting him out here, I developed a strong feeling that Enfield needed a marketing vice-president: a person who would be primarily responsible for directing the company into new markets. The job would involve making decisions about how to approach these markets from the standpoint of sales effort, distribution channels, pricing, advertising, and the whole spectrum of marketing functions.

"I don't know of anyone better qualified than you are. Would you like to have the job?"

"Are you kidding? Of course. I'd love to have the job!"

Brent continued. "In your new capacity, the sales manager will report to you. Assuming that you'll select one of your present salespeople to replace you, you'll need to hire a new salesperson."

For the next few minutes they discussed her new responsibilities. Barbara then shook hands with Brent, and as she was leaving, she said, "Thank you so much for this opportunity, and for your confidence in me."

"Thank you Barbara for the great help you've been to me while I've been here, and I'm grateful to you. I know you can play a major role in the future growth of Enfield."

38

● ●

During the previous three weeks, Brent had been interviewing prospective candidates for the job of president of Enfield, after they were screened by Alan and Richard.

At 8:30, Brent arrived at Enfield and went directly to Richard's office. Richard was going through his mail, and Brent asked, "Richard, do you have time to talk with me?"

"Sure, Brent. Come on in."

Before Brent sat down, he closed the office door.

"What's the problem?" Richard asked.

"No problem," Brent said lightly. "Relax, and quit being so paranoid. I'm not going to fire you."

"Very funny," Richard said as he leaned back in his chair and propped his feet on his desk.

"Richard, I've decided who should be the next president of Enfield."

"You have!" Richard exclaimed as he took his feet off the desk and sat up straight. "Who is it?"

"Alan Braswell."

"Alan Braswell? Are you out of your mind? You and I have talked at length about his managerial deficiencies. We're in agreement about how much he still has to learn, and now you're proposing to make him president?"

"Do you want the job?"

"Hell no!—but why Alan?"

"Because you and I *do* see Alan the same way, and you can continue to help him smooth out his rough edges and make sure he doesn't stray into the wrong part of the forest."

"How can I possibly do that? As long as I'm answering to him, he can do as he pleases. It will be the same kind of problem I had with Scott."

"But you wouldn't be answering to Alan—he'd be answering to you."

"I'm sorry, Brent. It must be too early in the morning—would you run that by me again?"

"Richard, you wouldn't be answering to Alan, because I want to kick you upstairs and make you chairman of the board. In that capacity, Alan would be answering to you. We might even raise your salary a couple of bucks."

"This is insane! I can't believe what I'm hearing. How did you ever persuade the Wilsons to go for this scheme?"

"I haven't told them about it."

"Now I know you're crazy. They'll *never* go along—and you know it. Don't you remember our conversation about the spat Alan and Connie had over the #4000 series, and about the dividends being discontinued, and how Helen insinuated that Alan had caused Scott's heart attack? Besides, the Wilsons think Alan is much too abrasive."

"Richard, I know he's somewhat abrasive, but he's improved dramatically during the past three months."

"I agree, but Helen doesn't know that."

Brent paused, then said quietly, "Richard, it really doesn't matter what Helen thinks about Alan being president."

"Why not? She and her daughters control the stock."

"Not any more."

"What do you mean?"

"They sold their stock."

"To whom?"

"To me."

Richard stood up. "I don't believe it. When did that happen?"

"Thursday—I'm now the majority stockholder of Enfield."

"Good God! Then why aren't *you* going to be chairman of the board?"

"No way—I've got other fish to fry."

Richard started pacing slowly back and forth behind his desk. Brent could almost hear the gears turning in Richard' head as he began to warm up to the practicality of this plan.

"Brent, do you really think we can make it work?"

"It'll be a walk in the park," Brent said with a smile. "Look Richard, you and I have agreed that Alan Braswell is one of the brightest young managers we've ever seen. Sure he's a little abrasive, but he's highly trainable, and he's a quick study. As you've pointed out, if you give him constructive criticism, he listens and usually reacts positively."

"But who would take my place?"

"Larry Butler. We agreed after we interviewed him that he's not ready to be a CEO, but he should make a good executive vice president."

"What if he won't accept? We interviewed him for the job of president."

"But he will accept—I've already asked him."

Richard was quiet for a few seconds, then said, "When we interviewed Ralph Crenshaw for president, I was very impressed with his background in finance. I wonder if he might be a possible candidate to take Alan's place as financial vice president?"

"I think that's an excellent idea—That's why I talked with him about the position over the weekend. He said he would accept if we offered him the job."

"You're too much!" Richard exclaimed.

Brent continued, "I'm also making Barbara the marketing vice president, and I want her to select a new sales manager to take her place."

"Great idea!" Richard replied. "But what's this going to do to our costs of management overhead, and our costs in the sales department?"

"Financially, it will be insignificant as a percentage of sales, because we'll only be adding two additional positions to the payroll—chairman of the board and vice president of marketing. I haven't been on the payroll, and Scott went off when the insurance company started making disability payments to him.

"Although we'll raise Alan's salary in his new position, he'll still be making considerably less than Scott did, and the difference will offset the raises for you and Barbara. So the *net* increase in our payroll will be the cost of Butler, who'll replace you, and the cost of a new salesperson, to replace whoever Barbara chooses as sales manager.

"From the standpoint of people count, we'll be adding Butler, Crenshaw, and a new salesperson, and I'll be leaving, so that's a net increase of just two people."

"What does Alan think of all this?"

"He doesn't know yet. I wanted to talk with you first, because you're the key to making the whole plan work. I wouldn't do this without you here to guide Alan and help him with his further development.

"Richard, if you don't have plans for lunch, could we get together with Alan and go over all of this?"

"Of course. I have an appointment at 11:00, but we could meet after that. How about 12:30?"

Brent stood. "That's fine. I'll call Alan and see if he's available. If you don't hear otherwise, we'll meet you at 12:30 at the River Room."

As Brent stood to leave, Richard said, "Right now, I believe I'll go out for a few minutes and take one of those famous walks along the river path that you and Stanley used to take. I need to do some thinking—and let all of this sink in."

"That's sounds like a good idea."

"Brent, I'm very excited about this promotion, but what if I let you down?"

Brent smiled. "Richard, I have total confidence in you, but just in case, I'm going to monitor your results. Although I plan to spend very little time here, I've made a list of the reports I'd like to receive on a regular basis."

Richard then appeared hesitant as he said, "I never planned to mention this to you, but shortly before Stanley died, he told me how you once saved my job—I'll always be indebted to you for that."

"What are you talking about?"

"Stanley said that several years ago, he had decided to let me go because of my reluctance to take on more of his responsibilities that involved innovative risks. But he said you convinced him that I had a valuable place in the organization."

"Okay, now I remember, but Stanley never gave me any hint that he was thinking about terminating you, or that I'd convinced him he shouldn't. I took a strong position at the time that I thought he was making a serious mistake by trying to mold you in his own image, and instead, he should take advantage of your long suits, which were very complementary to his.

"You've always made it clear that you don't want to be the CEO, but you *do* have strong managerial skills in areas Stanley didn't have. Alan doesn't have them either—and may never have them. I bring still another dimension to the equation at Enfield by being more of an entrepreneur than either you or Alan, and whenever you feel

I can help you, I'll try to make myself available. By shoring up our marketing efforts with Barbara as vice president, and with the addition of Crenshaw and Butler, I feel very good about Enfield's future."

As Brent opened the door to leave, Richard extended his hand. "I'll do my best for you, Brent."

"You always have, Richard. You're a good man."

Monday, 9:45 A.M.

Brent returned to his office and called Alan.

"Alan, could you get together with Richard and me for lunch today?"

"Yes, I can. In the cafeteria?"

"No, I'd like to talk with you away from the plant. Richard is going to meet us at the River Room at 12:30. How long can you spare?"

"I don't really have anything pressing this afternoon."

"Good. I'll come by your office around twelve."

"I could be in trouble now," Alan thought as he hung up the phone. He had never been to lunch with Brent except for the day at the Colonial Inn. His first reaction was that Brent might demote, or perhaps even fire him, now that Brent was leaving.

Then he said aloud, "That's not Brent's style. If that's what he was up to, he would come to my office, and he wouldn't have Richard present. Besides, I answer to Richard — I've got to stay calm — He probably just wants to discuss what will happen after he leaves on Friday."

However, Alan was concerned about the preconceived bias against Brent that he had displayed when Brent had first come to Enfield. He was also concerned about being too closely identified with Scott. He knew now that Scott was the source of the company's problems, not Stanley Wilson or Brent.

At twelve o'clock, Brent appeared at Alan's door. "Are you ready?"

"Yes," Alan replied, trying to act unconcerned. They took Brent's car, and as they drove along the river toward town, Brent directed the conversation to how the Boston Red Sox might do in the forthcoming baseball season.

Alan could not have cared less about the Red Sox, and he was becoming increasingly more apprehensive because it was uncharacteristic of Brent to take this long to come to the point. Alan was relieved when they arrived at the restaurant and he saw Richard. Maybe now he would find out what was on Brent's mind.

After they were seated at a window table with a view of the river, Brent said, "Alan, as you know, I still plan to leave Enfield at the end of this week, because of other commitments. I also feel that I've reached a point of diminishing returns in any further contributions I believe I can make to the company.

"The reason Richard and I wanted to have lunch with you today is to hear your recommendations about who should be the new president of Enfield."

Alan gave a silent sigh of relief that this was what Brent wanted to discuss.

"Well, of those we've interviewed, I'm most impressed with Ralph Crenshaw and Larry Butler. Although they're different in personalities and aptitudes, I believe either one would do a good job. If I had to choose one of them now, I'd pick Crenshaw, because Butler's financial background isn't as strong as Crenshaw's."

"I don't agree with your choice. I would probably pick Butler," Brent said, "but there's another candidate I would like to suggest."

"Who is it?"

"You."

"Me?" Alan responded with a shocked look on his face. "Why me?"

"Because my intuition tells me that you're the best candidate, and that you have the ability to do an outstanding job. Over the past few weeks, you haven't been intimidated by me, and you've been willing to take strong positions that were contrary to mine. However, except for the time you threatened to quit, you haven't been stubborn. Even then, you displayed the flexibility of being able to change your mind when necessary.

"You're bright, learn fast, and are aggressive—probably too aggressive in my opinion, but Richard can probably help you with that and also help you learn to be an effective CEO. Richard is being promoted to chairman of the board, so you would still be answering to him. He, in turn, will obviously answer to the stockholders."

"Oh," said Alan as he slumped back in his chair.

"Why should that bother you?" asked Brent. "You answer to Richard now, and you two seem to get along very well."

"Answering to Richard doesn't bother me. I'm concerned about the Wilsons. I'm on their blacklist since my run-in with Connie at the last stockholders' meeting, and the Wilsons probably even believe I brought on Scott's heart attack."

"Don't worry about the Wilsons. I bought their stock on Thursday."

"Damn!" Alan exclaimed and fell silent as he tried to absorb the impact of these changes.

Finally he asked, "Why aren't *you* going to stay on as president?"

"I was tempted, but it's not what I really want to do. After being a practicing manager for many years, my primary objective now is to focus on the further development of other managers.

"Are you interested in the position or not?"

"I'm more than interested. I would jump at the chance if you think I can handle the responsibility."

"What do you think?"

"Well, we've already discussed, and I've acknowledged, some of my managerial deficiencies. Although I've improved, I'm not too comfortable with the idea of taking on the responsibilities of president."

"Your candor is predictable and admirable," Brent said with a smile. "It's normal for a manager to be uncomfortable about a new job, because of the unknown challenges that may lie ahead. When I came to Enfield 12 weeks ago, I was confident about my management ability but didn't become comfortable about handling my new responsibilities until I actually started doing the job."

At that point, Richard described the plans for bringing in Crenshaw and Butler and making Barbara Lansing the marketing vice president. Brent added that he would still be monitoring Enfield's results and would be available to help if needed.

"With all of this having been said, do you still want the job?" Brent asked.

"I certainly do! This is very flattering and I feel honored. I welcome the challenge and will give you my best efforts."

As they had lunch, they discussed plans for making the transition after Brent left.

During the drive back to Enfield, Alan said, "Brent, I want to express to you again how much I appreciate this opportunity. I also owe you an apology for having you figured so wrong when you first came to Enfield. Without you, I'm certain the company would have failed. I was afraid to say this to you before now, because it might have sounded self-serving and appear that I was just trying to enhance my own position with you."

"I appreciate your sentiments, Alan, but it was a team effort, and those of you in the management group did the work."

"I hear what you're saying, but Richard and I had lunch together one day last week, and we talked about all of the improvements you've initiated at Enfield during the past 12 weeks, and we made a list. It's pretty impressive," he said, as he referred to a typed list in his notebook. "Richard and I see you as being responsible for

1. Discontinuing the #4000 series, which was losing money and was a distraction.
2. Identifying our niche in the marketplace, and changing the marketing direction of the company by focusing on selling smaller orders, which are more profitable than the more competitive larger ones.
3. Increasing the prices on our products without losing customers.
4. Cutting back on personnel and eliminating those people who were not pulling their weight.
5. Effectively dealing with the bank.
6. Significantly reducing overtime in the plant by gearing our production output to our average level of sales instead of our backlog of orders.
7. Initiating an incentive pay plan for some of our production employees that increased our production while reducing our percentage of labor cost.
8. Having regular management meetings that have caused us to all start pulling in the same direction and have kept everyone better informed.
9. Making us realize that our real market value is our management and marketing expertise.
10. Establishing better company policies and procedures.
11. Teaching us valuable management lessons.

"Then today you said you were creating the position of marketing vice president, which I believe will greatly enhance our growth.

"I also want to apologize to you for being so abrasive and argumentative at times. I've been very outspoken and haven't hesitated to disagree with you on many occasions. I wouldn't have blamed you for resenting it, and you could've made things rough for me, but you've convinced me that you don't operate that way."

"Alan, as your manager, I've never taken personally any criticism or disagreement from any of the management group. If I had, management wouldn't be so much fun. When it's no longer a game for me, I'm going to find a new occupation."

39

Friday morning, May 3

• •

Brent said to himself, "It hardly seems possible that it was only 13 weeks ago today that I received Helen's urgent phone call and went to Westport to meet her. Now the company is in surprisingly good shape, I'm the majority stockholder, and this is the last day I'll be running Enfield."

Although the rumor mill had been active, only Brent, Richard, and Alan knew who would be the next president.

A company meeting was scheduled in the plant that afternoon at 4:45 for the purpose of announcing the promotions of Richard Thompkins to chairman of the board and Alan Braswell to president of the company.

The past 13 weeks had been the most satisfying of Brent's career. Although he had built a successful business on his own, it took place slowly over a span of several years. The experience at Enfield had been like a time warp in which he was able to compact similar experiences into a three-month period.

He felt very nostalgic. Even though he would periodically return to Enfield while he was a major stockholder, this would probably be the last day he would sit in Stanley Wilson's old leather-covered chair. He would not sit in front of the rolltop desk again and look up at the framed quote: "When the great leader's work is done, the people say, 'We did it ourselves!'"

Brent walked over to the window and looked at the hills. The beautiful warm spring day added to his sense of well-being as he thought about the past weeks. He thought of Stanley Wilson again, and of how often Stanley had expounded on his leadership philosophy: wanting people to feel they had succeeded on their own without his help.

Brent vividly remembered the first time they had talked about this philosophy, and how he had challenged Stanley's desire not to receive more of the credit. Stanley had said, "Brent, it seems un-

271

natural to you now, but I'm sustained by my own sense of accomplishment. Getting the credit no longer motivates me, and I like to think this is an indication that I've reached another plateau in my maturity as a manager—a plateau you haven't reached, by your own admission. You can't relate to the way I feel now, but one day you'll remember this conversation and be able to appreciate what I'm saying."

"I do now, Stanley," Brent said aloud, as tears came to his eyes. Although he was alone in the room, he was embarrassed by this uncharacteristic display of emotion. This was a poignant and satisfying experience for him, because he now felt that in some measure he had repaid a debt to his late friend.

He was confronted with one more unpleasant task. Scott Wilson had phoned Brent first thing that morning to ask if he could come to Enfield and meet with him. According to Helen, Scott had been sullen and appeared depressed after he found out that she and his sisters had sold their stock to Brent. Scott apparently felt they had betrayed him by allowing Brent to acquire control of the stock.

A few minutes later the phone rang. It was Mary Hastings. "Brent, Scott Wilson is here to see you."

"Okay. Show him to the conference room and tell him I'll be there in a minute. And Mary—don't offer him any coffee."

"This could be rough," Brent muttered to himself. This was a confrontation he would rather have avoided.

Normally Brent would have gone to the reception room, escorted his visitors to his office, and then offered them coffee. However, he did not perceive this as a friendly visit, and he chose to meet in the conference room because he would have felt on the defensive if they had met in what had formerly been Scott's office.

"What can I do for you?" Brent asked coolly as he entered the conference room and took a seat without shaking hands.

Scott stared at Brent. "I wanted to say to your face that just because I dropped my lawsuit against you, don't think I'm going to take what you've done to me lying down."

"Just exactly what have I done?"

"You've finally gotten what you wanted. You've acquired control of my company and replaced me as president. You talked my mother and sisters into selling you their stock, with part of the consideration being an interest in a nonexistent shopping center, which may never get off the drawing board. In the process, you've put me in a bind because I'm left with 15 percent of the stock in Enfield, which no one would buy."

"You're wrong about the market value of your stock. I'll buy your stock today for the same price per share I paid your mother and sisters."

Scott was shocked by this unexpected offer, and before he had time to respond, Brent continued. "You're also wrong about your assumption that I've replaced you as president. On the contrary, this is my last day at Enfield."

"Then why did you buy controlling interest?"

"I didn't want Kilgore to buy Enfield, close the plant, and sell the land, which is precisely what they would have done—and I don't believe your father would have wanted that.

"Enfield is a fine organization with a lot of good employees, and they deserve a chance to keep the company operating. Later, I plan to sell the stock back to the employee stock ownership trust, assuming the company does what I expect it will do."

Scott was clearly unnerved and embarrassed when he realized how wrong his assumptions had been. There was an uneasy silence before he asked, "Are you serious about being willing to buy my stock in Enfield?"

"Of course. If you'll call Charles Dickey and tell him to draw up the necessary papers, I'll give you a check and we can wrap it up."

Scott paused again, then asked, "If you aren't going to be president, do you mind telling me who it will be?"

"Alan Braswell. However, I'm making Richard chairman of the board, and he can help smooth out some of Alan's rough edges."

"I think that's an excellent idea. Richard's a great coach, but he never wanted to play quarterback. They should make a great team.

"Brent, I've made this very awkward for both of us. I owe you an apology. I realize now what a great service you've done for my family and for the company. I also know I wasn't cut out to run this organization. It's too bad it took a heart attack to make me realize it.

"I'm very happy I came out here today and that you cleared up some things for me. I had a lot of time to think while I was recuperating at home. I've decided to move to Seattle. I'm looking forward to getting back to the Northwest and my wife is delighted because she's from Vancouver. We met when we were at the University of

Washington. It would've been ironic if I'd left Connecticut feeling bitter, when as it turns out, there's no reason for me to feel that way."

"May I ask what you're going to be doing in Seattle?"

"I'm going to join my former college roommate as a partner in his industrial design firm. This is what I've really wanted to do ever since I graduated, but I felt an obligation to work with my father at Enfield.

"This isn't easy for me, but I also apologize for the resentment I've felt toward you through the years, because of the relationship you had with my father. You were like the son he always wanted me to be."

Brent was silent for a minute while he gathered his thoughts. "Scott, what you just said means a lot to me and I also confess to a feeling of resentment toward you, because *you* were Stanley's son. However, I'd like to put all of that behind us."

"We can as far as I'm concerned. I'd like for us to be friends."

"There isn't anything I'd like better, because I loved your father and I feel a real kinship with your family—even if I'm an outsider."

"Since you are leaving Enfield today, do you mind telling me more about your own plans?"

"Not at all."

Brent described his plans to write and speak about management and to continue to do management consulting. Then he told Scott about the meeting that afternoon to announce the changes in the management of Enfield. As they both stood and shook hands, Scott said, "Alan should be an excellent choice for president, and I'm sure Barbara and Richard will do well in their new jobs."

Scott hesitated, then added, "I don't mean to be presumptuous, but I'd be glad to make the announcement about Richard and Alan this afternoon, if it would help smooth out the transition and show a united front."

"I'd appreciate that very much, Scott, because it will avoid what could've been a rather awkward situation."

They agreed that Scott should be at Enfield around 4:30. Then Scott said, "Thanks again, Brent, for everything. I realize now that without you, Enfield would *not* have survived."

"Scott, what you've said today is more than enough thanks for anything I've done."

Friday, 4:45 P.M.

As everyone in the company gathered around a temporary platform in the center of the plant floor, Brent watched quietly from the doorway of Mike Cline's office at the back of the plant. He stood with his hands in his pockets, leaning against the doorjamb. He was again thinking of Stanley Wilson.

Richard stepped up on the platform and opened the meeting. "As you know, Scott Wilson has been away from Enfield for the past three months due to illness. I'm happy to report that he is well on the way to a full recovery, and he is with us today. Please join me in welcoming him."

There was loud applause as Scott stepped up on the platform. He briefly, but warmly, thanked the employees for their concern and good wishes during his convalescence. Then he said, "The purpose of this meeting is to make some announcements that I believe will be of interest to all of you.

"On behalf of the stockholders of Enfield, it gives me great pleasure to announce that Richard Thompkins has been elected chairman of the board to succeed my mother, who has resigned this position."

After the applause subsided, Scott continued. "It has been very rewarding for me to work with all of you at Enfield, but because of my health and my desire to pursue other interests, I have resigned as president of the company." As a low murmur rippled through the crowd, Scott felt a lump in his throat as he continued. "Three years ago, I succeeded my father, who founded Enfield and served as its president for 45 years. Now I'm happy to announce the name of your new president and chief executive officer—Alan Braswell."

The crowd was briefly stunned by the unexpected announcement. Then there was enthusiastic applause as Alan stepped up on the platform and approached the microphone.

Alan made a few comments about being honored to be the new president of Enfield, and he asked for the support of the group. The meeting was then adjourned without any reference to Brent, as Brent had previously requested.

As the meeting was breaking up, Richard made his way through the crowd to Brent who was still standing by Mike's office. They remarked on how well the meeting had gone, then Richard asked Brent if he would accompany him to the conference room.

As they entered the room, Brent saw the other members of the management committee, as well as Scott, Helen, Connie, and Sandra Wilson. There were hors d'oeuvres and bottles of chilled champagne on the conference room table.

The champagne was poured, and Helen made a gracious toast to Brent expressing gratitude to him on behalf of the Wilson family and those of the management group. Before he could respond, Richard laughed and said, "Brent, please don't tell us again that 'We did it ourselves.'"

Brent smiled and told the group how much he had enjoyed working with them. Then Scott presented him with a large gift-wrapped package and said, "Brent, we all decided that my father would've wanted you to have this." Brent unwrapped the package to find the framed quotation that had hung over Stanley's rolltop desk for almost half a century: "When the great leader's work is done, the people say, 'We did it ourselves.'"

Brent was very touched, and his voice quavered as he said, "I can't think of anything I'd rather have. I'll always treasure this as a reminder of all of you."

As the reception broke up shortly afterward, everyone shook hands with Brent and wished him well.

Richard stayed behind after the others had left and asked Brent if he could walk with him to his car.

"Thanks, Richard, but I need to go back to my office and finish cleaning out my desk."

"Well, I'll just say good-bye now. We're going to miss you around here!"

"I'll miss being here, but I'll stay in touch—and you know how to reach me."

They shook hands again and Richard left the building as Brent returned to his office for the last time. Instead of switching on the ceiling lights he turned on the small lamp on the rolltop desk, leaving most of the office in semi-darkness. Leaning back in Stanley Wilson's old chair, he said aloud, "Well, Stanley. Who would've ever thought our chance meeting on the train would have led to this? You were a good friend, and I still miss you."

As he picked up his briefcase and started to turn off the lamp for the last time, his eyes fell on another quotation under the glass on Stanley's worktable: "We cannot hold a torch to light another's path, without brightening our own."

Brent thought, "You held the torch to light my path, Stanley, and I tried to hold the torch for those who followed you. When I did, it brightened my own path.

"Good night, Stanley!" he said as he switched off the lamp and walked out of the darkened office and down the deserted hallway, ending his stay at Enfield Manufacturing.

As Brent got into his car, he carefully propped Stanley Wilson's old plaque against the passenger side of the front seat. He drove through the parking lot and slowly rolled to a stop at the plant gate. Charlie MacIntyre, the guard, strolled over to the car.

"Have a nice weekend, Charlie!"

"You too, Brent! Will you be coming back now that the Wilson family has chosen Alan Braswell to take Scott's place as president?"

"No, Charlie. I guess I'll be moving on."

"Well, then good luck to you!—Hey! Isn't it great the way the gang in the front office was able to keep things going so well while Scott was out sick? I'm glad that Alan is the new president. He's a good man and I believe he'll be able to pick up right where Scott left off."

"I think you're right, Charlie! Good night!"

Brent Powell smiled as he drove through the gate and into the darkness. He glanced down at the plaque and said aloud, "You were right, Stanley! When the great leader's work is done, the people *do* say, 'We did it ourselves.'"

If you would like to contact the author about speaking engagements, seminars or consulting assignments, please contact:

Everett T. Suters
501 Peachtree Battle Avenue, N. W.
Atlanta, Georgia   30305
(800) 241-7308
(404) 873-5043 FAX

QUICK REFERENCE INDEX